# The Politics of the
# Powerless

# The Politics of the Powerless

## A Study of the Campaign Against Racial Discrimination

BENJAMIN W. HEINEMAN, Jr.

Published for the
INSTITUTE OF RACE RELATIONS
by
OXFORD UNIVERSITY PRESS
LONDON
· 1972

*Oxford University Press, Ely House, London W.*1

GLASGOW NEW YORK TORONTO MELBOURNE WELLINGTON
CAPE TOWN IBADAN NAIROBI DAR ES SALAAM LUSAKA ADDIS ABABA
DELHI BOMBAY CALCUTTA MADRAS KARACHI LAHORE DACCA
KUALA LUMPUR SINGAPORE HONG KONG TOKYO

ISBN 0 19 218178 5

Printed in Great Britain by
Western Printing Services Ltd, Bristol

# Contents

# Preface

In America, the symbolic catalyst for civil rights legislation was the 1963 march on Washington; 200,000 demonstrators massed at the Lincoln Memorial during August to hear Martin Luther King, then the embodiment of the civil rights movement, announce his dream of a United States free from prejudice and discrimination, in which black and white could live together as equals.

In Britain, the symbolic catalyst for the anti-discrimination legislation of 1968 was the publication of the P.E.P. report, a survey issued the year before that documented a fact well known to immigrants and sensitive observers: British society discriminated against coloured newcomers and against their children.[1]

Neither of these events was, of course, responsible wholly (or even in large part) for the subsequent pieces of legislation that emerged (the 1964 Civil Rights Act in the United States, the Race Relations Act of 1968 in Britain). Yet both events are rightly seen, I believe, as representative of the processes of change occurring in the two countries.

In America, the march has been viewed popularly as one of the proudest moments of the civil rights movement—a broad (if crudely defined) coalition of forces that included substantial portions of newly politicized black communities and important segments of white, 'liberal' America (parts of major pressure groups—unions, churches, the Bar, universities—and of the two major political parties). This coalition and its concerned response to the dramatic battles of the Southern civil rights struggle were of great importance in the efforts to legislate against discrimination. In Britain, no such coalition existed, although this book is concerned primarily with the attempt to form one. The P.E.P. report was to prove in Britain what was widely known in America: discrimination existed. The report was to foster legislation inspired in part by an American example. The legislation that did result was primarily

due to the energies of a Minister at the centre of British Government
and to relatively technical manoeuvrings in Whitehall and at
Westminster. It was not the response of Government to pressure
built up by a broad-based alliance of forces.[2]

It can be argued that both the march on Washington and the
publication of the P.E.P. report occurred during broadly similar
periods in the life of race relations in the respective countries,
during what E. J. B. Rose (following Adlai Stevenson) has called
'the liberal hour'.[3] During these periods, the fact of widespread
discrimination was brought forcefully before the public; a wide
spectrum of political forces decided that the law should no longer
tolerate such discrimination; and means were devised at a national
level for outlawing the questioned behaviour. To speak in schematic
terms again, this process occurred in America from about 1961 to
1964, in Britain from 1965 to 1968.[4]

The period during which a country is apparently united in its
resolve to assure equal rights in law (if not in fact) ended in America
with the massive urban riots that began in 1965; the apparent
agreement about the nature of equality and the route to its attainment was shattered. In Britain, the period ends with another round
of discriminatory legislation in the immigration field during 1968
and the evocative speeches of Enoch Powell whose mastery of
classical languages separates him from George Wallace, but whose
rhetoric in his native tongue sounds strikingly similar to the appeals
made by the former Governor of Alabama to those lower- and lower-
middle-class people who may be affected by the drive of coloured
minorities towards relative equality in fact. The conflicts, in both
countries, that the apparent consensus about anti-discrimination
laws had hidden began to emerge as the processes of basic social
change were seen to be of greater complexity than the passage and
implementation of anti-discrimination legislation.

The sketch above obviously has no pretentions to systematic
comparison for this book is hardly a cross-cultural study. Yet the
parallels and dissimilarities adumbrated above are important background for what follows, partly because what happened abroad
influenced Britain, partly because I am American and events in the
United States influenced, inevitably, the way I would perceive
events in Britain. The important fact for our purposes is that both
countries went through two distinct periods. First, one in which
anti-discrimination laws were the focus of political activity regarding race relations. Second, one in which an emphasis on social

rights (social equality),[5] not just on civil and political rights, began
to emerge and cause conflict. Although these periods are similar in
certain broad respects, the two countries began to enter each period
at different times—Britain following the United States.

This book focuses on the immigrants and attempts to tell part
of their story. It deals with the organization that was at the centre
of the British 'civil rights movement' from 1965 to 1967, the
Campaign Against Racial Discrimination (C.A.R.D.). In Britain of
the mid-sixties, people with coloured skins, whose ancestors had
been enslaved, colonized, and educated by the British and whose
lands had been exploited and modernized, commingled with each
other and with their hosts—some of whom were of course the direct
descendants of the exploiters and the modernizers. With the
traditional signposts gone, relations between white and coloured
in post-colonial Britain were uneasy and uncertain to say the
least.

For immigrants interested in politics in Britain and for their
English supporters, one source of ideas that could be used for
understanding relations between coloured and white were the
various patterns of thought that might be grouped under the
enormously broad heading, Marxist-Leninist. Marxist-Leninist
ideas about the struggle against imperialism, the battle against
colonialism, and, increasingly, contemporary Marxist ideas of
national liberation served as ways of structuring an analysis of the
relationship between coloured and white in Britain and prophesying
(or commanding) the directions for change. A second source of
experience and ideas for those in Britain concerned about the
immigrants' position and eager for change was of course the
immensely complex and heterogeneous experience of the United
States with its race problem in the early part of the decade.[6]

Those immigrants and their allies who looked to America for an
experience analogous to Britain's recognized from the outset that
the situations of coloured citizens in Britain and Negroes in the
United States were fundamentally different. The sheer number of
blacks in America and their long and tortured history meant that
the experience would be different for Indian, Pakistani, and West
Indian immigrants who comprised a very small percentage of the
British population and who, in many cases, were not even sure they
wished to remain in the mother country.

Yet, in an age of instant communication (an age in which the
British Press gave much space to the internal problems of the

United States), a process, which might be called the 'international-ization' of race relations, was at work. To put it in general terms: the growing sensitivity within Britain to problems of race relations meant that events abroad of a racial character would be received with great interest by many who were—or would be—active in British race relations and who needed ideas and examples to guide their own thoughts and actions. Thus, insularity was not possible. When authority was required to undergird support for anti-discrimination legislation in 1965, the language of morals and lessons of experience from America were also used in Britain. When the 'liberal hour' seemed to have passed and outright anti-immigrant sentiment was increasing, the spectre of 'an apocalyptic rendezvous at some future super-Detroit' was said to have struck many people as at least a practical reason for new anti-discrimination legislation.[7] Riots must be staved off, and the horrible examples were con-flagrations in America's urban centres, not disturbances in Notting Hill.

A result of 'internationalization' in the British context might be called the 'telescoping effect'. Actors in Britain might be influenced by events in America (we have not yet examined how in any detail), which could be part of a different stage of development. Events in America that occurred at nearly the same time as decisions were made by actors in Britain were parts of another broad phase of race relations. The fact that America was at a different phase thus had a telescoping effect: actors in Britain would be navigating through one phase—establishment of a legal frame outlawing discrimina-tion—already aware, through America's example, of the limitations and problems that lay ahead.

For example, C.A.R.D. began in late 1964. It was concerned with establishing a framework of laws prohibiting discrimination in employment, housing, credit facilities, and public accommoda-tions, concerns similar to ones voiced by the civil rights movement in, say, 1962. But in 1964 and 1965, activists' attention in America had turned to 'community action' and 'community organizing'. So, in C.A.R.D., there were debates about whether legislative change or community organization should be emphasized. These debates might have occurred anyway, but they drew force from experience in the United States. Similarly, at the end of C.A.R.D.'s life, those who had been initially concerned with passing legislation were turning their attention to building up the immigrant 'move-ment' through multiracial community action. But by this time in

America the appeal of 'Black Power' separatism was receiving wide attention and causing much controversy. C.A.R.D. was again racked with debate and dissension.[8]

This is not to suggest that the example of America was determinative. Rather it is to say that because there were no clear guide-posts for British activists promoting the immigrants' cause, the American experience had a distorting effect since it was often assumed that British race relations would go through analogous stages (though obviously at later times). As we shall see, this telescoping process was important in the case of a relatively powerless organization of immigrants and white supporters. Such an organization had, initially, to survive on the strength of its ideas and its appeal. These were its main resource, the strength of its vision of a new society and the clarity of the route that should be taken to get there. The constant changes in America coupled with the difficult and imperfectly understood situation in Britain served to undermine these fragile resources.

Most of the research for this volume was undertaken during 1966–7, when I was a graduate student at Balliol College. After four years at an American university, the opportunity to study at Oxford seemed a mixed blessing: a chance to escape the surpassing problems confronting the United States, and to journey back into the past. For generations of Americans preceding me, studying at Oxbridge meant putting the cap-stone on a liberal education. Pursuing an undergraduate course of study (even after four years of college) was an experience to be prized. Part of the aura of educational superiority stemmed, no doubt, from Britain's political pre-eminence. Thirty years ago, what were known as world events all seemed to take shape in Western Europe, however far-flung were the ramifications of decisions made in London, Paris, or Berlin. How different, of course, the England I visited turned out to be. The student of British culture delighted in the venerable marvels of the cities and the matchless landscape: the Piers Plowman manuscript, Blenheim, the cathedrals at Wells and Salisbury, the Lake District, the streets of Blake's or Dickens's London, Brighton as it might have been seen by Turner. Yet in the centre of Britain's historic industrial cities—Birmingham, Newcastle, Leeds, Manchester—were residents of the modern Britain, the coloured immigrants from India, Pakistan, and the West Indies, many of them living of necessity in dilapidated terraced houses that once had been the pride of the nineteenth century, emblems of an individual's liberty and a nation's strength. Now Britain struggled to adjust to its unaccustomed role as a lesser power.

The country also struggled with its unaccustomed race problem, an awkward remnant from a more grandiose past. In the 'development age', relations between coloured and white were of great moment. Britain was a relative newcomer to internal problems of this kind, her multiracial complexion (on the present scale) acquired recently, her relations with the colonial territories hardly a model for the domestic future. Yet, in 1964, major politicians, with few if any exceptions, had no coherent position detailing the proper response to the increasing coloured population, beyond control of it.[9] At Oxford, it seemed more was known about race relations in Zambia or even Birmingham, Alabama, than Birmingham, England. The study of British race relations, outside of the Institute's 'Survey of Race Relations in Britain', was not being pursued systematically in the universities or by the Government. To an American, fresh from a country preoccupied with marches, legislative debates, and urban rebellions, Britain's bemused response to its own problem seemed strange. Yet, despite Britain's history of colonialism, the difficulties here did not seem as severe or intractable as those in the United States—at least to an observer just off the boat. The relatively short time that a significant coloured population had in fact lived in Britain meant that the country was still unscarred; hope could exist for genuine multiracialism. Oddly, any American reasonably well informed about his own country could come to Britain—perhaps as men from the Old World had once, long before, come to the New—feeling the weight of his continent's history and seeing a society that could, perhaps, avoid the errors and tragedy etched so starkly upon the United States.

As I write this five years later, that feeling is something of a mockery. This book will concentrate on the problems that beset an attempt to establish a political organization of coloured citizens. This limited perspective should not be a source of misinterpretation. Immigrants and their children are in political terms largely powerless. The prime responsibility for alteration of British society to a multiracial community rests with white citizens and political leaders. In 1966–7, there were grounds for guarded optimism about the developing race situation in Britain. This can no longer be said. The Labour Government passed another discriminatory immigration Bill, watered down the second attempt at anti-discrimination legislation, and made only a halting start, with its Urban Programme, at facing the problems of immigrants massed in the large cities.[10] The Conservative party, newly enshrined in power, seems more concerned about beating off the claims of Powellism than taking any affirmative action. (Even today, it is announced in this country that Britain intends to resume arms sales to South Africa.) Because of the likelihood that leaders will not act in the interest of coloured people, the importance oi a powerful political group to represent immigrants and their children emerges even more forcefully today than in 1965.

As a foreigner *and* researcher, I must doubly thank those who were kind enough to share information and to help me find my way. This book, especially, results from the generosity of other people since I was dependent on interviewing to glean much of the material presented here. Deep-felt thanks are therefore owed to everyone whose name appears on the list of interviewees on pp. 233–4.

Special acknowledgement of assistance are due to those who gave extraordinary amounts of time and freely shared their knowledge on a wide range of matters concerning race in Britain: in the Campaign Against Racial Discrimination itself (during 1966–8), Hamza Alavi, Ranjana Ash, Michael Dummett, Julia Gaitskell, Selma James, Anthony Lester, Ian McDonald, and Dipak Nandy; in the Standing Conference of West Indian Organizations, London Region, Jeff Crawford; in the Federation of Pakistani Organizations, Tassaduq Ahmed; and in the National Committee for Commonwealth Immigrants, Martin Ennals.

The co-operation of A. Sivanandan, librarian, Institute of Race Relations, was most helpful in preparing parts of this manuscript.

Thanks are owed also to Steven Lukes, Fellow of Balliol College, for his help and encouragement.

Finally, I would like to thank Nicholas Deakin, formerly assistant director of the Institute's 'Survey of Race Relations in Britain', for his assistance in making contact with many of the principals in this narrative and for his suggestions and advice. It will be a mark of racial progress in Britain, I suspect, when Nicholas's name does not appear in the prefaces of all books on race relations. Its occasional absence should signify such an intensification of interest and concern in the country that he simply cannot be involved in all projects being mounted.

Of course, none of those named above are responsible for any errors in the material which follows.

Research for the bulk of the manuscript was carried out in 1966–7. Writing occurred during the summer of 1967 and covered Chapters Two to Four. This material in slightly different form was then submitted in fulfilment of degree requirements for a Bachelor of Letters at Oxford and an initial decision was made by the Institute of Race Relations and the Oxford University Press to publish. During the autumn of 1967 a major upheaval occurred within C.A.R.D. The group that had controlled the organization for two and a half years split apart, and C.A.R.D. underwent a substantial change which led to a severe diminution of its activities and effectiveness. In order to round out the history of the organization, I returned to Britain in the winter of 1968 to research the events of the previous months. The results of that effort are embodied in Chapter Five.

The focus of my efforts was initially on the Campaign Against Racial Discrimination itself: what was C.A.R.D. established to do; how successful had it been in achieving its goals; what kind of constraints had prevented the accomplishment of those objectives that had not been attained? Available records concerning the organization were canvassed; actors familiar with C.A.R.D. were interviewed. The contours of C.A.R.D. shaped the bulk of my research.

In order to move beyond straightforward goal analysis, to give the work comparative value, and to put it into a more systematic framework, I adopted the vocabulary and perspective of pressure group analysis. This was done for several reasons. First, C.A.R.D. was a fascinating and unique example of a pressure group. Because of its highly diverse membership, it did not (as will be discussed) fit neatly into the traditional categories of pressure group analysis: it was trying to organize and create strength among its constituents at the same time that it sought to bargain for their interests through public policy lobbying. The tension between the organizing function and the public policy pressure function would bring to the surface implications about the efficacy and justness of Britain's group politics.

Second, the adoption of the pressure group framework stemmed from a personal conviction that studies of race relations had neglected political relationships based on influence and power. In political terms, individuals who suffer discrimination simply do not have the power to alter their situation. Power normally must be exercised through organized groups. The process of developing such organizations to affect the other institutions, which determine the quality of life in either a local or national community, seemed central to any process of change that was to improve conditions for immigrants. Third, the use of pressure group vocabulary should help this book to function as a background paper for those who would attempt again to 'organize the immigrant/coloured community'. Hopefully, this volume offers some lessons through its recording of C.A.R.D.'s adventures (and misadventures).

There are, of course, limitations in giving primary attention to the activities of C.A.R.D. The impact of certain broad determining forces could not be properly assessed. For example, this book was written before the Institute of Race Relations' massive study, *Colour and Citizenship: A Report on British Race Relations*, was prepared (although it is published afterwards). It could not, therefore, take advantage of the Institute's important research. Thus important perspectives are touched upon in all too cursory fashion, e.g. the structure of immigrant communities in particular cities, the nature of immigrant politics in the homeland, economic and demographic profiles of the newcomers, the intricacies of Cabinet manoeuvrings, and the actions of other British pressure groups concerned with race relations. This book must be wedded with more detailed analysis of these subjects, both in *Colour and Citizenship* and elsewhere, to provide a more complete account of immigrant politics during the period under discussion.

Further, there is the methodological limitation inherent in pressure group studies stemming from the process of gathering information. A good deal of the material in this book comes from interviews, and the number of variables in informal, relatively unstructured interviewing are legion. A tape recorder was used to insure accuracy of quotes, but the interpretative skills required in any historical reconstruction are especially challenged when there is a personal relationship (the interview) between the writer and those whom he presumes to write about, especially when that writer is both foreign and white. Basically, the interviews were an attempt to establish some of the undisputed facts about the organization's history. They were also used to uncover what issues had concerned the particular interviewee—what her or his position had been, what was the basis of the conflict, what were the motives of the opposition, what was at stake? This was in keeping with ever-present tension between C.A.R.D. as an incipient movement and C.A.R.D. as a lobbying organization in London. Obviously, I am alone responsible for the reconstruction and the reader is invited to exercise his critical sense as he follows the story. This paragraph will not satisfy rigorous methodologues, but, in any event, I only claim a limited portion of what historians and political scientists at their euphemistic best call the Truth.

New Haven, Connecticut
26 July 1970

## NOTES

1. Political and Economic Planning, *Racial Discrimination* (London, P.E.P., 1967).

2. See Chapter 3. Also E. J. B. Rose and associates, *Colour and Citizenship* (London, Oxford University Press, for Institute of Race Relations, 1969), Chapters 26–7.

3. Rose *et al.*, pp. 10–11

4. Ibid.

5. For purposes of discussion, this study will at this point follow Rose *et al.* in their use of T. H. Marshall's definition of citizenship in his work *Citizen and Social Class* (Cambridge, Doubleday, 1960). See Rose *et al.*, op. cit., pp. 17, 27–8. For a discussion of the concept's limitations, see Chapter Six.

6. Of course, for some, analyses of the events in America would depend on a Marxist-Leninist framework.

7. Rose *et al.*, op. cit., p. 11.

8. See Chapter Four.

9. Rose *et al.*, op. cit., pp. 229–30.

10. Ibid., pp. 405–15, 547–9.

# CHAPTER ONE

# Introduction: The Politics of the Powerless

The Campaign Against Racial Discrimination was founded in December 1964 to speak for a social and political movement that did not exist. It was to energize and unify disparate groups of coloured immigrants at the same time that it presented a united front in pressing for the alteration of national policy. It was to make those who had power act for the benefit of immigrants while it sought simultaneously to develop power among those who were powerless.[1]

Although divided into three major nationality groups (Indian, Pakistani, and West Indian), the nearly one million coloured immigrants were conjoined by a common feature of their life in Britain. A high percentage suffered from the effects of racial discrimination.[2] Although certain journalists, academics, and Members of Parliament spoke out in the interest of immigrants, no political organization, no pressure group, represented all three immigrant nationalities to the Press, the political parties, the local authorities, Parliament, and the executive. The brute fact of discrimination, thought the founders of C.A.R.D., would bring Indians, Pakistanis, and West Indians together to form such an organization.

From one point of view, fighting discrimination is seeking to overcome a lack of political and economic power. If a person suffers discrimination as a member of a distinctive group, it suggests that neither the individual nor the group has the power to counteract the discriminatory practices, or the will or skill to utilize potential political influence to alter conditions. As newcomers, members of a lower economic class (generally speaking), and victims of discrimination, coloured immigrants suffered from compound problems of powerlessness. Discrimination against minorities implies that they suffer from social inequalities as a group and this in turn suggests that they will be plagued by an unequal distribution of political resources.[3]

The paradox of an organization representing a movement that did not exist is reflected in the two central functions that C.A.R.D. tried to perform from its inception. As a campaign against racial discrimination, the organization would try to change the pattern of public policy at national and local levels by:

eliminating discriminatory legislation (regarding immigration controls);

insuring equal opportunity in vital areas like employment and housing through passage of anti-discrimination legislation;

pressing for broad social and economic policies that would promote social equality for all people in lower income classes;

policing the administration of existing social and economic programmes to make sure that immigrants were not adversely affected by them.

C.A.R.D. would also try to mobilize, organize, and represent immigrants and their children. In terms of the number of people involved and the level of consciousness desired, this may be seen as an attempt to create a political and social movement. This movement might seek formal elective or political party power for its members in certain areas. Its main functions would be to:

aid in the performance of the organization's pressure group function;

fight discrimination in ways other than alteration of public policy;

promote equality through organizational efforts in community development;

serve as a conduit into British society while at the same time working to alter that society.

C.A.R.D. would thus have two broad sets of relationships: with those in the immigrant communities and within the immigrant organizations that it wanted to mobilize, and with those who had the power necessary for the alteration of public policy. The articulation of interests by a group like C.A.R.D. is critically important because it marks the boundary between British society and the British political system.[4]

In one sense, then, C.A.R.D. would attempt to become a pressure group in the British political system. C.A.R.D.'s distinctive attributes meant that it did not fit neatly into definitional categories used to classify pressure groups by recent writers on British politics.[5] And it was those distinctive attributes—those characteristics which pointed up its differences from other pressure groups—that had a major impact in determining the conception of the organization, the nature of its functions, and its effectiveness in performing them.

In traditional pressure group analysis, groups have been classified in broad terms by the nature of their aims, membership, functions, and influence. With regard to aims, a distinction is made between the groups which promote a general cause and those which protect the interests of a particular section of society.[6] Yet C.A.R.D. would attempt to promote the general cause of social equality within Britain and also try to protect (and represent) the interests of immigrants by urging anti-discrimination measures. This duality of aims stemmed from two fundamental aspects of immigrants' lives. First, they were (and still are) an underprivileged group in British society.[7] Second, as coloured immigrants, they were beleaguered by difficulties arising from their race (discrimination) and newness (adaptation to the new society). Put another way, immigrants suffered from the societal problems of bad housing, overcrowded schools, poor jobs, and overtaxed social services in a manner that is intensified by their newness and by the discrimination directed against them.[8] To phrase it still another way, immigrants suffered from problems of race and problems of class.

Thus, C.A.R.D.'s aims were to defend an interest (coloured immigrants and their children) against discrimination and to promote the cause of general social reconstruction and social equality in Britain through emphasis on the need for the public and private sectors to provide better housing, jobs, education, medical care, and other social services for a number of British citizens, not just immigrants. Presumably, by advancing the cause of greater social equality C.A.R.D. would help remove or counter some of the causes of discrimination.

Clearly related to the broad distinction in aims is the differentiation in types of membership. Pressure group writers have defined membership by objective characteristics for members of an interest group or by shared attitudes for a group promoting a cause (for example, the poor or the aged as opposed to all those who favour unilateral disarmament).[9] Again C.A.R.D. fit into neither classification. It was to be a coalition comprised of those who could be described by objective characteristics, coloured immigrants, and of whites from the host society opposed to discrimination on the basis of colour.

A third distinction is made by pressure group writers between the broad functions of the two types of group. By definition, the function of an 'interest' (or 'sectional') group is to speak for its 'class' or 'type' of people 'with authority'.[10] Such a group is representative in two ways. Its leaders are 'representative' of the class or type of people organized and these leaders 'represent' the interests of that class in a bargaining process. The attitude (or 'promotional') group must unite a variety of different 'classes and types' of people so as to further a cause endorsed by a broad spectrum of opinion. C.A.R.D. would try to perform both functions.

That it would attempt to do so stemmed from the nature of power that pressure groups command in the political system. Regarding the organizations classified under the sectional heading, there are two broad types of group as defined through function by Samuel Beer: producer and consumer blocs.[11] A prominent feature of current British politics is the legitimization of collectivities, predominantly political parties, as the structures through which the battle for the state's power is fought. Yet it is a commonplace that the pressure group configuration shapes the struggle for power. Beer notes two main features in the politics of post-war Britain: the realities of governing that led governments and parties to bargain with organized producers; and the realities of winning power that led them to bid for the support of consumer groups that could be singled out from the bloc of voters.

It was primarily because the government attempted to control or manage the economy that the producer groups acquired power to influence policy. On the other hand it was mainly because programs of the welfare state appealed to groups as consumers that governments and parties were incited to appeal for their support by means of these programs.[12]

The producer groups were able to influence public policy through a system of 'functional representation'. Such a theory of representation finds the community divided into various strata, regards each stratum as having a certain self-conscious unity, and holds that they ought to be represented in the government.[13] Members of each stratum perform functions within society. Recognizing this function and the common interests attendant to it, members of the stratum, say, working men, act as a unit and find the group to be a sphere of moral fulfilment and an instrument of political action. Because the government needs the advice, acquiescence, and approval of the groups to manage the economy,[14] these collectivities gain influence.

Ultimately they are able to bargain and negotiate with the government on issues which affect them.

But immigrants in 1964 did not have much influence in the producer group sense. They often held unskilled or semi-skilled positions; they were, by and large, not organized in unions; they often worked in industries with the weakest unions (construction, woollens, catering); and they suffered discrimination in seeking entry to jobs or trade unions.[15] Of course, very few immigrants owned productive resources, and those productive resources in immigrant hands were of small scale. Thus, they were neither organized as a producer group nor did they have the full protection offered to white labourers by the trade unions.

Consumer groups (defined by Beer generically as a 'number of voters whose material well-being is affected in some way by some measure of government action, actual or prospective') gain power through a different sort of political relation. In an electoral system where differences between parties are not great, these collectivities have broad power through a system of parliamentary representation in which party government is the dominant feature.[16] Immigrants, although clearly consumers, were not in 1964 organized electorally and, in fact, from what can be determined in local studies, had (and have) an extraordinary low rate of voter registration.[17] Moreover, immigrants as a voting (consumer) group were not treated as a special bloc by the political parties (in contrast, for example, to another group which is powerless in a functional way, the pensioners). Thus, as part of a system of functional or parliamentary representation, immigrants as a sectional interest had little power. They did not benefit from the system of influence that is informally recognized in Britain's political culture.

Not only did immigrants have little power as either a producer or consumer group, they were, because of their status, colour, and political weakness, subject to hostile pressures from other producer and consumer groups, counter-pressures which would only reduce still further the possibility of immigrants exercising influence with the Government as a 'sectional' group. Given the set of political relationships that parliamentary and functional representation suggest, it follows that other sectional groups may, if antagonistic, prevent a government which was disposed to take action favourable to immigrants from so doing. To be specific: If the government wanted to press for anti-discrimination legislation in employment, the producer groups could possibly veto or at least significantly alter it. Industrial Ministers, for example, might oppose legislation, since it would complicate their already difficult relationship with employers and trade unions.[18]

If the government was convinced that consumer groups, i.e., voters, were antagonistic to immigrants, it might be either indifferent to the needs of the coloured immigrant or hostile to them. The pattern of the introduction of 'race' into the general election in 1964 and the retreat of the Labour party from a position of principle regarding immigration control are notable examples of this process.[19]

If immigrants had little power as a 'sectional' group in 1964, their influence in a 'promotional' sense, too, was limited by significant factors. As mentioned, the main function of a promotional group must be to gain supporters from other status, power, or class groups in its attempt to advance a cause. The capacity to perform this function depends in large measure on the political culture. As Richard Rose has written, 'the relationship between pressure group demands and cultural norms is of fundamental importance in analysing pressure groups'.[20] A group like C.A.R.D. would not only have to promote a cause publicly that could attract allies if it were to be a 'promotional' group, but it would also have to avoid exciting widespread opposition among other influential segments of the population. The point here is not to analyse the nature of racial prejudice and racial discrimination, to trace their impact on the social structure and the political culture, and, through these systems, to delineate their impact on the political system. It is only to suggest that the evidence that many Britons were colour prejudiced and practised discrimination indicates that a deep conflict could develop between the norms of behaviour commended by a group like C.A.R.D. and the attitudinal and behavioural patterns in other segments of society.[21] Thus, barriers of a fundamental nature stood in C.A.R.D.'s path if it was to attract and arouse wide support in a public pressure campaign.

Because C.A.R.D. did not fit neatly into the analytical categories used by political scientists and was in those terms an anomaly, the organization's efforts would be suggestive about the functioning of the British political system. It has been said during the past few years that the immigrants' experience in British society is revealing (diagnostic if you will); the interaction between the coloured immigrants and the social system would indicate 'weaknesses' and 'failures' of structures and institutions.[22] A corollary of this proposition is that C.A.R.D. would indicate 'weaknesses' within the British political system, a system marked by the exercise of collective influence, especially through pressure groups.

The use of the terms 'weakness' and 'failure' suggests a normative perspective. But writers dealing with British pressure groups have tended to blend together normative and descriptive perspectives in their analyses.[23] It has not always been clear whether they were just describing and presenting systematically a phenomenon of great importance in the British political system or whether they were not also commending the functioning of pressure groups as a good aspect of current democratic practices, one that could be justified from a normative perspective, i.e. from the perspective of prescriptive political thought. In the time-honoured vocabulary of political theory, were these writers describing the way the pressure group system is or commending to their readers that this was the way current democratic practices ought to be. And, if the latter, what was the effect of the description of the way the system is? Was the brute fact of the existence of the pressure group system a form of justification for it? At the least, it can be said that the writers generally did not make clear their normative bias for the pressure group system. Nor, *a fortiori*, did they advance normative justificatory arguments as to why such a system was good.

Wolff,[24] among others, has begun the task of making explicit the normative implications of the systems described by pressure group analysts in general:

Pluralism [a political system marked by pressure groups] is a theory of the way modern industrial democracies work . . . it is also an ideal model of the way political society ought to be organized, whether in fact it is or not. . . . As a normative theory . . . pluralism must be defended by appeal to some principle or virtue or ideal of the good society.[25]

Without ever describing adequately the complexity of the modern democratic polity, Wolff none the less notes three justifications for the pressure group basis of politics. The first, stemming from the pre-industrial period, is the justification of tolerance. Pluralism is an argument for groups, originally religious groups, tolerating the existence of other groups and competing with them for power through legitimate means rather than through use of force. Second, pluralism is seen as a 'morally neutral means for pursuing political ends which cannot be achieved through traditional representative democracy'.[26] Since, in an industrial state, relations between governed and governor are necessarily attenuated, interest groups, which make up the social order, must approximate democracy in their internal workings, articulating the interests of the individuals that comprise them. Third, stemming from a view of the relationship between personality and society, is an argument that the 'human personality in its development, structure and continued functioning is dependent upon the social group of which it is a significant member'.[27] In sum, pluralist democracy is defended, says Wolff, because it:

constitutes the highest stage in the political development of industrial capitalism. It transcends the crude 'limitations' of early individualistic liberalism and makes a place for the communitarian features of social life, as well as for the interest group politics which emerged as a domesticated version of the class struggle. Pluralism is humane, benevolent, accommodating and far more responsive to the evils of social injustice than either the egotistic liberalism or the traditional conservatism from which it grew. . . .[28]

Yet on the level of normative argument, Wolff is highly critical of the alleged group basis of contemporary democracy. First, if politics in such a system is a contest for power among social groups, and redistribution of goods and services among groups is the basic process at work, then certain principles of equality or fairness or aesthetics may be ignored in the struggle between collectivities and the polity as a whole may suffer.[29] Second, strong groups will inevitably be favoured over weak ones, and this is bad since the continued weakness of certain segments of the population may be contrary to the principles of equality, justice, or fairness which should be realized in the social and political arrangements of a modern state.[30]

This second criticism has been noted by writers concerned with the British pressure group system (although the normative implications of it have not been explored by them). Finer has warned that the strongly mobilized will be more likely to have their demands acted upon than the weakly mobilized.[31] It is difficult to counter this except by trusting the web of 'institutions, procedures and shared beliefs to secure some measure of distributive justice'.[32] Mackenzie, in the introduction to a special issue of *Political Quarterly* devoted to pressure groups, noted that weak groups 'may be trampled'. One of the potential dangers, he writes, of the party and pressure group system is that they may fail to 'secure the organization of unrepresented interests, such as children, consumers, the deaf. . . .'[33] Surely, if he were writing today, rather than in 1958, he would include immigrants in that catalogue.

The analysis of Wolff (and of other pluralist critics) is incomplete, since he does not present a necessarily complex description of social and political reality (how accurate is it to talk about the group basis of the modern democratic state?) and because his normative 'thought' is a series of loosely linked ideas and not a systematic social and political theory. None the less, failing in that Herculean task, he is suggestive in noting the 'normative' blindness of pressure group writers.

A similar questioning of the normative implications of descriptive systems is found in the sociological writings of John Rex and Robert Moore, a similarity that links up with the criticisms directed against pressure group writers.[34] Until recently, the basic vocabulary for describing the interaction between the races in British society was found in the concepts: assimilation, accommodation, integration.[35] The role of the immigrants was seen to be one of adjustment and adaptation—either through assimilative or integrative processes— to British society. The implied assumption was that these processes were good (and that the host society was a relatively stable entity and thus necessarily the way it was: the immigrants would have to change, to adapt, and to adjust). Yet, Rex and Moore seriously questioned this approach in their excellent study of Sparkbrook.[36] They emphasized instead the continuing struggle for power and property in an urban social system, given the perceived scarcity of resources and differing value systems (e.g. views of equality or the proper role of government) held by different actors in the process of conflict (however much these actors might share certain core values necessary for the mere existence of social and political institutions— a belief held generally 'in democratic processes'). For Rex and Moore, the role of the immigrant group as an actor in this process is critical:

What we have to discover is what kinds of primary communities immi- grants form in order to obtain some sort of social and cultural bearings and also what relationships exist between their community structure as a whole and the complex system of class conflict and status which we refer to as the host society.[37]

Rex and Moore claim that prejudice results as much from social systems as from personality development and that 'once we under- stand urban society as a structure of social interaction and conflict prejudiced behaviour may be shown to fit naturally into or even be required by the structure'.[38] A similar perspective has been suggested by van den Berghe, among others.[39] And, as will be discussed in Chapter Two, the traditional vocabulary of race relations and the assumptions underlying it have been attacked by immigrant groups themselves as giving a false impression of their own goals and the actual situation in Great Britain. The development of a different set of descriptive tools raises normative questions. If the social system induces prejudice and encourages discrimination, if the conditions that are considered undesirable from the immigrants' perspective are not the result of wilful individualistic behaviour but conditioned, in fact encouraged, by systemic forces, how is that 'system' to be altered? Put another way, if 'integration' into 'existing' society is not desirable, what is the ideal of 'cultural diversity' which should prevail in the 'new' society?

Thus, a history of C.A.R.D. would be a piece of description that would fit into the pattern of other accounts of the British political system. Could C.A.R.D. succeed in gaining and exercising influence in traditional ways? The experience would also inevitably raise normative questions. If C.A.R.D. could so gain influence, was that good for all the immigrants? If it could not, what did that suggest about a system of power distribution that had seemed good, fair, or just? This general point might be stated more formally as a series of issues:

Does the nature of conflict within the British political system—characterized as it may be by the exercise of power through collectivities—necessitate the creation of a pressure group like C.A.R.D. which would attempt to exercise influence on behalf of the immigrants?

How would such a group attempt to gain and exercise power?

If it could not gain power given existing policies and practices within the system as presently structured and operated, should special support be given to the effort (presumably in either direct or indirect fashion by government) so that it might succeed in operating within a pluralist system of competing groups?

Or, rather, should the system of influence be altered in some more fundamental fashion?

In this volume, the answer to the first issue raised is assumed to be affirmative. I say 'assumed' because to demonstrate that point would require a complicated and sustained argument outside the scope of this book. As suggested above, I assume that in 1965 the immediate (through general) goal for individual immigrants was to attain all the rights of full citizenship—social, political, and civil.[40] I assume that under prevailing conditions in 1965 the attainment of such rights had been frustrated.[41] I assume further that given the political and social conflicts at both national and local levels, a political organization, a group effort, was required to exercise power to alter these conditions. Otherwise, coloured immigrants and their children would not attain the full scope of rights that should constitute British citizenship.

As has been noted, this last point is supported, at a local level, by the analysis of Rex and Moore. Given their view of urban society as a number of overlapping and competing systems of social relations, they suggest the necessity of groups to mobilize power in order to compete for scarce resources. In housing, for example, the local authority administers its own estate and the exercise of influence by an individual group on that government is central to achievement of goals desired by a particular section of that society. To compress their complicated argument, immigrants are concentrated in zones of transition because of the system of housing allocation. In their desire to achieve domestic property and position for themselves and their family, it is functionally imperative that the immigrants' groups should not suffer discrimination. Yet the poor conditions of life in the twilight zone, the prevalence of discrimination in housing outside the zone, and the disorientation of the immigrant serve to make him more and more dependent on the city's bureaucratic agencies and his own conjugal family. Further, large numbers of immigrants may not be involved in associational life. And immigrant organizations that currently do exist may not be oriented towards changing discriminatory patterns as they exist within the city. Rex and Moore conclude that as immigrants try to move outside their own enclaves and reach equality in housing in an area, the greater is the necessity for the application of social, economic, and political power.[42]

Similarly, the obvious conflicts at the national level and the inability (reluctance) of government to satisfactorily represent the immigrant point of view require the establishment of a strong pressure group. Finer has written that it is the responsibility of the government to see that the 'less strongly organized interests do not go to the wall'. Yet obviously the government, even if it wanted to, cannot represent the interests of immigrants. The government simply is not the body to do that: the immigrants must themselves make determinations about their preferences and policies, must try to make government act in their interest. A strong group is thus required both because government cannot adequately represent the immigrants' interest, given other conflicting claims on it,[43] and because immigrants and their children should achieve autonomy and independence by acting in their own interest.

Assuming then that the nature of conflict within the British political system necessitates the creation of an immigrant pressure group, the bulk of this volume will be concerned with answering the questions raised by the second issue: can immigrants and their children compete in the pressure group system? (Consideration of the other two issues will be deferred until Chapter Six.) Chapter Two discusses the formative period of C.A.R.D., examining the development of a conception of organization (C.A.R.D.'s goals, structure, and two main functions—influencing public policy and uniting immigrants with sympathetic members of the host society) in the context of initial activities and organization building. Chapter Three examines C.A.R.D.'s attempt—and its failure—to build an 'organization of organizations', an alliance of groups, predominantly from within Britain's immigrant communities, dedicated to the eradication of discrimination. Chapter Four details C.A.R.D.'s efforts to change public policy and the nature of its success in that area. Chapter Five describes the conception of a model organization that developed during the first years of C.A.R.D.'s existence and then analyses the forces that brought about the break-up of C.A.R.D. as it had previously been known. The Conclusion evaluates C.A.R.D.'s efforts, discusses the causes of C.A.R.D.'s failures, and considers the implications of its short history.

C.A.R.D.'s problems in performing its two central functions, the interrelationship between these functions, and the potential antagonism between them, provide the focus for this book. In trying both to promote a cause and to represent an interest, C.A.R.D. was to be a coalition, a union of nationalities, races, classes, languages, cultures, religions, and political beliefs. C.A.R.D. did not start with much conventional power as a promotional or sectional group and, as a voluntary association with resources limited initially to the idealism and intelligence of its members, was dangerously close to a Victorian anachronism in a collectivist age. C.A.R.D.'s distinctive characteristics which made it such an unusual pressure group, shaped the contours of the organization and determined its specific activities. For in the formative period, the outline of the organization was by no means clear. Legislation against discrimination was necessary; organizing and involving the immigrant in the C.A.R.D. structure were imperative. These two ideas, stated almost that simply, were the poles around which the Campaign Against Racial Discrimination took shape.

## NOTES

1. The League of Coloured Peoples attempted to unify coloured citizens in Britain before the Second World War. Its orientation was largely towards altering the colonial system. After the War, the League became inert and no attempt was made to join coloured people in efforts to affect British politics until the founding of C.A.R.D.

2. P.E.P., op. cit. See also Race Relations Board, *Report for 1966–7, Report for 1967–8* (London, H.M.S.O.).

3. For amplification of these concepts, see W. G. Runciman, *Relative Deprivation and Social Justice* (London, Routledge & Kegan Paul, 1966), Chapter III. A person's 'class' situation may refer to his location in the process of production, distribution, and exchange. This refers not merely to lack of capital but also to opportunities for accretion of advantage under the conditions of the commodity and labour markets.

4. G. Almond and G. Bingham Powell, Jr., discuss this point in *Comparative Politics: A Developmental Approach* (Boston, Little, 1966).

5. Samuel H. Beer, *Modern British Politics* (London, Faber and Faber, 1965); Harry Eckstein, *Pressure Group Politics* (London, Allen & Unwin, 1960); S. E. Finer, *Anonymous Empire: A Study of the Lobby in Great Britain*, second ed. (London, Pall Mall Press, 1966); Allen Potter, *Organized Groups in British National Politics* (London, Faber and Faber, 1961); Richard Rose, *Politics in England* (London, Faber and Faber, 1965); A. H. Birch, *Representative and Responsible Government* (London, Allen & Unwin, 1964); Jean Blondell, *Voters, Parties and Leaders* (Harmondsworth, Penguin, 1963).

6. See Blondell, op. cit., p. 160, for the distinction between 'protective' and 'promotional' groups; Finer, op. cit., p. 3, for the distinction between 'promotional' and 'interest' groups; Potter, op. cit., p. 25, for the distinction between those 'organizing sectional interests' and those 'organizing shared attitudes'.

7. For a discussion of immigrants' difficulties with regard to housing: Committee on Housing in Greater London, *Report of the Committee on Housing in Greater London* (London, H.M.S.O., 1965) (Cmnd. 2605); Elizabeth Burney, *Housing on Trial* (London, Oxford University Press, for Institute of Race Relations, 1967). Education: *Children and their Primary Schools* (London, Central Advisory Council for Education, 1967). Employment: Bob Hepple, *The Position of Coloured Workers in British Industry*, a report prepared for the N.C.C.I. conference on racial equality in employment (London, N.C.C.I., 1967); B. Hepple, *Race, Jobs and the Law in Britain* (London, Allen Lane, The Penguin Press, 1968); Sheila Patterson, 'Immigrants and Employment', *Political Quarterly* (January–March 1968). Welfare: Peter Townsend, 'Social Welfare and Equality', in A. Lester and N. Deakin (eds.), *Policies for Racial Equality* (London, Fabian Research Series, No. 262, 1967). For the cumulative effects of substandard conditions (a British variant of the culture of poverty theory), John Rex and Robert Moore, *Race, Community and Conflict: A Study of Sparkbrook* (London, Oxford University Press, for Institute of Race Relations, 1967). For a summary discussion of these problems, Rose *et al.*, op cit.

8. National Committee for Commonwealth Immigrants, *Report for 1966* (London, N.C.C.I., 1967), p. 9. For a discussion of the 'immigrant' perspective in British

race relations, see Michael Banton, *Race Relations* (London, Tavistock Publications, 1967). Generally, Rose *et al.*, op. cit.

9. Eckstein, op. cit., p. 9.

10. Potter, op. cit., p. 25.

11. Beer, op. cit., p. 309.

12. Ibid.

13. The social system could be divided up into groups according to class, status, or power. Each of these groups could 'function' in a particularly defined 'sub-system'. Beer has chosen to isolate certain groups according to the nature of their power. There are other methods of analysing a system of functional representation.

14. Beer, op. cit., pp. 319–39; Finer, op. cit., Chapter 4.

15. Hepple, *The Position of Coloured Workers in British Industry*, pp. 9–21, and *Race, Jobs and the Law*, pp. 64–88; P.E.P., op. cit., Section II; R. B. Davison, *Black British: Immigrants to London* (London, Oxford University Press, for Institute of Race Relations, 1966), Chapters IV and V; Rose *et al.*, op. cit., Chapter 19.

16. Beer, op. cit., p. 319.

17. Precision studies have not yet been conducted nationally on immigrant voter registration. For a general estimate at the time C.A.R.D. began and a discussion of selected case studies, see Nicholas Deakin (ed.), *Colour and the British Electorate, 1964* (London, Pall Mall Press, 1965); Rex and Moore, op. cit., p. 210.

18. Counter-pressure directed against efforts to amend the Race Relations Act of 1965 will be discussed in Chapter Three. See also Rose *et al.*, op. cit., Chapters 26–7. As Finer (op. cit., p. 27), has written: 'Organized capital and labour do not dictate public policy by massive and explicit threat. But because of their very position in the economy their co-operation must be won, rather than their services commanded. They do not direct, but they may veto.'

19. See Nicholas Deakin, 'The Politics of the Commonwealth Immigrants Bill', *Political Quarterly* (January–March 1968); Paul Foot, *Immigration and Race in British Politics* (Harmondsworth, Penguin, 1965); and the major national news-papers during the formulation of the Commonwealth Immigrants Bill of 1968. The phenomenon of Powellism is discussed in those papers and in Rose *et al.*, op. cit., pp. 535–46, 616–18.

20. R. Rose, op. cit., p. 130.

21. Banton, op. cit., Chapter 15; Ruth Glass, *The Newcomers* (London, Allen & Unwin, 1960); Clifford Hill, *How Colour Prejudiced is Britain?* (London, Gollancz, 1965); Rex and Moore, op. cit., Chapter III; Rose *et al.*, op. cit., Chapter 28.

22. Burney, op. cit., pp. 1–2; Rose *et al.*, op. cit., p. 33: 'In a divided society, the newcomer's function may be to show up the weaknesses in the structure of the societal community, and it is in this sense that he ultimately earns our attention, as the focus for the Condition of England question for this generation.'

23. Stewart, op. cit., Introduction; Eckstein, op. cit., pp. 7–8; Almond, op. cit., pp. 9–15 and Chapter IV, for a general account of pressure groups that does not directly confront the normative implications of such a system. For critics of the interest group writers, see Robert Paul Wolff, *The Poverty of Liberalism* (Boston, Beacon Press, 1968); Charles A. McCoy and John Playford (eds.), *Apolitical Parties: A Critique of Behavioralism* (New York, T. Y. Crowell, 1967). 'Critics' is used here in the sense of those writers who have basic normative criticisms to make of the pressure group system.

24. Wolff, op. cit., Chapter IV.

25. Ibid., p. 131.

26. Ibid., pp. 132–3.

27. Ibid., p. 134.

28. Ibid., pp. 160–1.

29. Ibid., pp. 158–9.

30. Ibid., pp. 154–6. Wolff discusses two roles for government in metaphorical terms in a system marked by a multiplicity of pressure groups: the 'referee' theory and the 'vector-sum' theory. Under the first conception, government mediates between conflicting groups, presumably insuring certain minimum fair procedures in their competition. In such a situation, large and strong will have an advantage over small and weak. Under the second conception, government makes policies that result from the interaction of pressure groups on the institutions of government itself. Again, the strong will be advantaged, according to this simple image.

31. Finer, op. cit., pp. 114–36.

32. Ibid., p. 121.

33. R. T. Mackenzie, 'Parties, Pressure Groups and the British Political Process', *Political Quarterly* (XXIX, January–March 1958), p. 15.

34. The work of political sociologists has done much to complement the critics of the pressure group writers. See Reinhard Bendix and Seymour M. Lipset, 'The Field of Political Sociology', in Lewis Coser (ed.), *Political Sociology* (New York, Torch, 1966).

35. Sheila Patterson, *Dark Strangers: A Study of West Indians in London* (Harmondsworth, Penguin, 1965), pp. 301–25.

36. Rex and Moore, op. cit., pp. 13–15: 'Once we have grasped the idea of urban society as a number of overlapping and sometimes contradictory systems of social relations it soon becomes clear that the commonly used vocabulary of race relations which includes such words as "assimilation", "integration" and "accommodation" is inadequate. Such vocabularies assume a "host-immigrant" framework in which the culture and values of the host society are taken to be non-contradictory and static and in which the immigrant is seen as altering his own patterns of behaviour until they finally conform to those of the host society.' This is not to suggest that the processes of assimilation, accommodation, and integration do not take place. Rather it is to suggest that, first, they may be a limited way of viewing interaction between immigrants and their children, and British society. Secondly, insofar as these processes are considered good, their normative aspects should be questioned. For an attempt to redefine the concept of integration to take account for cultural diversity that results from immigration, see Rose *et al.*, op. cit., pp. 24–6. However, the systemic conflict perspective of Rex and Moore is not followed in Rose (see Chapter Six, *infra*).

37. Rex and Moore, op. cit., p. 14.

38. Ibid., p. 12.

39. Pierre van den Berghe, *Race and Racism: A Comparative Perspective* (New York, John Wiley, 1967).

40. See Preface, p. xvi, footnote 5.

41. Rose *et al.*, op. cit., Parts III and IV.

42. Rex and Moore, op. cit., pp. 11–41.

43. See p. 6.

# CHAPTER TWO

# The Genesis of C.A.R.D.:
# A Conception of Organization

## 1. ORIGINS

Dr. Martin Luther King, Jr., arrived in London on 5 December 1964, *en route* to Stockholm where he was to receive the Nobel Peace Prize for leadership of the United States' civil rights movement. Before leaving Britain, Dr. King preached at St. Paul's, spoke on American race relations at a meeting organized by Canon John Collins of Christian Action, and gave interviews to the Press in which he warned that Britain's deteriorating racial problems could become as tragic and intractable as America's unless they were publicized and attacked. On Monday, 7 December, the Negro minister met specially with thirty Commonwealth immigrants and a handful of white sympathizers.[1] After King left, the immigrants decided to found an organization that would speak with a united voice for all coloured people in Britain. Some of those present were leaders of immigrant organizations; some were just concerned about the delicate state of British race relations. Many had not expected to see Dr. King or each other that day.

Although the King meeting served as a catalyst, the impetus for the founding of the then unnamed organization came not from King but from a West Indian Quaker, Marion Glean. Mrs. Glean, a member of the Society of Friends Race Relations Committee and warden of William Penn House, was the founder of the Campaign Against Racial Discrimination's only direct lineal ancestor, a small organization called Multi-Racial Britain. To Mrs. Glean the political, social, and economic problems of the immigrant in Britain were similar to those of their relatives in Africa, Asia, and the Caribbean. Immigrants had to overcome the 'élitist' policies of Britain, much as the colonized had to overcome the autocratic policies of the colonizer. From her Quaker convictions came a religious commitment to equality and a belief in the efficacy and legitimacy of non-violent direct action. In past years, she had been active in the Campaign for Nuclear Disarmament and the Committee of 100.[2]

During the months before King's visit, she had been deeply concerned about the worsening racial situation that culminated in Patrick Gordon Walker's defeat at Smethwick. The Smethwick campaign underlined two aspects of British race relations which she found particularly disturbing. First, liberal elements within British society had been unable to prevent the passage of the discriminatory Commonwealth Immigrants Act of 1962 and had, in her view, failed to promote the interests of coloured newcomers.[3] Second, the disorganization of existing immigrant groups made it difficult to combat increasing prejudice and discrimination.[4]

Mrs. Glean's concern was shared by Theodore Roszak, the recently appointed editor of *Peace News*. As an American, Roszak was accustomed to a closer link between the peace movement and those active in civil rights. He was disturbed by the pattern of discrimination in Britain which could lead to the stark conditions prevalent in America's Northern industrial cities. In the weeks before the general election, he ran a series of statements from immigrant leaders which answered the question, 'Is Race an Issue?'. Mrs. Glean, in her article, suggested that the problem would only be seen from the proper perspective—as a struggle for equality, not a debate over the necessity of immigration controls—when those who suffered discrimination protested publicly.

Following the general election, Mrs. Glean got in touch with Alan Lovell and Michael Randle, pacifists and former members of the Committee of 100 who were closely associated with *Peace News*. They had seen her article and were eager to help found an organization that would be predominantly immigrant in membership. Mrs. Glean then contacted several other friends who had written for the radical weekly, among them Ranjana Ash (an active member of the Movement for Colonial Freedom), C. L. R. James (West Indian author and critic), and Barry Reckford (West Indian playwright and actor). These people in conjunction with Randle and Roszak came together informally in the group called Multi-Racial Britain. Neither the white nor coloured members of M.R.B. were directly connected with the immigrant communities through immigrant organizations, although Glean, Ash, and James were friendly with many immigrant leaders. Rather, the founders of M.R.B. were active in organizations and causes on the left wing of British politics.

Despite Mrs. Glean's generalized desire to involve immigrants and immigrant organizations, no real attempts were ever made. Meetings and seminars were held, issues discussed. But M.R.B. was essentially a forum for debate; it never expanded. The only action taken by the group was a hurriedly organized lobby of Parliament to oppose the extension of the Commonwealth Immigrants Act of 1962. The failure of the lobby demonstrated to the coloured members of M.R.B. that the contacts made by Lovell and Randle in their work with C.N.D. and the Committee of 100 could not be transferred to another group.

Towards the end of November, as Multi-Racial Britain limped forward, Bayard Rustin, the American civil rights leader and strategist, came to London to help plan Martin Luther King's visit. Rustin, a conscientious objector during the Second World War, had known Michael Randle from the British Peace Movement,[5] and through Randle was put in touch with Marion Glean. They agreed that the base of a British anti-discrimination organization should be broadened by using the drawing power of King. They also decided that King should meet with 'black faces'.[6] Randle and Roszak were in agreement with Rustin and Mrs. Glean that the new movement, however nebulous its form for the moment, should be led and controlled by immigrants, although given support by whites.

Yet because of confusion about who was responsible for inviting immigrants, plans for the meeting were not carried out. When King arrived in London on Saturday, 5 December, it was left to Mrs. Glean to gather people together within forty-eight hours for a Monday morning discussion. As a result of the last minute arrangements, many people outside London could not be reached or could not come. The London influence, which would necessarily have been strong, was thus especially marked. None the less, the narrow bounds of Multi-Racial Britain had been stretched and more organizations were represented. In addition to members of C.N.D., the Committee of 100, and the Movement for Colonial Freedom, there were members from the Indian Workers' Association, Southall, the Standing Conference of West Indian Organizations, London Region, the West Indian Student Union, the British Caribbean Association, Anti-Apartheid, the National Federation of Pakistani Associations, and the Council of African Organizations. Also present were prominent immigrants like Dr. David Pitt, a West

Indian G.P. who had run as a Labour candidate in Hampstead in the 1959 general election, was on the Executive of the London Labour party, and sat as a member of the Greater London Council.

At the Hilton Hotel, King and Rustin urged the group of coloured immigrants to oppose any discriminatory legislation and to put pressure on the Government for sound policies by uniting in effective protest. As King said the next day in a B.B.C. interview:

I think it is necessary for the coloured population in Great Britain to organize and work through meaningful non-violent direct action approaches to bring these issues to the forefront of the conscience of the nation wherever they exist. You can never get rid of a problem as long as you hide the problem, as long as you complacently adjust yourself to it.[7]

During the meeting, King did not exhort the immigrants directly; he merely asked questions about the racial situation in Britain. But, as he drew analogies between Britain and America using an evangelical style with elaborate metaphors, his language and the inherent drama of the U.S. civil rights movement had the effect that Marion Glean had wanted.[8] An *ad hoc* committee which would serve as the nucleus for an umbrella organization to co-ordinate the anti-discrimination efforts of organizations in the immigrant communities was formed by a group of people who had come together mainly out of curiosity and who were not unanimously in favour of creating a militant civil rights organization modelled after certain American groups ('militant' meaning at this time a group willing to undertake protests through direct action).

At the second formal meeting of the C.A.R.D. nucleus—held on 20 December at Marion Glean's house and attended by eighteen people—only Michael Randle was white.[9] He and the seventeen immigrants—including four from the Standing Conference of West Indian Organizations and two from the Indian Workers' Association, Southall—established subcommittees for policy, finances, and the legislative campaign, after a long and confused debate about directions in which the organization should move. The last subcommittee was to 'investigate the areas that are available to us in the mounting of a major campaign to present to the British government and people our views on the type of anti-discrimination bill that is needed in Britain'.[10] It was given the only specific task because the need for legislation was clear to the founders, because the Government was planning to introduce a Bill of its own, and because those present could not agree on other policies.

At the next full meeting, held on 10 January 1965, the name of the organization—the Campaign Against Racial Discrimination—was officially adopted. Thirty-three people attended this meeting, with about one-third representing immigrant groups. London was still dominant, and about a sixth of those present were white. One of the Englishmen attending was Anthony Lester, a young barrister who had been educated at Cambridge and Harvard Law School, and was an acquaintance of Ted Roszak. Lester had been on a Society of Labour Lawyers subcommittee which had been drafting anti-discrimination legislation for the National Executive of the Labour party. He was critical of the committee's final report on the grounds that the proposals were too narrow in scope and potentially ineffectual in enforcement.[11] He had also been to several meetings of Multi-Racial Britain, and because of a trip to the United States during the dramatic summer of 1964 and his experience teaching coloured students at night school in London, was personally concerned about the formation of an anti-discrimination group.

The main task of the meeting was to hear the initial reports of the subcommittees, adopt a set of aims and objects, and choose an Executive Committee *pro tem*.[12] In voting for E.C., David Pitt and Marion Glean received the highest number of votes. The other six members were London intellectuals who, with one exception, had not been active in existing immigrant organizations. Following Pitt and Glean in the voting were Richard Small, a law student, aid to C. L. R. James, and former officer in the West Indian Student Union; Gurmukh Singh, member of the Committee of 100 and a researcher at the University of London; Selma James, the white wife of C. L. R. James; Anthony Lester; Dr. Ranjana Ash; and Autar Dhesi, a factory worker and member of the Southall Indian Workers' Association (who held a graduate degree from an Indian university and during the spring of 1966 left London to become a lecturer at the University of Leeds).[13]

During this meeting, as at the earlier one, there was sharp debate over the question of how far the new organization should cooperate with existing organizations and institutions in British society. This was not a debate between black and white, and it was not very well focused. There was general distrust of the Labour party because of its decision to extend the Commonwealth Immigrants Act and because it had failed to make clear the need for strong anti-discrimination legislation. Patrick Gordon Walker, after his defeat by Peter Griffiths at Smethwick in the autumn, was trying to secure a seat in Parliament in the Leyton by-election and people were concerned about whether C.A.R.D. should take a stand in favour of a political party during the campaign. In the course of the discussion Marion Glean argued against working closely with the Labour party and the trade unions.[14] David Pitt, while not suggesting direct co-operation with the Labour party, asked for the enlistment of allies among the more sympathetic elements of British society.[15]

Despite the dispute over the question of co-operation, the members were able to adopt a set of aims and objects. C.A.R.D. was:

To struggle for the elimination of all racial discrimination against coloured people in the United Kingdom.

To struggle for the elimination of all forms of discrimination against all other minority groups in the United Kingdom.

To be concerned about the struggle of oppressed people everywhere.

To seek to co-ordinate the work of organizations already in the field and to act as a clearing-house for information about the fight against discrimination in Britain.

To oppose all racially discriminatory legislation or that inspired by racial prejudice, for example, the Commonwealth Immigrants Act of 1962.

To work for the ratification of the United Nations Bill of Human Rights by the Government of Great Britain.[16]

The members of C.A.R.D. decided to postpone the national founding convention until July. C.A.R.D., it was felt, must prove itself through activities before seeking formal recognition from Commonwealth immigrants and British sympathizers. The conception of the organization was still to be worked out.

The image of C.A.R.D. that emerges from an outline of the first days is of an organization that developed haphazardly around one idea: opposition to racial discrimination in Great Britain. Those involved in C.A.R.D. at the outset brought to the organization a number of models from their own experience with other organizations. Perhaps model is too elegant and sophisticated a word. They were familiar with the mistakes, achievements, and experiences of left-wing organizations and civil rights groups in both Britain and the United States. This knowledge naturally influenced their thinking about the type of organization that was to develop—and the problems to avoid. Contradictory strains were clearly present.

For example, the efforts of American Negroes to secure equal rights through public demonstrations served as an inspiration for many who attended the initial meetings, especially those engaged in direct action through C.N.D. Yet to a number of immigrant leaders the prospect of public demonstrations in Britain was un-thinkable—immigrants would not march, the country would not approve. A similar ambivalence centred around the idea of a mass organization. Many admired the capability of C.N.D. to induce large numbers of people to demonstrate publicly against nuclear armaments. Yet there was a feeling that a yearly demonstration, no matter how large the number of participants, would not serve the needs of a developing, ongoing organization.

No one put down systematically how their past experience influenced their thinking about goals, strategies, structure, func-tions, organizational procedures, or mistakes to be avoided. It is difficult to make a point-by-point comparison of the various shades of opinion; people's thoughts were not that coherent. In the early stages of policy formation C.A.R.D. heard echoes of C.N.D.; the Committee of 100; the trade unions (both in terms of centralizing the power of numerous union locals in a large federation and creating the independent, grass-roots organizations of the shop stewards); the American civil rights movement (ranging from the more militant Congress for Racial Equality and the Student Non-violent Coordinating Committee to the more moderate National Association for the Advancement of Coloured People—including its legal action subsection—and the Urban League); Quaker pacifism, direct action, and non-violence; anti-imperialism (repre-sented in such groups as the Movement for Colonial Freedom and Anti-Apartheid); a variety of more generalized political beliefs ranging leftward from orthodox Labour party reform thinking all the way to Maoist doctrine.

These perspectives, especially when put forward by strong per-sonalities, were not very compatible, even though all strongly opposed discrimination. At the outset, those involved in the organization were predominantly professionals—intellectual, know-ledgeable about left-wing, radical politics (and often active in them), searching for a new cause now that nuclear disarmament was no longer seen as so important an issue. Sympathetic with the problems of immigrants, many members of the new group, including the coloured ones, did not have direct contact with the working-class Pakistani or Indian or West Indian. There was a propensity for argumentation and discussion. As a variegated coalition, hastily assembled, C.A.R.D. was to work out its idea of organization—the group's structure, function, aims, alliances, emphasis—at the same time that it undertook the practical tasks of beginning operations and building an organization. This put a severe strain on those who were trying to perform concrete tasks in the moments they could spare from their occupations.

## 2. TOWARDS A CONCEPTION OF ORGANIZATION

In January, the Campaign Against Racial Discrimination began regular activities by choosing a set of officers. In a vote among its members, the Executive Committee selected David Pitt as chairman; Victor Page (a West Indian dentist who had been co-opted), treasurer; Ranjana Ash, recording secretary; Selma James, organizing secretary; Richard Small, press officer; Anthony Lester, chairman of the legal subcommittee. The E.C. itself was enlarged by seven members during the new few weeks. A place reserved for the Standing Conference of West Indian Organizations was taken by that group's vice-chairman, Mrs. Frances Ezzreco; another, reserved for a Pakistani, was filled by Allam Ir Kabir, a critic, author, and member of East Pakistan House. There were five co-options. Page, Hamza Alavi (a businessman, author, and member of the National Federation of Pakistani Associations), and Kojo Amoo-Gottfried (past president of the Council of African Organizations) were immigrants. Nicholas Deakin (at the time assistant director of the 'Survey of Race Relations') and Roy Shaw (business executive, C.N.D. member, and former manager of David Pitt's Hampstead parliamentary campaign) were also included at Pitt's suggestion to further broaden C.A.R.D.'s membership, to attract liberal Englishmen to the organization (and, in Shaw's case, to inject organizational skill into C.A.R.D.).

During the first month of C.A.R.D.'s operations, the legal subcommittee formulated legislative proposals. In addition to Lester and some white friends of his who were lawyers, the committee included two West Indian law students, Richard Small and Fitzroy Bryant, both of the West Indian Student Union. When the legal subcommittee's suggestions were presented to the Executive Committee, there was sharp disagreement. The legal group had unanimously recommended conciliation machinery as the first stage in the enforcement of an anti-discrimination law, following practices in other countries. Criminal sanctions would be a last resort. Some members of the Executive wanted C.A.R.D. to urge an immediate criminal penalty for any infraction of the law. It was decided to place the question before the full C.A.R.D. membership. At this time the E.C. and the subcommittees were responsible to a monthly meeting of members. These meetings, often conducted in London's Conway Hall with a mixed audience and lengthy, noisy debates, were a prominent feature of C.A.R.D. until it became a delegates organization at the national founding convention in July.[17] At a heated general meeting held on 7 February 1965, Lester and Small held sway. Conciliation machinery which they supported as the most effective means of enforcement was narrowly approved, and a series of resolutions embodying C.A.R.D.'s legislation proposals were passed. The first said simply: 'CARD is opposed to all forms of racial discrimination and calls for legislation as one means of fighting it.'[18]

The passage of the resolutions at the membership meeting and the approval of another, similar resolution several weeks later, at a public meeting announcing a campaign to petition Parliament for adequate legislation, firmly committed C.A.R.D. to the shaping of public policy. The public meeting, held on 20 February, was called not only to affirm C.A.R.D.'s support for broad anti-discrimination laws but to launch the organization into British politics. The presence of Colin Jordan stalking the corridors outside Friends' House and the sight of National Socialists being forceably ejected from the floor by burly stewards amidst the glare of flash-bulbs caused great excitement, ensured unity behind the legislative proposals, and strengthened the resolve of the fledgling organization.[19]

The original members of C.A.R.D. were unanimous in their agreement about the necessity of legislation as one of the first steps in combating discrimination. Less clear than the function of changing public policy through the assumption of a pressure group role, but no less necessary in the view of most C.A.R.D. members, was the development of an organizational structure that would involve immigrants. This would help C.A.R.D. in fulfilling its pressure group function by demonstrating that C.A.R.D. in some sense 'represented' immigrants and could command their allegiance and support. Such mobilization would give C.A.R.D. power, although the nature of that power or how such power was to be used was problematical. Other more specific functions were necessarily unclear. The means of combating racial discrimination were numerous; the task of co-ordination, unification, and stimulation, vague. The desire to create an organization to an extent preceded any precise delineation of its functions. Here, the influence of the Student Non-violent Coordinating Committee, transmitted especially by Marion Glean and Selma James, was felt. A crucial part of the informal credo of this American civil rights organization during the first part of the decade was the reluctance to impose programmes devised by leaders on the members of the organization: 'the people are to decide'.[20] Thus, for some, only when C.A.R.D. had been able to gain the support of the mass of immigrants could it begin to evolve specific functions under the general aim of combating discrimination. C.A.R.D.'s job was to encourage immigrants to tell C.A.R.D. what problems they had and wanted solved. But in the months that followed the legal proposals and resolutions, despite the concern that working-class immigrants be given a large voice in the creation of C.A.R.D., the founders were involved in continuous discussion about organization which was at times angry, at times agonizing.[21]

The main formal record of the developing conception of organization is found in a series of 'Statements of Future Work' prepared in April by Selma James, Marion Glean, Ranjana Ash, and Nicholas Deakin; also, in three different drafts of a 'Summary of Future Work' statement ultimately distributed at the founding convention in July; and in an essay on the C.A.R.D. constitution prepared by Hamza Alavi.

The main problem delineated in the 'Future Work' statements was how to build an organization and movement to represent immigrants in Britain: what form the movement would take; what would bring it into being; what would sustain it; who would direct it. It was not precisely what the formal C.A.R.D. structure would be, although considerations about it were intimately connected to any answer to the preceding questions. Nor was it a discussion of what functions C.A.R.D. would perform. Nor, most importantly (and most surprisingly), was it an analysis of the kind of power C.A.R.D. would try to acquire. The need for a good framework of laws was clear, but beyond that, the banner of anti-discrimination activities was followed by all with little differentiation of the meaning of the phrase. The development of the organization was paramount.

In an optimal situation, the leaders of an organization like C.A.R.D. would base its aims on a detailed assessment of the situation facing the people they were hoping to serve. If the main object of the organization was to end discrimination, for example, then it would presumably be necessary to understand the causes, incidence, and effects of discrimination before adopting a strategy to deal with it. If the unification, organization, mobilization of the immigrant community was desired (a community as varied and fragmented as that existing in Great Britain), then one would want to understand the structure, attitudes, responses, expectations, and leadership of the various components.

In the first six months of 1964, lacking time and information and trying to obey the confusing and contradictory lessons of the past, C.A.R.D. members were unable to theorize very acutely about the form that a movement to 'mobilize' immigrants of three nationalities would take. Such suggestions as did emerge during the discussion of organization were often inconsistent and blurred, ignoring the implications for necessary functions and the means of cohesion. They can be summarized as follows:

C.A.R.D. could:
1. Arouse the political consciousness of immigrants and define a set of immigrant interests without establishing formal relations between nationality groupings or particular organizations.
2. Establish an organization of organizations by:
   winning the support of existing immigrant organizations and co-ordinating their anti-discrimination activities;
   winning the support of existing immigrant groups and directing and stimulating their activities;
   winning the support of sympathetic British organizations in combination with the above.
3. Establish a mass movement:
   either by appealing through immigrant organizations to their membership (implying that national C.A.R.D. could ask for support from these individuals);
   or by developing individual membership in the national organization.
4. Establish local C.A.R.D. groups, comprised predominantly of local C.A.R.D. members, as part of a national C.A.R.D. structure.
5. Establish an organization that was a combination of 2–4.

Each of the various memoranda began with an awareness of the need for conceptual clarity. Each made an apostrophe to the lack of information that bedeviled the writers. And each mentioned the need for careful planning and careful thought to deal with complex problems and many-faceted communities.[22] The C.A.R.D. 'theorists' agreed on the following points:

First, they believed that the basic premise for operations should be that C.A.R.D. would 'mobilize the coloured community on its own behalf' and 'unify the immigrants' groups themselves'.[23] Key phrases and words like 'mobilize', 'on its own behalf', and 'unify' were not further defined or discussed beyond their single sentence usage, although Marion Glean warned that: 'We must not . . . take it for granted that unity will come, that it will be easy to achieve, or even that identity of interests breeds respect.'[24]

Second, they believed that C.A.R.D.'s essential task in unifying and mobilizing was to establish lines of communication to the *immigrant communities*. For Marion Glean this meant a survey of the organizations in the various communities, joint entertainment and cultural activities, a conference of writers and artists. Mrs. James urged that C.A.R.D. prepare a pamphlet, publish a news-letter, organize public meetings, and hold a round-table conference with existing immigrant organizations.

Third, they felt that C.A.R.D. must work closely with the existing *immigrant organizations* and establish 'firm links' with them. There was a general belief that C.A.R.D. had a great deal to learn from these groups about anti-discrimination work and that C.A.R.D. 'must find out from them how they would like us to coordinate our work with theirs'.[25]

Fourth, they agreed that C.A.R.D. must build up support among the mass of *immigrant workers*. As Selma James wrote: 'Ours is a new organization which is attempting to involve new people, some who never (or only at work) have been involved not only in organizations, but in the life of the country.'[26] Glean, Ash, and James also made a corollary point: C.A.R.D. should be an organization directed by immigrants.

We must always be aware that what the coloured community which suffers discrimination wants for itself and its organization is not easy to discover. It is easier to act for, rather than with and through the coloured community. This memo has rejected acting for, and is proposing to act through and with.[27]

We must be willing to *share* our initiative with the man in the street.

This must be *his* cause. Leadership should be as light as is compatible with organization.[28]

Fifth, they felt that C.A.R.D. should be broadly based and should bring in a wide variety of organizations sympathetic towards those who opposed racial discrimination. C.A.R.D. could encompass people from different political parties, holding different political philosophies. Racialism was the enemy and 'C.A.R.D.'s standpoint must be broad and flexible enough to unify heterogeneous elements'.[29]

Sixth, although C.A.R.D. should in one capacity act as a pressure group, they believed it must be a pressure group arising from the immigrant community. The basic criterion of C.A.R.D.'s development should be the extent to which C.A.R.D. could gain the confidence of large numbers of immigrants. By this standard the success or failure of the organization should be judged.

Seventh, until adequate legislation banning racial discrimination in places of public accommodations, employment, housing, and credit facilities was passed, they felt C.A.R.D. should work to alleviate the burdens of discrimination. This would occur through seeking information about discriminatory situations, publicizing them, and negotiating with those who practised discrimination. Marion Glean strongly urged that, when necessary, direct action techniques like picketing, sit-ins, and economic boycotts be used to solve problems of discrimination. She warned that law was a 'slow and conservative' process, that C.A.R.D. needed to develop strong communities of immigrants, that it should not become so concerned with legal problems that it failed to create a strong organization and solve the real problems of immigrants. Drawing an analogy from the United States she argued:

CORE (The Congress of Racial Equality) and SNICK [*sic*] (The Student Non-violent Coordinating Committee) were revolts against the old coloured, legalistic bourgeoisie of the NAACP (The National Association for the Advancement of Coloured People). . . . It would be a pity if CARD became the NAACP equivalent in Britain.[30]

The authors of these memoranda were people outraged by discrimination in Britain. They were not experienced organizers; they lacked contact with immigrant workers, local communities, and many immigrant organizations. Their ideas were only tentative gropings and it is fruitless to criticize them for lack of rigour or foresight. But it is important in understanding C.A.R.D.'s evolution to know on what implicit and potentially contradictory assumptions their vague desire for a movement was based. They assumed:

That the immigrant 'worker' would respond to a request to rise and oppose discrimination.

That the immigrants would want to participate in organizational and anti-discriminatory activities.

That the existing organizations understood the 'problems' at local level in some detail and were engaged in a 'battle' (a recurring metaphor) to eradicate those 'problems'.

That the existing immigrant organizations actually represented or could influence masses of immigrants.

That the desire to have immigrants participate in and, to an extent, direct the affairs of C.A.R.D. could be organizationally reconciled with the desire to let the immigrant organizations give C.A.R.D. the lead.

That C.A.R.D. should not do any direct organizing in communities in an attempt to establish local C.A.R.D. groups because it would antagonize existing immigrant organizations which would be doing the same kind of work anyway.

Of all these assumptions, the most fervently held was the belief in the need for C.A.R.D. to be a federal structure, working through already existing immigrant organizations. The extreme sensitivity about existing immigrant organizations is shown in the 'Future Work Summary Memorandum' in the section proposing a conference in London to explain C.A.R.D.'s role and dispel 'present feelings of uncertainty' among immigrant groups.[31] Promising to learn and assist, the Memorandum's author felt obliged to make clear that C.A.R.D. would restrict its activities to anti-discrimination work, looking to immigrant groups 'to play a major part in determining C.A.R.D.'s policy', and expecting those groups to 'take an active part in all of C.A.R.D.'s work'.

Beneath the professions of faith in the efficacy of immigrant organizations to provide a source of strong support for C.A.R.D. was the fact that for people like Ranjana Ash and Selma James ties existed with at least two immigrant groups. Mrs. Ash was closely in touch with the Indian Workers' Association, Great Britain, and Mrs. James with the Standing Conference of West Indian Organizations, London Region. They were both eager to have these organizations, which were run by people whom they knew, join C.A.R.D.

Richard Small's belief in the need for the support of immigrant groups was based partly on his past experience and contact with Standing Conference, but he, like the others, while ready to admit the possible deficiencies of the existing organizations, felt loyal to them and believed that C.A.R.D. should first try to help them develop as a means of furthering its own growth. He wanted a flexible approach.[32]

To Hamza Alavi, to work with the immigrant organizations was to choose one of the horns of a dilemma. He felt that it was 'perhaps too early to hope that an organization can be brought into existence in which the entire rank and file of the immigrant communities take part directly'. Relationships with existing organizations were vital to building a mass base since a mass campaign could only be conducted with the help of 'progressive leadership'.[33] He was aware too that merely having immigrant organizations come into C.A.R.D. did not mean that there would be effective participation, co-operation, or organizational evolution. Yet, since it was necessary to avoid antagonizing immigrant leaders, it was felt that C.A.R.D. initiatives in immigrant communities would have to be forestalled out of deference to the existing leadership.[34]

Additionally there was emphasis on the belief that immigrants of three different nationalities could be brought into a multiracial group because of the discrimination in British society. Oppressive patterns of behaviour would give common cause to Pakistanis, Indians, and West Indians and serve to unify them. A number of other ideas or metaphors were loosely mentioned by C.A.R.D. members as a means of creating cohesion among immigrants and raising political consciousness. Besides offering relief from discrimination, C.A.R.D. might try to engage immigrants and immigrant organizations by promoting equality, using this 'idea' as a form of appeal; securing freedom from repression, joining people together through the promise of conflict with oppressors (however vaguely defined); stressing the unity of the working classes— clearly not a strategy which would appeal to immigrants exclusively, but an important one since the vast majority of immigrants were workers; fighting anti-colonialism, posing British society with its pattern of discrimination as an analogue to the pre-independence days in the home country; stressing colour unity, establishing unity by developing and utilizing colour consciousness; citing cultural excellence and uniqueness, emphasizing the community of the East or the spirit of the Caribbean; appealing to national loyalty;

promising participation in the organization, promoting intra-organizational democracy, securing direct involvement of the individual immigrant; promising the provision of welfare services, the development of economic power, and the development of electoral power. All these appeals would have implications for the kind of organization to be developed; yet none of these 'images' were systematically developed into strategies for joining the immigrants or gaining power; none were used, that is, as the premise from which a coherent conception of C.A.R.D. could be developed.

## 3. ACTIVITIES: THE PARLIAMENTARY LOBBY

The concurrent discussions about the development of the organization and about its activities were both characterized by an uneasy consensus. During the six months from the adoption of the C.A.R.D. name on 10 January 1965 to the founding convention in late July, C.A.R.D. was active in two areas only: lobbying for amendments to the Race Relations Bill and building up the organization. The first task, as suggested above, had been sanctioned even before work began on the second. During the spring of 1965, the Government was planning to introduce legislation which banned discrimination in public places and outlawed inflammatory racial literature and speech. The enforcement of the Bill's anti-discrimination sections was likely to be accomplished by criminal sanctions. The Bill was not introduced until 7 April, but C.A.R.D. members had correctly predicted that it would not be adequate in two important respects: scope and means of enforcement. The proposals approved by C.A.R.D. urged extension of the law to housing, employment, insurance, and credit facilities and asked for a change in the method of enforcement so that criminal sanctions were only used as a last resort following conciliation efforts, a civil action, and a contempt order from the final court.

The actual lobbying operation will be discussed in Chapter Four, but it is important to note that except for some debates in the Executive Committee in January about technical legal questions, C.A.R.D., in subcommittee, on the Executive Committee, and at a mass membership meeting, approved the legislative proposals and tacitly accepted the need for lobbying activities. Throughout the founding period much time was spent by David Pitt, Anthony Lester, the Legal Committee members, and Richard Small as press officer, in putting C.A.R.D.'s views to the Government and the public. Letters and a summary of the C.A.R.D. proposals were sent to every M.P.; deputations and letters were sent to Cabinet Ministers, the Attorney-General, and the Prime Minister;[35] committee sessions attended; members briefed.

Besides the formal lobbying at Westminster, in Whitehall, and on Fleet Street, a petition campaign was started to 'muster enough support to convince the Government to amend their proposals to our requirements'.[36] Twenty thousand forms were printed and in the optimistic first days a target of one million signatures was set. The idea for the petition was essentially Pitt's. To him it served two functions: it would be palpable pressure in support of C.A.R.D.'s legislative proposals and it would allow C.A.R.D. to canvass at the local level and make itself known to immigrants. Pitt's basic conception of C.A.R.D.'s structure was that it would be 'not unlike the Labour Party'.[37] The organization would have both group and individual affiliations and, like a political party, would canvass its constituents to discover grievances which would then be funnelled back to a national executive for the necessary action. Roy Shaw, the manager of Pitt's Hampstead campaign and a Labour party ally, was appointed chairman of the Petition Committee.

Others in C.A.R.D. were less enthusiastic about the proposal. It seemed an indirect way to build up the organization. Some felt that there were overtones of an Easter March: gathering signatures constituted 'mass activity' but it was not an effective means of rooting C.A.R.D. in the local communities or pressing for legislation. Hamza Alavi wanted to use the petition in a compromise fashion to help establish the organizations. He thought that if C.A.R.D. organized a series of meetings around the country with a variety of speakers, one could attract local immigrants and immigrant organizations and develop the nucleus of a C.A.R.D. coalition in various localities by bringing in a variety of people on the pretext of supporting the petition.[38] But an effective linking of the petition campaign and development of the C.A.R.D. structure never took place. Most members of the E.C. tolerated the campaign; they neither supported nor opposed it—it was a concrete suggestion which might have some value. At that stage, in early February, people like Ranjana Ash, Selma James, Marion Glean, and Richard Small, those most vocal about the need for local development, 'didn't have any other set of proposals that the Executive Committee could act on'.[39]

Petition forms were distributed through immigrant groups and other interested organizations; teams canvassed in neighbourhoods.[40] By June the campaign had fallen 985,000 signatures short. The 15,000 names collected were never presented to the Government because the number was so small.[41] The campaign failed partly because the C.A.R.D. leadership was only lukewarm about the project and did not want to devote much of their own time to its successful implementation (Pitt and Shaw were themselves desultory in their efforts), and partly because the C.A.R.D. office was not efficient in co-ordinating efforts. Nor were the immigrant organizations themselves very dedicated in their solicitations. It would not be the last time that C.A.R.D. relations with other groups would be frustrating and unfruitful.

Other than the petition campaign, no C.A.R.D. activities required major policy decisions. Money was raised; individual membership sought sporadically (400 people had joined by the end of June); affiliations from organizations solicited (twenty-eight by June agreed to support C.A.R.D.'s aims and objects); speeches made; meetings held; C.A.R.D. explained to the Press; support given to striking Indian and Pakistani workers at Courtauld's plant in Preston; a long memorandum on 'Racial Discrimination in Great Britain' prepared for the Commonwealth Prime Ministers Conference in June; plans for the July convention formulated; a constitution written and discussed.[42] On none of these questions was there any serious disagreement. No real debates arose over the allocation of C.A.R.D.'s meagre resources.[43]

## 4. ISSUES: THE VERBAL WAR

Yet for all the apparent agreement, the first six months developed into a 'nightmare situation'.[44] Meetings and discussions were marked by severe factionalism and bitter infighting. Personal attacks became commonplace on the Executive Committee. The mass membership meetings were often undermined by embarrassing acrimony between members of the E.C. People began to do their work outside the Executive, unwilling to raise issues and questions for fear of endless doctrinal battles. One group accused another of wanting a complete breakdown of the organization.[45] In a counter-accusation, the second group charged that the first was doing everything possible to block and frustrate initiatives.[46] By the month before the founding convention, the organization was dead-locked. As a former E.C. member said: 'The Executive Committee became a horrible bottleneck. Meetings were exercises in frustra-tion.'[47]

Depending on whose perspective one adopted, the organization was rent by a host of divisions; rhetorical dichotomies were in-voked on numerous occasions. To the members of the effective working majority—Pitt, Lester, Deakin, Shaw, Singh, Alavi, and Page—C.A.R.D. was split between the realists, who wanted legis-lation as a first (although by no means only) step towards fighting discrimination, and the romantics, who were going to raise up the coloured masses with a clarion call; between those who favoured meaningful reform and those who wanted a total, immediate (and impossible) restructuring of society; between pragmatic idealists and impractical ideologues; between those who wanted to take advantage of existing institutions and the structure of power in society to seek social change and those who wanted to frustrate existing institutions to create an atmosphere 'for revolution'; between flexible liberal-radical reformers and rigid doctrinaire adherents to a variety of Marxist-Leninist philosophies.

To the dissidents—Small, Ash, James, Glean,[48] Ezzreco—C.A.R.D. was divided between the militants and the moderates; between those who favoured the mass approach and those who were élitists; between those who aimed for non-partisan inde-pendence and those who were in collusion with the Labour party and had ambitions to rise within its ranks; between those who were in sympathy with the working class and those who were middle class; between black radicals and white liberals (if a coloured person voted with the working majority he demonstrated 'white liberal' attitudes); between those who favoured full participation of the immigrant in the organization's decision-making processes and those who favoured bureaucratic centralism; between those who sought major institutional and structural change in British society as a concomitant of anti-discrimination work and those who were piecemeal reformers, interested only in tinkering with the existing social and political relations; and, for some, between those who were anti-colonialists (anti-imperialists) and those who were paternalistic neo-colonialists.

Yet, in a sense, these emotive dualisms were chimera, relics from past battles and other struggles, the baggage of former conflicts between those on the 'left wing' and those in 'the left centre' of

British politics, or of conflicts between various civil rights groups in the United States. In a polarized situation they could be hauled into action like some ancient cannon, loaded and discharged with properly imprecise and bloody effect. The ostensible dichotomies as uttered by both the dissidents and the working majority did not necessarily have much to do with the harsh reality of organizing immigrants nor with the rather simplistic substantive discussions within C.A.R.D. itself.

Among the dissidents, several prominent members were distinctly associated with 'radical, left-wing' politics. Mrs. Glean, as mentioned, was a Quaker, active in C.N.D., and an advocate of non-violent direct action for C.A.R.D. Mrs. Ash was a Marxist and was reportedly a member of the Communist party in Britain. Mrs. James's husband was a Marxist author noted for his social and political writings about the West Indies who had been an International Socialist; both were members of an American socialist group called Facing Reality. Pitt, Lester, Deakin, and Shaw were active Labour party members. Yet these divisions must be qualified. Hamza Alavi, the most systematic Marxist of all members of the C.A.R.D. Executive Committee at this time, was firmly associated with the working majority.[49] So was Gurmukh Singh, a former member of the Committee of 100. And Victor Page, who also voted regularly with the majority, through his associations with a local West Indian group, the Brockley International Friendship Council, might be said to have had the most contact 'with the masses' of any of the Executive at the time. None the less, despite these qualifications, it is critically necessary to understand the general political experience and orientation of the main actors in both factions since they undoubtedly account for much of the vicious factionalism and for the images and rhetoric used to bludgeon the opposition.

Paradoxically, these differences in the context of C.A.R.D. policy-making were very vague. Although there were deep divisions between the two groups in terms of style, rhetoric, and general political belief, these differences were never directly manifested in divisions over specific, explicit proposals for action. The major problems facing C.A.R.D. at the time, as perceived by both factions, were to establish C.A.R.D. in the immigrant communities and to amend the forthcoming Race Relations Bill. Each faction became associated with one of these tasks: the dissidents with developing C.A.R.D. as a group, the working majority with improving the Government's proposed legislation. Each recognized the value of the other's work. Underlying the paradox was a fundamental confusion, in both camps, about what type of power C.A.R.D. was to have and how it was to gain that power.

Yet, for the dissidents the assumption by C.A.R.D. of a pressure group role posed severe problems. Conscious of how powerless coloured immigrants in Britain were, the dissidents at times acknowledged the supreme importance of anti-discrimination laws both as a declaration by the Government that discrimination could not be tolerated and as a means of securing equal opportunities. Yet, at other times, the concept of equal opportunities was viewed with antipathy as a patronizing slogan. Equal opportunities for what? For gaining entrance into a society that was viewed with distrust if not contempt? The dissidents, given their political beliefs, did not want to fight for the elevation of coloured people into the delusory Utopia of middle-class British society. Moreover, how could immigrants get laws passed, since they were, in broad economic and political terms, without power? Being powerless and therefore to an extent dependent on the goodwill and actions of liberal and sympathetic members of the host community caused deep resentment among the dissidents. Both because of their own previous experience and because of their view of the experience of Negroes in the United States and the colonized coloured people in the Third World, they did not want to have to rely on the white man.

Further, they were uncertain whether laws should be changed by protest or by parliamentary politics. Since the immigrants lacked cohesion and organization, parliamentary lobbying was obviously necessary if laws were to be changed. At times the dissidents recognized this, as their general support of C.A.R.D.'s legislative proposals and activities showed.[50] Yet, given their objective of making immigrants a political force, which for some on C.A.R.D. would be the catalyst that could unite the British working classes and bring about 'structural' change, they were not sanguine about parliamentary activities.

Thus, there was a curious ambivalence. Although acknowledging that the aim of legislation was an important one, and lobbying necessary, the dissidents began to see these efforts as in some sense destroying the C.A.R.D. that they wanted to develop. There came to be an opposition in their minds between C.A.R.D.'s function as a pressure group and as founder of 'a grass-roots movement'. They were united in speeches in what they did not like about the pressure group role. They did not want a 'traditional bureaucratic organization run from the top down'; they did not want the immigrants to be given hand-outs; they did not want to hover and orbit around Parliament 'in customary pressure group fashion'.[51] As Richard Small said: 'We didn't want a passive organization with a strong Executive Committee, moving through contacts and winning victories through journalists whom you happen to know.'[52] For a variety of personal and political reasons these people were embittered about the treatment that the immigrants had received in Britain and were prone to angry and acid outbursts against others in C.A.R.D. who seemed at all conciliatory towards or involved with the 'Establishment'.

What the dissidents did want was to root an organization in the immigrant communities, to develop a movement of coloured people, to involve people on their own behalf, to have a group of immigrants that was strong and independent, and could control its own destiny without 'domination' by whites (although not necessarily without white support) and also, given the working-class nature of the immigrant community, without 'domination' by the middle class.[53] United in what they opposed, they were only generally aware of what they sought. And, as noted, they never came to grips with the kind of power that the ideal C.A.R.D. would exercise. On this point, they were strangely silent, unable to articulate much beyond a desire for direct action protest. Although the dissidents were certainly familiar with Marxist analyses of political and social problems, they never expressed clear steps which could be taken to gain economic power or join C.A.R.D. with the working classes. They had no blue-prints, only hopes and a predilection.

The working majority on the other hand was concerned about a concrete and immediate problem. They wanted to build up the C.A.R.D. organization—just as the dissidents wanted the passage of anti-discrimination laws—but they were aware that C.A.R.D. had no power and that allies were needed. They were eager to avoid the mistake of ignoring the chance to take immediate, substantive measures in the policy field. Amending the Government's Bill was a necessary first step in shaping race relations in Britain. It was to the fulfilment of that task that they devoted their energies, responding to the short-term imperatives of the political situation, not to the long-term problem of developing power for C.A.R.D. itself.

Thus, in the course of the spring debates, the function of C.A.R.D. as a pressure group was set by the dissidents in opposition to the need for C.A.R.D. to function as the catalyst for a movement that involved immigrants. A choice between the basic functions was never faced nor was it necessary to face it at this time as a discussion of the issues separating the two groups will indicate. Debates took place both in the Executive Committee and in the membership meetings, and it is important to remember that the working majority only effectively controlled the E.C. The attendance at membership meetings fluctuated and changed. That voting patterns were irregular in these meetings is all one can say with certainty.[54]

Some of the debates were essentially over symbols. For example, at the January meeting that elected the Executive Committee, the question was raised whether the new organization should have as part of its name the phrase 'Campaign for Equality' or 'Campaign Against Discrimination'. Those who were to become dissidents on the Executive argued against some who were to become part of the working majority that the immigrants should not politely show they were for equality, but angrily oppose discrimination. After lengthy and heated discussion which set tempers at the ready, it was decided that immigrants should demonstrate their opposition to the discrimination practised by members of British society.[55]

Similarly there was a bitter debate in the first days about whether C.A.R.D.'s first aim and object should express opposition to prejudice and discrimination directed at all minority groups or just to prejudice and discrimination practised on the basis of colour. To the dissidents this became an extremely important issue: they were fearful that whites and moderates would shy away from forcefully telling British society of the need to combat colour discrimination for fear of alienating liberal opinion. To some of the most sensitive, the desire from whites, particularly Lester, to generalize the aims and objects seemed to confirm their fears.[56]

To Lester, the reasons for having the generalized aim appear first was a matter partly of principle and partly of practicality. He did not want to 'write discrimination into the temporary constitution' and he was concerned about the need for raising funds for C.A.R.D. especially among wealthy Jews in Britain.[57] Since both aims were to appear in the constitution anyway, it clearly was not an issue of great importance, but the hypersensitivity of some coloured people coupled with inexperience and lack of understanding of this sensitivity meant that the issue was seen as an important one, reflecting fundamental positions.

A dispute over the organization's attitude towards the Commonwealth Immigrants Act 1962 seemed to be of more substance. Two questions were involved. First, whether C.A.R.D. should specifically state in its aims and objects opposition to the Act and express a desire for its repeal. Second, whether at the 7 February meeting at which the C.A.R.D. proposals for anti-discrimination legislation were approved, a resolution also should be passed criticizing the 1962 Act.

The dissidents felt strongly that C.A.R.D. should publicly oppose it. It was discriminatory. C.A.R.D. was an organization founded to combat racial discrimination. Therefore it should condemn the Act and demand its repeal. To people like Pitt, Lester, and Deakin, opposition to the Act in January 1965 was pointless. Race was a major consideration in British politics, immigration a most sensitive issue. The Government was not likely to change its policy on immigration from the Commonwealth. They felt that it was better to press for anti-discrimination legislation.[58]

At the first meeting at the Hilton Hotel with Martin Luther King, David Pitt had expressed doubts about the importance of opposing the Act. Yet later the same day at the mass meeting sponsored by Canon Collins, Pitt had spoken out sharply for the repeal of the discriminatory legislation, in keeping with the tone established by King.[59] At later C.A.R.D. meetings, however, when the question about a strongly-worded aim condemning the Act was raised, Pitt resisted its inclusion in the constitution. None the less, despite the chairman's vacillation, those in favour of inclusion were victorious at the 10 January membership meeting.

Despite this victory for the dissidents, at a meeting of the Executive Committee three weeks later, it was decided that a resolution condemning the Commonwealth Immigrants Act 1962 would not be submitted at the membership meeting called to approve C.A.R.D.'s legal proposals. The working majority felt that it would appear contradictory to ask for repeal of legislation at the same time C.A.R.D. was asking for the passage of new laws. It might also be unproductive since it was clear that the Government was in the process of moving to a harsher position on racial questions.[60] To the dissidents, the Executive's action was seen as a retreat, a sop to a reactionary Government, a remote decision taken against the wishes of the membership (tiny though it was). In retrospect, the issue had a high symbolic and emotional content, but was tangential to the major activities and direction of C.A.R.D. The Government's policy probably could not have been altered by a co-ordinated and sustained campaign—which none of the dissidents were proposing—let alone by a single resolution from a small, unknown group. The future lobbying activities of C.A.R.D. in support of the legislative proposals would not have been affected by the resolution. A single statement condemning a Government Act passed among many other legal proposals would probably not have had much effect on an immigrant community which had lived with the discriminatory legislation for three years without taking concerted action, and whose political consciousness did not seem high.

To the dissidents, this issue, while essentially one of posture and therefore in a certain sense insubstantial, was at another level of great importance. They believed that the mass of immigrants were as militantly angry as they were, and as sensitive to the implications of political parry and thrust, and thus they were eager to have C.A.R.D. appear sufficiently tough and uncompromising. In this belief they were undoubtedly influenced by their own friends and the more vocal and radical members of immigrant organizations who attended the monthly meetings and with whom they were in regular contact.

Similarly, the working majority was concerned not to have C.A.R.D. appear too woolly and wild-eyed and, therefore, to be consigned to the nether world of the British political fringe where its advice would not be heeded. Thus they were eager, probably over-eager, to avoid taking any angry rhetorical positions just for the sake of establishing a posture and a tone for the organization.

Much was said at the time about the distinction between militants and moderates in C.A.R.D.—a distinction relevant only in terms of the desire of one group to appear militant,[61] and of the other group to appear moderate (or, more accurately, reasonable, technically proficient, knowledgeable, responsible). These differing desires were based on differing immediate goals—to organize, to amend legislation—and on the expectations that each group had about the people who were central to the achievement of these objectives. The dissidents assumed that the 'immigrant'—few people in these debates differentiated between nationality or community or occupation—was bitter about the harsh treatment he had received in Britain and disillusioned about the promises of the liberal community. This 'immigrant' would respond to a militant stand on the 'issues'. The working majority assumed that those who possessed influence—Ministers, Civil Servants, the Press, M.P.s—would tend to see C.A.R.D. as a fringe group, that any posturing would encourage this tendency, and that, as a result, C.A.R.D.'s credibility would be undermined. Both groups were extremely sensitive as to real or imagined reactions of others outside C.A.R.D.—and relatively insensitive to the attitudes and suspicions of those inside.

The flash-point came in late May. An *Observer* article entitled 'Anatomy of a Lobby' heaped fulsome praise on Anthony Lester for his role in the successful effort to force the Home Secretary to amend his own Bill and substitute conciliation machinery for criminal sanctions as the primary means of enforcing anti-discrimination legislation. 'This is a spectacular victory for Anthony Lester and his co-lobbyists', it trumpeted.[62] The article also suggested, although it did not say so explicitly, that Lester, as a member of the Society of Labour Lawyers, had managed to use C.A.R.D. effectively as a vehicle for publicizing amendments to the Race Relations Bill. Lester had clearly been interviewed by the *Observer*'s anonymous correspondent.

This aroused the fury of the dissidents. Many of the things that they feared seemed substantiated in the pages of one of the country's major papers. Suspicious of the close, clandestine relationships which Lester and his aides had established during the lobbying activities, they discovered that C.A.R.D. was being portrayed as a satellite of the Labour party. Further, they were incensed that the aversion of a major legislative débâcle was being misrepresented as a triumph, one which apparently satisfied immigrants and for which C.A.R.D. could properly accept plaudits. Moreover, Lester had violated a technical and (little-observed) rule established by the Executive Committee stipulating that all interviews should be cleared through Richard Small as press officer. The image of a C.A.R.D. they abhorred had appeared in print; that the report was inaccurate regarding C.A.R.D.'s role was less important.

Fearful that there would be misunderstanding among immigrants generally and more particularly among those people who were attending the C.A.R.D. monthly membership meetings, the dissidents were able to gain the support of some of the working majority and issue a special Executive Committee statement which was distributed at the next general meeting and sent, over David Pitt's signature, to the *Observer*.[63] Deploring the impression given by the article that C.A.R.D. felt any victory had been won by the recent lobbying and that C.A.R.D. was being used 'by a number of groups for their own purposes', the statement went on to say:

We have always said that CARD is not just a new organization but was attempting to build a new kind of organization based on the experiences and ideas of coloured peoples in Britain who will win the support of British people sympathetic to them. But we reject the creation of an organization dominated by British liberals.[64]

Despite Lester's protestations that the article was extremely inaccurate and that he too disapproved of its implications, the breaking-point had been reached.

The situation was further complicated by David Pitt. He had clearly demonstrated his desire to be an M.P.; he had close contacts with the Labour party; and he was also—of all the people on the Executive—the one most wedded to the conception of a centralized organizational structure. He had never liked the inefficient ordeal of the monthly membership meetings, preferring to set policy from the E.C.[65] And he was distrusted by the dissidents because those members co-opted to the C.A.R.D. Executive had been suggested by Pitt and tended to vote with him against the dissidents. Often late to meetings, occasionally stentorian in manner, he was not the person needed to bind over C.A.R.D.'s widening divisions.

After the publication of the *Observer* article, C.A.R.D. effectively came to a standstill. The dissidents did not trust the lead of the working majority. The working majority, many of whom were sympathetic to the general organizational aims of the dissidents, would not follow their uncertain lead down to the grass roots. Personal relationships deteriorated as pejorative epithets were used freely with anger.

Basically, underlying the issue war was a problem that existed for dissident and working majority alike: what to do lacking power, what to do to develop power, what kind of power to develop, and, if power was obtained, how to exercise it. Differing political ideologies, different perceptions of what C.A.R.D.'s immediate priority should be, and abrasive personalities compounded by the absence of an individual leader who could command universal respect were only used, in the end, to avoid confronting the underlying issue. Underneath the bombast and the echoes from past conflicts was the question, not whether to 'organize' immigrants, but how to organize them and for what purposes. How could immigrants be brought into C.A.R.D.? What aspects of the British social and political systems required the existence of a group? How were conditions to be altered by the functioning of such a group?

It was an unformed argument that stemmed from equally nebulous and unformed assumptions about immigrant organizations, work at the community level, and the way that an image of C.A.R.D. would be projected into the immigrant communities. Thus the issues, although not important in a certain substantive sense, should be seen as part of this argument, an argument in which only one side really participated. The dissidents believed implicitly that a radical, political consciousness existed among many immigrants and could be both sparked and harnessed by an uncompromising C.A.R.D. stand. Such a stand would appeal to the immigrant's sense of oppression, and arouse him. This was in keeping with their thinking as outlined in the memoranda on future work. The lines between the groups were thus drawn on issues that affected C.A.R.D.'s image and on rather instinctive guesses as to the level of political consciousness in the immigrant communities and how to appeal to that consciousness. The debate on how to organize never really developed, however, foundering on the brute fact that neither group had much, if any, experience in grass-roots work, in building a movement or a strong organization among people who were strikingly different from those who took to the road in Aldermaston marches. Little effort was made to gain such experience.

Although very little organizing was done in the immigrant communities at the time, any attempt at building an anti-discrimination organization to represent immigrants could have raised real problems of choice: for example, which type of appeal would most effectively bring in the immigrant. Should an organization be built on the desire to fight discrimination; or organized along class lines to fight a structure of housing discrimination which may have a systematic bias not only against coloureds but also against poorer whites? Should organizational unity be based on colour alone, concentrating on the development of pride and independence to counter feelings of apathy or inferiority? Or would the simple provision of welfare services encourage the immigrant to join the organization? Or should the value of participation of immigrants supersede the benefits accruing from the provision of welfare services? This raises the further question of whether one can separate the form and procedures of an organization from what it does. Further, an analysis of the dynamics of community power in a particular locality is vital to the cperations of a local group. That in itself may be a source of deep division within an organization, both as to whether such an analysis should be undertaken at all and in what terms it should be framed. Further, the way of gaining economic or electoral power could be debated. When an organization enters actively into the immigrant communities, these kinds of question have to be faced and substantial conflicts between those who must work at the national level to change public policy and those in contact with the immigrants at the neighbourhood level might well develop. The dissidents, in a rough, imprecise way, raised some of these considerations, which would remain central to the development of C.A.R.D. They wanted sectional power, being concerned about the danger of white influence if the promotional group route was chosen. But they offered few ideas about how political, economic, or cultural strengths could be evolved, shying away from the implications of C.A.R.D.'s powerlessness as a consumer or producer group, yet wary of violent action by the immigrants.

In C.A.R.D.'s formative period, division, polarization, and paralysis came from questions begged and from crude expectations of what would happen, not from questions framed and analyses of what was happening. Such difficulties will always be present in a fast-developing political action group. In a fragile coalition like C.A.R.D., they had particularly destructive effects. The period of sharp disagreement illustrated that in a multiracial, multi-nationality coalition, debilitating factionalism could obstruct the work of the organization even before such work could give rise to divisions based on real choices about the present. For example, the dissidents were all West Indian: they distrusted more established West Indians—Pitt and Page—as well as Asians and Englishmen. But the 'verbal war' did not yet demonstrate that the substantive functions with which each group became associated were incapable of being yoked. It merely avoided the question of power in a confusion of promotional and sectional roles; attacking each other was easier for the two factions than attacking the question of developing influence and facing the reality of powerlessness.

## 5. CONSTITUTION AND CONVENTION: A COMPROMISE STRUCTURE

The symbol of the confusions and contradictions with which C.A.R.D. struggled during the formative period was the constitution. The complicated and unwieldy formal structure represented an effort to embody several different conceptions of organization in one set of rules. The constitution's authors tried to combine provisions for a federal structure—an organization of organizations—with a role for individual mass membership, not necessarily based on the membership of immigrant organizations. It was an attempt to provide a flexible framework for a coalition of undetermined forces. It also tried to reconcile the desire for central control with the need for membership participation in the organization.

The constitution committee[66] did not begin work until mid-March, nearly three months after the first meetings of C.A.R.D. Its models were the constitutions of the Anti-Apartheid Movement, the Movement for Colonial Freedom, the National Council for Civil Liberties, and the American civil rights organizations: a federal structure supported by affiliated organizations. A basic factor distinguished C.A.R.D. from M.C.F., Anti-Apartheid, and the N.C.C.L.: these organizations derived their support from other organizations sympathetic towards the work of the central organization, though engaged in quite different fields of activity. To the C.A.R.D. Executive Committee, however, a large measure of support was to be derived from organizations themselves directly involved in the same field of work. As Hamza Alavi wrote:

CARD's work will be complementary to theirs and will strengthen their work. . . . CARD's organizational structure must lend itself to the task of co-ordination of such work. Wherever possible, CARD should stimulate and support such work rather than try to duplicate it.[67]

To implement the aims and objects[68] of C.A.R.D. there would be three main bodies: the Annual Delegates Conference, the National Council, and the Executive Committee (which would have appropriate subcommittees and a secretariat). Membership was of two main classes: those who belonged through affiliated organizations; individual members.[69]

The annual conference was to have two types of delegate, following from the membership division: representatives from affiliated organizations, the number depending on the size of the organization; individual members. The last category was to be determined by a complicated procedure whereby a number of 'individuals' in a given area, at the initiative of the Executive Committee, would call meetings of the individuals in the 'area' and this group, depending on its size, would send a proportionate number of people to the annual conference. Other individual members, whether they had participated in an area selection committee or not, were allowed to attend and speak at the conference as observers.

The Annual Delegates Conference was presumably the highest policy-making body in C.A.R.D. Its main functions were to elect a C.A.R.D. chairman and a National Council. The N.C. was to meet every three months and was, like the delegates conference, to have two types of membership: fifteen general members nominated and elected at the conference; thirty representative members, three from each of ten types of affiliated organization (African, Arab, Indian, Pakistani, West Indian, interracial, Jewish, trade union, student, and other). Groups in each category could nominate individuals to be elected representative members at the conference.

The National Council, headed by the chairman elected at the annual conference, was from its members to elect a vice-chairman, secretary, and treasurer, all of whom would sit with the chairman on the Executive Committee.[70] It also selected the Executive Committee's other ten members from within its own ranks. The Executive Committee was presumably to carry out the policy of the National Council.

In effect, then, C.A.R.D. was an attempt to combine the various alternative structures suggested in the typology above. This indiscriminate lumping together of forms was in keeping with the most dominant ideas of the working majority whose members—especially Pitt, Lester, and Alavi—had been influential in preparing the constitution.

Pitt had always felt that the primary need of C.A.R.D., given the organization's inevitable lack of power, was to bring together the victims of discrimination and members of the host community who were against discrimination. Following the Labour party model, he wanted group and individual membership. But rather than just having a national executive and an annual conference, the stratagem of a national council was devised to allow more concrete participation both for groups and for individuals. But in Pitt's mind the National Council, although ostensibly the policy-making body of C.A.R.D., would in fact approve policy that the Executive Committee had initiated.[71]

Pitt, Lester, and Alavi were also concerned that the constitution achieve three negative aims. They did not want C.A.R.D. to become London-dominated; white-dominated; or political-party dominated.[72] There was a great fear that C.A.R.D. would become a debating forum for white London intellectuals if it remained a membership organization. One of the reasons for devising the elaborate delegate system, which specified group representation, was to prevent this development. (Political parties were not allowed to affiliate.) Again, at this stage, individuals were more certain about what they wanted to avoid than what they wanted to promote. In one sense, the constitution should have been an anathema to the dissidents. To work properly, C.A.R.D. would have to be an elaborate bureaucracy. The Executive Committee would effectively run the organization since the National Council would only meet four times yearly. And the participation of individual members of the immigrant community was made extraordinarily difficult. It would be cumbersome to call area conferences and send delegates to the annual conference. Besides, individual delegates were only eligible for election to fifteen of the forty-five National Council seats.

Yet, as with other specific proposals made during C.A.R.D.'s early months, the constitution went largely unopposed. Richard Small, who among the dissidents was most knowledgeable about legal drafting, was dismayed when he saw the constitution. He could not understand how C.A.R.D. could function by effectively excluding members from participation in the organization's activities. Yet he did not argue against it before the national convention. There was simply no time. Besides, he could not pose an alternative.[73] 'There should have been a debate', but there was none.[74]

The dissidents, although a single word has been used to describe them, were hardly a united group. Despite mutual allegations of conspiratorial machinations, neither faction had ever really come together to think out a coherent position or to plan a strategy for shaping the organization to their ideas. On the constitution, like other matters, the dissidents made some instinctual assumptions. They hoped that the structure of C.A.R.D. would develop as C.A.R.D. developed and they were not concerned about how the formal structure would shape the activities and success of C.A.R.D. in making contact with the immigrant community. Further, as we have seen, they were themselves hardly clear about how 'immigrants were going to be mobilized on their own behalf'. Thus, given their commitment to the existing immigrant organizations, and given the tension between having, on the one hand, formal participation of these groups in the work of the organization and, on the other, active participation of individual immigrants, they were unhappy about the constitution but not at all sure about how to amend or recast it.

At the national founding convention, held in Conway Hall on 24–25 July 1965, there was very little attempt to change the tentative structure suggested by the constitution committee and approved by the Executive Committee. The convention was attended by 230 individual C.A.R.D. members and 100 delegates or observers from affiliated organizations.[75] After six months of development, C.A.R.D. claimed 400 individual members and thirty-one affiliated organizations.[76] Anyone who was a paid member could vote. During the two-day convention, attendance fluctuated between 200 and 300. There are no precise figures but observers estimated that roughly half present were coloured, and half white.

The major constitutional debate was stimulated by Richard Small who wanted the £1 individual membership fee lowered to five shillings. The dissidents, trying to incorporate their idea of individual immigrant participation in C.A.R.D., felt that the reduction in fees would have the desired effect. The emotions of the past months boiled over and there was bitter disagreement over the issue. Members of the working majority argued that C.A.R.D. would not be able to pay the administrative costs—mailing material and establishing lines of communication—unless there was sufficient income from membership subscriptions. David Pitt argued that a £1 sacrifice was not too much to ask, only further angering the dissidents and their supporters by what they regarded as his callous disregard for the difficult economic position of working-class immigrants. Small's amendment carried and the fee was reduced.

In another attempt to allow participation of individual immigrants, Small tried to incorporate the tentative idea of local C.A.R.D. groups into the constitution. A set of Standing Orders had been prepared by the constitution committee to establish local C.A.R.D. committees, outlining aims and objects, and suggesting a number of general steps that could be taken at the local level against discrimination. The orders were not approved because it was felt that the affiliated organizations would mistake this as a declaration of C.A.R.D.'s intent to usurp their role. Small's last-minute amendments simply gave the National Council the powers to create special C.A.R.D. area representatives or area committees as it deemed necessary.[77]

Beyond these debates, no real questioning of the constitutional structure took place. A gaggle of resolutions was passed.[78] Some condemned Government policy on immigration, others the recently passed Race Relations Bill, others the Department of Education and Science Circular (7/65) which suggested the dispersal of immigrant children from schools with a high colour concentration; some scored all three. Local work was discussed. C.A.R.D.'s proposals to publish a news-letter, to hold regional conferences on subjects of local interest, to act as a central information agency, to act as a co-ordinating body, and through these to establish a base in the coloured communities, were all put forward.

The mood of the convention was one of anger. As one person from Leicester who had not previously been involved in C.A.R.D. activities put it:

What was evident was that there is a new mood of bitterness among immigrants. This came out in speech after speech . . . [people] will be satisfied with nothing less than their full rights. . . . What emerged was the overwhelming feeling that race relations in this country have steadily deteriorated in the last two years. It was clear that the immigrants present at the Conference were not prepared to apologise for their colour or their origins.[79]

These were highly intelligent, sensitive, and well-informed people who were bitter about the shift in the Labour party policies and tired of having the word immigrant equated with the word problem. They resented what seemed to them to be the patronizing language of the Government, official bodies, newspapers, and other mass media. They complained of the unwillingness of officials and official bodies to consult the immigrant communities over measures intended directly for them. And they deeply resented the popular feeling, as they interpreted it, that 'immigrants were people *to* whom you did things, *for* whom you did things, but whom you would never dream of consulting'.[80] Many of these people at the convention, the intellectual immigrants and their white supporters, had a major problem: to transmit their legitimate anger and desire for change to tens of thousands of immigrants who suffered under the humiliations and hardships of discrimination, to bind them together in a movement that could speak with that united voice so desperately sought, in quest of concrete policies that could change the quality of individual lives.

The strongest advocates of grass-roots organization would no longer be active in C.A.R.D. Richard Small, discouraged and dismayed by the events of the past months, decided not to run for the National Council, refusing to sit on the raised platform with the Executive Committee at the convention. Selma James was barely elected to the National Council and failed to be selected for the Executive Committee. Of the dissidents' most articulate and persistent spokesmen, only Ranjana Ash remained. But she resigned as recording secretary and the post of organizing secretary was left unfilled. David Pitt, as chairman, was unrivalled as the leading immigrant on C.A.R.D. and of the Executive and he was the least interested in local C.A.R.D. development.

Yet the tension within C.A.R.D. was broken. With the election of a new National Council and an Executive Committee that was less divided,[81] there was a sense of relief and expectation among C.A.R.D. members.[82] The work of the organization could now proceed unhampered by the long and bitter intra-organizational feuding. Anti-discrimination work and organization building could truly begin.


## 6. A PARLIAMENTARY PRESSURE GROUP?

Only a few days following the national founding convention the press of events again caught up with C.A.R.D. In early August, the Labour Government published a policy statement on *Immigration from the Commonwealth*, commonly referred to as the White Paper. The second part of the document discussed future immigration control policy. It proposed stiffening the already discriminatory measures embodied in the Commonwealth Immigrants Act 1962. The White Paper was bitterly attacked for continuing and strengthening the earlier measures and for outlining new powers of detainment and deportation which were interpreted as giving the Government dangerous arbitrary authority.[83]

In the third part of the White Paper, the Government noted that the presence of coloured immigrants 'creates various social tensions in the areas where they have concentrated' and declared its intention to help remove these tensions and problems so that 'individual members of every racial group can move freely in society without any form of discrimination being exercised against them'.[84] As a means of fulfilling this pledge, the Government endorsed the work of the Commonwealth Immigrants Advisory Council and the National Committee for Commonwealth Immigrants. The C.I.A.C. was set up in 1962 to provide information for the Home Secretary and had sent him a number of reports.[85] The National Committee, founded in April 1964 on the recommendation of the C.I.A.C., was also charged with providing information and advice to the Government and with co-ordinating a network of voluntary liaison committees (working under many different names) established in various localities throughout the country (often by the Council of Social Service) in an attempt to improve relations between the immigrants and the host community. The Government pledged to combine the functions of both groups in a reconstituted National Committee for Commonwealth Immigrants.

The White Paper posed two problems for the new organization: C.A.R.D. had failed to amend the Race Relations Bill and it therefore wanted to lay the groundwork for a further extension of anti-discrimination laws but was instead forced to turn its attention to a holding action designed to prevent the proposed stiffening of immigration controls. Secondly, the reconstitution of the National Committee for Commonwealth Immigrants—the expansion of its activities and the broadening of its membership base—made it necessary to decide whether C.A.R.D. should co-operate with the semi-official body.

But before there was any discussion, a decision was taken for C.A.R.D. In September, David Pitt and Hamza Alavi announced that they had accepted invitations from the Prime Minister to become members of the National Committee. This set off a new round of recriminations and disputes within C.A.R.D. (discussed in Chapter Three). Two major issues were raised. Should C.A.R.D. members co-operate with and participate in a committee established by a document which approved (and proposed to extend) a discriminatory immigration policy? Should C.A.R.D. Executive Committee members make such important decisions without referring back to the National Council for advice?

Pitt and Alavi argued that although the National Committee was reconstituted in a document which perpetuated a discriminatory Government policy, none the less, the Committee's functions were

aimed towards improving relations between the races and formulating a more enlightened internal policy. The shape of the Committee's thinking might be influenced and Pitt's feeling was that, if
given the ear of the Government, one had the responsibility to
'whisper into it'.[86]

Regarding the organizational problem, in a letter sent to all
C.A.R.D. members, both Pitt and Alavi argued that they were
joining the National Committee in their 'personal capacities' and
that therefore they did not have to consult the National Council.[87]
The letters requesting them to join had been marked 'confidential'
and under the circumstances they did not think they could open the
question publicly. Moreover, Pitt had already been active on the
N.C.C.I., and no one on C.A.R.D. had previously questioned the
propriety of his membership.

A new and bitter argument swept C.A.R.D., with new dissidents
and new alliances evident. None the less, although there was a
continuous and prolonged debate lasting for several months, the
decision on C.A.R.D.'s final position towards the National Committee was postponed, and Pitt and Alavi began attending meetings.
Soon after, a number of C.A.R.D. Executive Committee members
accepted invitations to join the various specialist panels of the
N.C.C.I. and more C.A.R.D. manpower was devoted to serving it.

With the dissidents in disarray, with the exigencies created by
the White Paper, and with the evident need for preparing further
legislation and policing the soon-to-be-appointed Race Relations
Board, C.A.R.D. became more and more concerned with the
formation of public policy. As with the problem of amending the
Race Relations Bill during the spring, the need here was clear. The
more difficult and nebulous task of unifying immigrants was easily
left in abeyance. As the formative period came to an end and
C.A.R.D. began normal, routinized operations under its new constitution, the national pressure group function was, in a promotional
sense, ascendant.

## NOTES

1. Interview with Ranjana Ash (15 March 1967).
2. Letter to the author from Marion Glean (2 June 1967).
3. For a review of the early interpretations of the Act, see Institute of Race
Relations *News Letter* (January 1963), p. 4.

4. Letter to the author (2 June 1967). Mrs. Glean gave two other, more personal and more immediate reasons for her desire to establish an immigrant organization. First, the Friends Race Relations Committee on which she served seemed ineffectual and timid. Second, she became disillusioned with the good intentions of British 'liberals' after a meeting with David Astor, Editor of the *Observer*, to discuss extension of the Commonwealth Immigrants Act, 1962. 'I considered that the arguments used there in support of restrictive immigration were outright racialist. . . . All [those present] were active in some branch of race relations. All, with the exception of me, were also English. I drew my conclusions from these two groups . . . immigrants could not depend on the members of the host community to represent their interests.'

5. Christopher Driver, *The Disarmers: A Study in Protest* (London, Hodder, 1964), pp. 50, 111, for a brief discussion of Rustin's role in the Campaign for Nuclear Disarmament.

6. Interview with Ranjana Ash (15 March 1967).

7. Quoted from *Peace News* (11 December 1964).

8. Interview with Richard Small, C.A.R.D.'s first press officer (10 May 1967).

9. Minutes of C.A.R.D. membership meeting (20 December 1967). The organization was still unnamed.

10. Minutes of C.A.R.D. membership meeting (20 December 1967).

11. See Keith Hindell, 'The Genesis of the Race Relations Bill', *Political Quarterly* (October–December 1965), pp. 393–4.

12. Letter to the author from Marion Glean (2 June 1967).

13. Minutes of C.A.R.D. membership meeting (10 January 1965). One place was reserved for Standing Conference, one for the National Federation of Pakistani Associations. There were to be five co-options.

14. Minutes of C.A.R.D. membership meeting (10 January 1965).

15. Interview with David Pitt (29 May 1967).

16. C.A.R.D. constitution *pro tem*, passed 10 January 1965.

17. Attendance at these meetings grew from thirty in January to nearly one hundred in June. At the membership meeting on 27 June, for example, there were ninety-five in attendance, of whom ninety were from the London area.

18. Minutes of C.A.R.D. membership meeting (7 February 1965).

19. *The Times* (22 February 1965).

20. For a discussion of the development of the Student Non-violent Coordinating Committee, see P. Jacobs and S. Landau (eds.), *The New Radicals* (Harmondsworth, Penguin, 1967), Chapters 1 and 3.

21. Interview with Hamza Alavi (14 May 1967).

22. For example, Selma James, 'Thoughts on Future Work', a paper presented to C.A.R.D. Executive Committee: 'It is vitally necessary first to consider the objective state of race relations and to make an analysis of the role coloured immigrants have played in British society . . . it is imperative that C.A.R.D. should deal with these questions in depth in the near future. From this flows our idea of the kind of organization C.A.R.D. should become and its role in British society.'

23. Selma James, 'Thoughts . . . .' Marion Glean, 'Suggestions for the Future Activities of C.A.R.D.', paper presented to C.A.R.D. Executive Committee.

24. Marion Glean, 'Suggestions . . . .'

25. Ranjana Ash, 'Ideas'.

26. Selma James, 'Future Work: Summary Memorandum (Second Draft)', presented to C.A.R.D. Executive Committee.

27. Selma James, 'Future Work (Second Draft)'.

28. Marion Glean, 'Suggestions . . . .'

29. Hamza Alavi, 'Some Thoughts for Discussion', a paper presented to C.A.R.D. Executive Committee by the Constitution Subcommittee.

30. Marion Glean, 'Suggestions . . . .'

31. Second and Third Drafts.

32. Interview with Richard Small (18 May 1967).

33. Hamza Alavi, 'Thoughts . . . .'

34. Interview with Hamza Alavi (7 May 1967).

35. Letters from David Pitt to Sir Frank Soskice, Home Secretary; the Right Honourable Lord Gardiner, the Lord Chancellor; Sir Dingle Foot, Solicitor-General; Sir Elwyn Jones, Solicitor-General; Harold Wilson (10 March 1965). Wilson refused to see a C.A.R.D. delegation.

36. Letter from David Pitt to C.A.R.D. members (February 1965).

37. Interview with David Pitt (29 May 1967).

38. Interview with Hamza Alavi (7 May 1967).

39. Interview with Richard Small (18 May 1967).

40. Report of the C.A.R.D. Petition Subcommittee (7 March 1965).

41. Secretary's Report (July 1965).

42. Ibid.

43. Minutes of C.A.R.D. membership meeting (27 June 1965). At this point, C.A.R.D. had raised £851 7s 4d, spent £618 13s 5d, leaving a balance of roughly £240. The major expenditures had been for office equipment and publishing costs.

44. Interview with Anthony Lester (16 February 1967).

45. Interview with Anthony Lester (11 March 1967).

46. Interview with Ranjana Ash (15 April 1967).

47. Ibid.

48. Mrs. Glean left C.A.R.D. in February 1965 when she went to Paris to work for the United Nations. Except for Small, the core of the 'dissident' group (as I have termed it) was comprised of women. Mrs. James was a white American.

49. Interview with Hamza Alavi (7 May 1967): 'In broad political terms I was much closer to them [the dissidents] than I was to David [Pitt]. It was only through the attacks and debates that I moved to the other side. They were fruitless and stultifying.'

50. Interview with Selma James (7 March 1967): 'They prepared proposals that were fine, just what was needed and if they wanted to play around with Parliament it was quite all right with us. That's just part of what C.A.R.D. should be doing; there were other more important things to be done.'

51. Interview with Richard Small (10 May 1967).

52. Ibid.

53. They were themselves middle class in terms of occupational or educational criteria.

54. The voting patterns in the Executive Committee can only be discerned in most general terms since the Minutes of the Executive Committee have disappeared and since votes were not recorded. There was a hard core of dissidents: Small, Ash, James, Glean (before she left for Paris). They were supported by Ezzreco (although she did not come to meetings often) and by Kabir (although he too attended E.C. meetings only sporadically). The dissidents could thus count on a minimum of three and a maximum of six votes. There was also a hard core that comprised the working majority: Pitt, Lester, Deakin, Singh, Alavi, Shaw, and Page. This is not to say that there was not substantial disagreement among this group and a variety of opinions. They just tended to vote together on the specific issues that arose during the spring. Two members of the E.C., Amoo-Gottfried and Dhesi, came rarely and did not seem to be firmly identified with either group.

55. Interview with Anthony Lester (11 March 1967).

56. Interview with Selma James (7 March 1967): 'This was an important argument. One which we had many times afterward. There was a refusal to concentrate on colour, a desire to remain nebulous. Once you emphasize colour, people know

what you are for and identify with your particular perspective. You look at the world in a particular way and attract a type of person. People who were opposed to this were concerned about alienating white opinion.'

57. Interview with Anthony Lester (11 March 1967).

58. Interviews with Anthony Lester (11 March 1967); Selma James (7 March 1967); Nicholas Deakin (1 November 1966).

59. Letter to the author from Marion Glean (2 June 1967).

60. Interview with Anthony Lester (11 March 1967).

61. This statement must be qualified. During the first months, the dissidents were as concerned as the members of the working majority that C.A.R.D. be accepted in the political life in Britain and not be viewed as a fringe group. For a discussion of the nervous, uncertain mood of C.A.R.D. members and British politicians in the first months, see Colin McGlashan, 'Integrating Britain's Anti-Racialists', *Observer* (25 January 1965).

62. *Observer* (30 May 1965).

63. Letter to the Editor, *Observer*, from David Pitt (16 June 1965). At the end of a polite, subdued letter, Pitt wrote: 'But the Government's Race Relations Bill is a shambles . . . just a piece of window dressing. The suggestion that the proposals contained in this absurd bill is somehow a victory for C.A.R.D. and its associates, although well meant, is in fact deeply wounding and to give the impression that the organization has been used by certain individuals in order to achieve this end is like rubbing salt in the wound.' The letter was not printed.

64. C.A.R.D. Executive Committee statement (24 June 1965).

65. Interview with David Pitt (29 May 1967).

66. It was chaired by Hamza Alavi, with a fluid membership, including Pitt, Lester, and Ian McDonald, who drafted the constitution.

67. Hamza Alavi, 'Notes for Discussion'.

68. The aims and objects adopted in January had been changed slightly. As adopted in July, they were:

(1) To struggle for the elimination of all racial discrimination against coloured people in the United Kingdom.

(2) To struggle for the elimination of all forms of discrimination against minority groups in the United Kingdom.

(3) To use all means in our power to combat racial prejudice.

(4) To oppose all forms of discrimination on the entry of Commonwealth citizens into the United Kingdom.

(5) To oppose all legislation that is racially discriminatory or inspired by racial prejudice.

(6) a. To seek to co-ordinate the work of organizations already in the field and to act as a clearing house for information about the fight against discrimination in Britain.

b. To establish and maintain links with organizations outside the United Kingdom having aims and objects broadly similar to CARD's.

69. C.A.R.D. constitution (July 1965).

70. An amendment passed at the Annual Delegates Conference, 1966, provided for two vice-chairmen.

71. Interview with David Pitt (29 May 1967).

72. Interview with Hamza Alavi (14 May 1967).

73. Interview with Richard Small (10 May 1967).

74. Interview with Hamza Alavi (14 May 1967). The constitution was debated for two days but although there was disagreement over the wording and shape of various clauses, no major changes were suggested.

75. Sending delegates:
British Caribbean Association; Cardiff Inter-Racial Council; Committee for

Tamil Action; National Federation of Pakistani Associations; Indian National Association (Leamington); Indian Workers' Association (Southall); Islington International Friendship Council; Labour Worker; London School of Economics West Indies Society; Manchester Colonial Sports Club; Oxford Committee for Racial Integration; Society of Friends Race Relations Sub-committee; Standing Conference of West Indian Organizations; Student Conference on Racial Equality: Simon Community Trust; Pakistan Immigrant Socialist Group; Sheffield Coloured Workers Association; Council of African Organizations; United Social Club; West Indian Student Union; East Pakistan House; London Majlis.

Sending observers:

Student Campaign Against Racial Discrimination; Co-ordinating Campaign Against Racial Discrimination; National Council for Civil Liberties; Pakistan Friends League; Wood Green Young Socialists; Amnesty International; Wood Green Commonwealth Citizens Consultative Committee; Pakistan Welfare Association; Campaign for Social Justice.

76. Secretary's Report (July 1965).

77. C.A.R.D. constitution (July 1965).

78. Resolutions submitted to the National Founding Convention of C.A.R.D. (24–25 July 1965); Agenda, C.A.R.D. Convention (July 1965).

79. Report to the Leicester Campaign for Racial Equality on the C.A.R.D. National Founding Convention from Dipak Nandy (August 1965). For a similar report see the *Guardian* (26 July 1965).

80. Ibid.

81. The members of the Executive Committee selected after the National Convention were: Pitt, chairman; Alavi, vice-chairman; Victor Page, treasurer; Jocelyn Barrow, secretary; Ranjana Ash, Oscar Abrams, Julia Gaitskell, Zacharia Choudhury, Anthony Lester, Lee Moore, Roy Shaw, Gurmukh Singh, K. Okwabi, Tony Brown, Tilden Francis, David Shipper, Walter Birmingham, R. Karapiet. Karapiet left C.A.R.D. in the spring of 1966 and was replaced by Martin Ennals. Dipak Nandy and V. D. Sharma were co-opted to the Executive Committee early in 1966. The rough characterization of the C.A.R.D. Executive Committee as 'middle class', 'intellectual', and 'professional' held as well with the second elected Executive as with the first. The main change was that although the E.C. continued to be a meeting-place for people of many political persuasions, these did not come into the E.C.'s discussions with the frequency that characterized the meetings during the formative period.

82. Interview with Michael Dummett (7 March 1967).

83. *Immigration from the Commonwealth* (London, H.M.S.O., 1965), pp. 6–9 (Cmnd. 2739). See also Institute of Race Relations *News Letter* (September 1965) for reactions to the White Paper.

84. *Immigration from the Commonwealth*, op. cit., p. 10.

85. The Commonwealth Immigrants Advisory Council published four reports before its functions were transferred to the National Committee for Commonwealth Immigrants: Housing (Cmnd. 2119, London, H.M.S.O., July 1963); Education and Information (Cmnd. 2266, February 1964); Employment (Cmnd. 2458, September 1964); Housing (Cmnd. 2796, October 1965).

86. Interview with David Pitt (29 May 1967).

87. Letter from David Pitt and Hamza Alavi to the C.A.R.D. membership (21 October 1965).

# CHAPTER THREE

# The Failure of Federation:
# The Movement Founders

The decision taken by David Pitt and Hamza Alavi to join the National Committee for Commonwealth Immigrants not only had internal repercussions within the C.A.R.D. Executive but also resulted in the withdrawal of the Standing Conference of West Indian Organizations from the C.A.R.D. structure.[1] In October, the Standing Conference Executive Committee decided that either Pitt and Alavi would resign from the National Committee, or Conference would disaffiliate from C.A.R.D.[2] Since both C.A.R.D. executives were publicly committed to the N.C.C.I., this was an effective announcement of disaffiliation by the West Indian group, and the formal step was confirmed in February 1966 in a vote of the general monthly meeting of Standing Conference.[3]

The withdrawal of the West Indian organization symbolized the failure of the 'organization of organizations' idea to catch hold and exist as a successful strategy by which C.A.R.D. could unite all those groups which were sympathetic to a campaign against racial discrimination. This idea had a dual focus: to bring in all British organizations sympathetically disposed to the immigrants' cause, and to bring in all existing immigrant organizations. As has been noted, uniting the existing immigrant organizations was considered by far the most important task by many inside C.A.R.D. Yet it was this second function that C.A.R.D. failed to perform from the start.

The organization of organizations idea, the welding together of British and immigrant organizations in a federal structure, envisioned that C.A.R.D. would have three types of relationship with the already existing groups. It would co-ordinate efforts already launched against discrimination; it would act as a clearing-house for information; and it would participate with organizations in initiating further efforts to eradicate discrimination. It was also assumed that C.A.R.D. would stimulate those currently inactive in anti-discrimination work—presumably the British organizations, but also some immigrant groups—to dedicate themselves towards a new goal.

The concept of combating discrimination and, by implication, improving the quality of life of individual immigrants was never worked out explicitly, as we have seen in Chapter Two. But there were three broad areas for action in the minds of those who were involved in C.A.R.D. in the formative period:

First, to change public policy at a national level. The major tasks here would be to:

work against discriminatory laws;

promote laws that insure equality of opportunity and combat discrimination;

promote social reform legislation and argue for its proper implementation;

try generally to change attitudes of the public, especially those who have influence.

Second, to work against discrimination at a local level. In 1965 a number of activities were seen as possible:

registering voters so that immigrants could act politically against discrimination;

testing discrimination as a means of understanding its mechanisms and identifying the discriminators;

publicizing discrimination; policing the Press; countering racist propaganda;

negotiating with employers and trade union branches for fair employment practices;

protesting housing conditions or rents; negotiating with the proper official or property owner;

lobbying local councillors, M.P.s, and other officials for support of anti-discrimination policy in their areas;

improving relations with the local community.

Third, to promote equality through community development at the local level. Work to insure that immigrants could achieve economic and social development and security through:

obtaining access to the proper welfare services;

organizing collectively to build economic and social strengths.

Each of these sets of functions needed an organization to implement the implied goals, although the nature of the organization might differ according to which goal was being stressed.

Those concerned with developing the organization were thus eager to involve four types of group in the work of C.A.R.D.:

1. Multiracial organizations already involved at the local level in anti-discrimination work: voluntary liaison committees associated with the National Committee for Commonwealth Immigrants; local anti-discrimination groups like the Leicester Campaign for Racial Equality;

2. Sympathetic British organizations not directly involved in anti-discrimination work (though often multiracial) operating at national level: groups like the Movement for Colonial Freedom, Anti-Apartheid, the National Council for Civil Liberties, trade unions; and at local level: groups like constituency parties, Trade Councils, trade union branches, church groups.

3. Immigrant organizations that operated at a national or regional level and claimed to represent members of one nationality group —Pakistanis, Indians, West Indians: the Indian Workers' Association, Great Britain; the National Federation of Pakistani Associations, Great Britain; the Standing Conference of West Indian Organizations, London Region. These groups would be involved in a range of activities and the proportion of time, money, and effort devoted to anti-discrimination work would vary.

4. Immigrant organizations operating at the local community or city level: a variety of cultural, social, religious, sporting, or economic organizations that would be organized along nationality lines and might or might not be affiliated to the nationality's umbrella organization and might or might not be involved in anti-discrimination activities.

In the first blush of optimism during C.A.R.D.'s early days, it was hoped that the nationally recognized immigrant organizations, and through them Pakistani, Indian, and West Indian organizations at the local level, would become the heart of the new organization. This hope was in turn predicated on the belief that the national immigrant organizations would become roughly analogous to trade unions and that, subsequently, C.A.R.D. would in some sense become a Trades Union Congress for immigrants.

Both as a pressure group trying to change public policy at a national level and as an organization representing a nascent movement wanting to effect change at the local level, C.A.R.D. needed to mobilize and develop organized power. Given the federal nature of the C.A.R.D. structure, mobilization might be gauged by the capacity for unified decision-making and action that would have the approval of the various member groups. How much an organization like C.A.R.D. had such capacity for unified behaviour, how far it had succeeded in mobilizing power, depended on its degree of concentration and its level of cohesion.[4]

Concentration may be measured on two co-ordinates. One dimension is 'density', that is, the percentage of members in the existing universe of groups that could associate with C.A.R.D., which had in fact done so. As Beer has pointed out, a high degree of density is compatible with a low degree of unity because the organized are divided into many separate bodies. A second dimension of concentration is thus amalgamation, 'taking this to mean how far the organized have been brought together in one body, whether by outright merger, federation or similar arrangements'.[5] A further dimension of concentration which is of importance in race relations is representativeness: how many immigrants and their children (who are of the proper age) of the total who are able to participate in a given area, in a particular primary organization, actually do so.[6]

Cohesion does not measure and describe the characteristics of the groups acting in tandem but rather the factors which bind them together in the larger organization. Roughly speaking, groups could have helped C.A.R.D. to co-ordinate efforts, to disseminate information, and to fight discrimination because they were bound by sanctions, by consent, or by participation in support of C.A.R.D.'s activities.

Members of the C.A.R.D. Executive who thought about the problem in both the formative period and in the months following the national founding convention were, of course, aware that the immigrant communities were not particularly well organized. They knew that many immigrants were not involved in groups dedicated to improving their life in Britain and that where there was amalgamation, the national umbrella organizations had their own problems. They surmised it might therefore be difficult to gain a high level of individual participation in C.A.R.D. For example, the Standing Conference of West Indian Organizations claimed an affiliation of fifteen organizations with a total membership of 6,000 to 8,000. This represented only a small fraction of London's approximately 230,000 West Indians.

Still, it was hoped that the large national immigrant organizations would provide the framework for development. And there was the belief that although there was little concentration in any of the main immigrant organizations, there could be cohesion in an organization like C.A.R.D., not through sanctions, but through consent and participation—consent and participation based on the common cause of coloured immigrants in Great Britain, i.e. the deprivation, anger, and humiliation caused by discrimination. Cohesion through the consent and participation of the Pakistani, Indian, and West Indian national group structures (the I.W.A., the Pakistani Federation, the Standing Conference) would help local development, increase participation and organization building at that level, and through these developments and the process of further amalgamation and strengthening lead to the concentration that would be necessary if C.A.R.D. was to be a movement with momentum at the local level, a pressure group with the influence of numbers at the very least.

It is important to understand why this strategy failed, both to indicate the kinds of difficulty that C.A.R.D. had in developing as an organization, and to explain the nature of the internal constraints which hindered C.A.R.D.'s effective operation as a force against discrimination. Here it is necessary to be selective. This chapter will examine in detail the relation of the Standing Conference of West Indian Organizations to C.A.R.D. This will be followed by a brief discussion of C.A.R.D.'s difficulties in establishing relations with the Indian Workers' Association, Great Britain, and the National Federation of Pakistani Associations in Great Britain during the period 1965–7.

## 1. C.A.R.D. AND THE STANDING CONFERENCE OF WEST INDIAN ORGANIZATIONS

The West Indian Standing Conference, London Region, was one of the first groups to affiliate with C.A.R.D., but it did so reluctantly. Four people on the Conference Executive, Vernon Laidlow (chairman), Mrs. Frances Ezzreco (vice-chairman), Jeff Crawford (secretary), and Neville Maxwell (welfare officer), were especially concerned about the implications of joining the newly formed antidiscrimination group. Members of Conference had been present at all C.A.R.D. meetings since Martin Luther King's visit to London, and at the 10 January organizational meeting Crawford had been asked to serve on the C.A.R.D. Executive *pro tem*.

Crawford had declined both because he lacked the time and because he had serious doubts about C.A.R.D. He and other members of Conference discussed these concerns with Dr. David Pitt at a special meeting held early in February at Pitt's surgery on Gower Street in London.

The members of the Standing Conference told Pitt they wanted assurances that individual membership would not be allowed to outweigh—and outvote—the membership of the affiliated organizations. They were afraid that the group voice of Conference might be lost among the welter of individual tongues present in any large mass organization and that if C.A.R.D. began to solicit individual members it would begin to compete with Conference.

The Conference representatives also wanted assurances that C.A.R.D. would not be 'white-dominated'.[7] They wanted C.A.R.D. to be a group run and controlled by immigrants. Pitt explained that whites had a useful role to play in the organization that was envisioned. After some discussion about the nature of white involvement, the members of Standing Conference and Pitt agreed in general that whites were not to run the organization but should definitely assist immigrants in their fight against discrimination.

Lastly, Crawford, Maxwell, Laidlow, and Ezzreco asked that C.A.R.D. be forthright and 'militant' in its public opposition to discriminatory practices and in its efforts to counter them. They insisted that C.A.R.D. should in no way be tied to the Labour party. Victor Page, C.A.R.D. treasurer, was a member of one of the local groups affiliated to Conference[8] and eagerly wanted Conference to link up with C.A.R.D. Following the discussion with Pitt and subsequent talks with Page, Standing Conference affiliated.[9]

During the eight months that Standing Conference was formally associated with C.A.R.D., it had little to do with the activities of the organization. Conference was offered two places on the Executive Committee, but only one was filled (by Frances Ezzreco, who attended E.C. meetings infrequently). Standing Conference supported C.A.R.D.'s proposals to amend the Race Relations Bill and attended conferences held before and after the national founding convention to discuss the direction in which C.A.R.D. and the affiliated organizations should move. But a place for it on the committee drafting the constitution remained empty. Standing Conference simply did not have an interest in building up C.A.R.D.

In this, concerned members of Conference—Crawford, Maxwell, Laidlow, and Ezzreco—were fundamentally different from the

C.A.R.D. dissidents, Small, Glean, Ash, and James. The Conference members were wary of C.A.R.D. for a variety of reasons (some which they shared with the dissidents), but of central importance was their own uncertainty about how the development of C.A.R.D. would affect Standing Conference. This ambivalence made action difficult.

Through Selma James and Richard Small, both of whom were close to Conference members, the people from Conference developed a dislike for C.A.R.D. By the time of the national founding convention, the bitterness within C.A.R.D. had been communicated to Conference leaders who then saw the new organization as middle class, white-dominated, moderate, and controlled by the Labour party—criticisms identical to those made by the C.A.R.D. dissidents. When Selma James, the Conference's closest ally on C.A.R.D., was not elected to the Executive Committee by the National Council following the convention, suspicions were further aroused: David Pitt, they felt, had been manoeuvring behind the scenes. And finally, with Pitt's and Alavi's acceptance of positions on the National Committee for Commonwealth Immigrants, Standing Conference decided to leave C.A.R.D.

Yet, just as the nature of the split between the dissidents and the working majority was different and more complicated than the verbal dualities would suggest, so the departure of Standing Conference was much more than a militant, black, working-class organization leaving one that was moderate, middle-class, white-run, and gradualist. The Press, perhaps in an attempt to recreate a little of the bitterness, conflict, and drama of the American civil rights movement, played it this way.[10]

Standing Conference had hardly given C.A.R.D. a chance. Activities were just getting under way. Conference members had not tried to forcefully push C.A.R.D. in any direction. Although there were, as we shall see in this chapter, personal tensions between Pitt and the Standing Conference, their meetings were not frequent enough to lead to the personal breakdown that occurred on the C.A.R.D. Executive. Standing Conference leaders were not so concerned, as were some of the dissidents, with bringing in individual immigrants to C.A.R.D. and allowing them to participate, and were thus not so perplexed about the contradictions in the conception of organization that inevitably developed. Members of both the dissident group and the working majority have agreed that if Standing Conference had wanted to, given that the constitution was weighted in favour of organizations, it could have effectively controlled C.A.R.D.[11]

Further, if Standing Conference were indeed making an angry exit based on differences over fundamental questions about race relations, it would be reasonable to assume that they would have issued a statement, making public their critique and their reasons for leaving. Although they did write to David Pitt to demand that he and Hamza Alavi leave the National Committee, this issue was only one of a number of possible reasons for the rupture. None of the issues that had so agitated the dissidents on the C.A.R.D. Executive Committee, and through them the members of Standing Conference, were discussed. The letter announcing formal disaffiliation was short and vague.[12]

Shortly after Conference severed ties with C.A.R.D., it decided to 'affiliate' with the National Committee for Commonwealth Immigrants, although immigrant organizations had no formal ties with the N.C.C.I. and were not asked even to pledge formal support. This reversal in course came in the Conference Executive Committee during a heated meeting when it was decided to put the question before the delegates. The decision of the monthly meeting to 'join' the N.C.C.I. was communicated to the National Committee—much to the surprise of the N.C.C.I. staff—by Conference's public relations officer, Joseph Hunte, who was then a member of the N.C.C.I.'s Legal and Welfare Panel.

The peculiar shift in policy hardly seemed to square with the image of a militant black organization dedicated to a strategy of haughty isolation and confrontation. It seemed more in keeping with an organization unsure of its direction, ambivalent about its relationship to white Britain; a group of people coming together into what was in essence a forum for debate, a talking-shop. Yet the Standing Conference of West Indian Organizations during the first years of C.A.R.D.'s existence was at once both a 'militant' black organization and a talking-shop. It was the latter trying to be the former and we must therefore ask about Standing Conference: what were the operative reasons that explain why it left C.A.R.D.? Why did it never really make an effort to take over C.A.R.D., shaping it to its own demands and needs? In answering these questions, we can perhaps gain insight into two different problems faced by C.A.R.D.: the difficulties of working with West Indians at both the national and local levels; and, more generally, the problem of organizing the various nationality groups through the national organizations. To do this, it is necessary to sketch the development of Standing Conference since its inception in 1959. The major theme is a quest for independence; a minor theme is the problem of overcoming excessive disorganization.

## 2. A SHORT HISTORY OF THE STANDING CONFERENCE OF WEST INDIAN ORGANIZATIONS

The West Indian Standing Conference was formed as the result of a single infamous event, and it was not the creation of its own members.[13] These two facts—and the passive role that it implies for some of the founding members—form the back-drop for striking aspects of Conference which were to be noticeable in subsequent years: the desire for independence on the part of Conference officers and the lack of commitment to Conference from the leaders of the constituent organizations. The event which gave the impetus for the founding of Conference was the race 'riots' in Nottingham and in Notting Hill, in London, during the summer of 1958. These disturbances shocked many West Indians in Britain and focused their attention on a fact they had been trying not to confront: race relations in Britain were deteriorating, prejudice and discrimination were prevalent.[14]

Among those shaken and upset by racial violence in Britain was the High Commission of the then federated Government of the West Indies. The Migrant Services Division of the Commission, through its Community Development Section, decided that the problems facing West Indians in Britain (and London) were general ones and that collective action was necessary. Two Community Development Officers, Edward Burke and his assistant, Mrs. S. Gregory, were sent to London from the West Indies and in conjunction with the officers of the Migrant Services Division, especially Arthur Bethune, they helped bring in the leaders of West Indian social, religious, and cultural groups to start Standing Conference.[15]

During 1959, Standing Conference met under the leadership of the High Commission's officers and its work was 'inspired by the help of the Community Development Officers'.[16] By December, a constitution had been written and delegates from the constituent organizations were able to choose their own leaders. Still the High

Commission exercised great influence over Standing Conference. Meetings were held in the offices of the Migrant Services Division, whose officers attended meetings regularly, and the advisers on Community Development were actively involved with the leaders of the member organizations.[17]

The High Commission and the Migrant Services Division were then central to the lives of many West Indians in London. As Ruth Glass wrote in 1960: 'The Division's sphere of influence is incomparably greater than that of any one of the voluntary organizations run by and for West Indians. In considering the extent of social cohesion among immigrants, it is this official agency, above all, which must be taken into account.'[18] For many in Standing Conference, the High Commission provided not only a meeting place and aid through its welfare officers, but also reassurances. 'It was helpful then to know that we were under the protective wing of the Federal Government, to know that they backed us.'[19]

In accepting the constitution in December 1959, the leaders of the constituent organizations of Conference were also accepting a long set of aims and objects. In essence, Conference was established to be a channel of communication between the existing West Indian organizations in the London region, and between these organizations and the High Commission; to develop leadership among the West Indian community and to help these leaders with organizational problems;[20] to foster integration and improve relations between the races. Integration was left undefined and in practice efforts to achieve this goal consisted of discussion groups, research into problems that affected immigrants, e.g. housing and employment, and a number of social events held with members of the host community.[21]

The structure of the organization set forward in the 1959 constitution remained six years later. Roughly speaking, Conference was composed of independent constituent organizations, each with its own constitution, functions, executive committee, and sources of revenue. For a nominal fee, these groups affiliated with Conference upon acceptance of its aims and objects and sent three delegates to the annual general meeting where the Executive Committee was chosen. The Executive met regularly and with the aid of subcommittees carried out the business of the organization. It reported to the general monthly meeting, an assembly comprised of delegates from each of the member organizations. Also, the Executive met regularly with the officers of the constituent organizations, by-passing the delegates to the monthly meetings. By the middle of 1961, eighteen organizations had federated to Standing Conference.

In the early years, tension began to develop between the leaders of Standing Conference and the members of the High Commission. Burke and Gregory did not continue to work with Standing Conference and the relationship between the Civil Servants in the Migrant Services Division and the Conference officers was not amicable. There were no special flare-ups; just a vague feeling of uneasiness and the belief that the Commission did not recognize the independence of Conference and was trying to impose its will on the member groups.[22]

In 1962, Conference began to shift significantly. Two major events precipitated the change. First, after the voters of Jamaica indicated in the September 1961 referendum that their island would seek independence, the West Indies Federation broke up— an event that led to the death of the High Commission and its division into several parts. Second, in early 1962, the Commonwealth Immigrants Act was passed, severely reducing migration from the Caribbean to Britain. Confronted with the dual problems of independence from the High Commission and a discriminatory immigration policy, Conference was forced to evolve in the new directions discernible before the twin shocks of 1961–2. Standing Conference was now forced to adopt a new programme for independent action and develop a new concern about the cohesion of the West Indian community in London. At this time, a series of ideas, attitudes, and programmes evolved around the concept of a united West Indian community in Britain.[23] Similarly, the passage of the Commonwealth Immigrants Act and attacks from racialists like Sir Oswald Mosley and prominent politicians like Sir Cyril Osborne and Norman Pannell undercut, at least among some of the officers of Standing Conference, a belief in the goodwill of the host society and encouraged their desire to build up independent strength to counteract prejudice and discrimination and to insure integration in British society on the terms of 'equal partnership'.

These concerns were not always clearly articulated, nor was there unanimous acceptance, among the various sections of Standing Conference, of the general reformulation of the 'host-immigrant' problem and of the need for measures to change the disorganization and discrimination that were at the roots of the problem. The shift was first manifested in a change of mood after 1962. Suspicion, distrust of white intentions, anger at both the weaknesses of the West Indian community and the unfulfilled promises of life in Britain, became more prominent attitudes among a number of leaders in Conference.[24] These were coupled with renewed defensiveness about West Indians to people outside the community. Increased pride in the sometimes slender achievements of Conference, and increased criticism of the state of the West Indian community in London among those within Conference, were all part of an atmosphere that seems to have been created by some of the officers of Conference, especially Laidlow, Crawford, and Maxwell.[25] Further, there was a realization that a voyage back to the West Indies was not going to come immediately.

Most of us assumed we would come here and rake up the gold that covered the streets of London and make a little packet and get back home, buy small property, or a small farm and run it. But then realizing that we weren't going back, at least not for a long time, we had to give serious thought to our own development here.[26]

The fatalism and willingness to push ahead of some of the leaders can perhaps be explained by their fears that British attitudes would not change and that first-generation immigrants would not get a 'fair deal' in their lifetime and must therefore bear the brunt of discrimination so as to prepare the way for the second generation.

One manifestation of the shift in mood and the quest for independence was the departure of all whites from the Standing Conference Executive. In 1959, two out of six E.C. members were white; in 1960, three out of nine (more positions having been created); in 1961 and 1962, four out of nine. These Englishmen had come from multiracial organizations affiliated with Conference and in the early days, when close relations with the host community were a priority, the interracial manifestation of a Standing Conference aim was considered important. In fact, Miss Nadine Peppard, then working with the London Council of Social Service, could be asked to take the chair during the election of Conference officers.[27] But as the mood of the Conference changed, whites on the E.C. sensed that they were no longer needed or wanted and that in fact it might be best if they left.[28] After 1963, there were no 'European' members left on the Executive Committee.

The desire for independence was also manifested in Conference's relationship with the various High Commissions. Although the new constitution (rewritten after the break-up of the Federation) urged

Conference to 'work in conjunction with the Migrant Services Divisions of all the various governments of the West Indies as if it were a Federal Government',[29] and although speakers and observers from the Commission continued to visit the meetings of Conference, they did so irregularly, and advice was no longer sought frequently from any of the various divisions.

Another manifestation of the new mood was a distrust and suspicion of all outside research on West Indians in general and Standing Conference in particular. An editorial in *Teamwork* expressed this general dislike of research:

The 'racial' problem is rapidly developing into a vested interest sphere of activity . . . (and yet) there is precious little to show from all this hive of activity, and more often than not, the West Indian people's views are not even sought when these inquiries are being made. . . . We regret the need for 'experts' in the field of race relations. . . . A self-generating vested-interest clique could have the effect of perpetuating beliefs and attitudes which are harmful to us, unless they are genuinely concerned to alleviate the distressing condition under which we live our lives. The vast sums of money being spent in the pursuit of 'pure' knowledge on racial issues, could achieve much more if some of it were put to preventive or remedial use. . . . Some of this money must be spent on the back streets of the Notting Hills of Britain. . . . While we cannot stop these surveys, we would like to suggest two things: that a survey of West Indians' opinion be taken for a change and that some action be taken *now* on the knowledge which exists in abundance.[30]

The Institute's 'Survey of Race Relations' was not allowed to send an observer to the monthly meetings of Standing Conference. There was sharp criticism of Sheila Patterson's well-known study of Brixton, *Dark Strangers*. Parts of this book were criticized for suggesting that the West Indians could not, like Indians, Chinese, or Jews, 'integrate into British society', but would 'assimilate'. Discussing 'integrative social action', Mrs. Patterson argued that in the West Indian case its ultimate goal:

would seem to be not group integration but assimilation: first, because the West Indian migrant group is 'assimilating' in character, if not yet in intention; and, second, because to promote cohesive group integration beyond a certain stage might, in the present climate of race relations in Britain, lead to the establishment of a highly visible, lower class minority group with inferior rights and status. This does not mean that no efforts should be made to promote internal organization and control within the West Indian migrant group, but rather that this should be done as a transitional not a final measure.

She went on to say:

. . . if accommodation and assimilation are to be achieved, the West
Indian migrants must face the fact that they have to make a thorough-
going and sustained effort to adapt their behaviour and values in all major
spheres of life.[31]

To many in Standing Conference the word 'assimilation' was an
anathema, suggesting a process that denuded the migrants of their
culture, their past, and their self-respect and which offered them
acceptance within British society at the price of absolute conformity
to that society. This view was put forward in the manifesto of
Standing Conference, *The Power of Negro Action*, a 59-page pamphlet written and published in 1965 by Conference's welfare officer,
Neville Maxwell.

Angry at some of Mrs. Patterson's conclusions, Maxwell warned
against the 'ever present danger of having one's cultural, political
and economic course charted by a presumptuous outsider' and
castigated those who were pray to 'Anglo-centricity'. He distinguished between 'assimilationists' and 'integrationists' and charged
that the former simply wanted immigrants to accept blindly the
patterns of life and the customs of the host society, while asserting
that the latter hoped for 'internal organization and economic and
social development' as a base from which the West Indians could
build a community within British society.[32] He challenged Mrs.
Patterson's basic finding that West Indians were assimilating in
'character if not intention'. He wrote:

Whatever were the expectations and preconceptions of English Society
and English people held by West Indians on or shortly after their arrival
. . . the passage of time has witnessed a constructive and positive attitude
held by all thinking West Indians in relation to themselves and the society
around them. No West Indian unless he is dreaming, now goes around
piously seeking to be accepted by the native people as *Dark Strangers* all
along conveyed.[33]

The new mood, the new view of the High Commission, the
feelings against research, all formed the background for a new
attitude towards the concept of integration. The 'tea and bun'
approach to good relations between the races which had prevailed
after the Notting Hill riots was no longer considered to be of any
importance. Social mixing at 'functions' was felt by some officers
of Conference to be only a bitter symbol of the failure to have real
opportunities and thus real integration into British society.[34]

Maxwell generally defined 'integration' as taking place in a multi-racial society 'wherein minorities, though fully organized as a community, participated with the majority in the facets of life *for which they qualify*'. The key word in achieving integration was partnership: 'Integration must of necessity be a game for two . . . each respecting the other's dignity as a human being and recognizing merit where it exists—with no reservations.'[35] This concept of equal partnership (a basis for an integrating process that insured the self-respect and self-sufficiency of both communities) implied that the West Indian community would have to develop its own strengths before concerns about integration could be meaningfully confronted.

It is impossible for West Indians to segregate themselves from the rest of the community. Our everyday existence depends on the broadest possible inter-relationship with the other peoples of this country; but what was needed at this stage was for West Indians to give more thought to helping themselves. Opportunities will not be given freely. West Indians have got to fight for whatever they want, and this could only be done successfully through organizing. However people cannot be organized in an abstract sense: they must be organized in a positive manner for positive reasons.[36]

Put in baldest terms: integration as seen by the more political leaders of Standing Conference was to be based on power, not on tolerance and goodwill.

Maxwell suggested activities that would help West Indians develop the necessary strengths to integrate. Economically (and most importantly), credit unions, consumer co-operatives, investment societies, housing and business associations were to be developed. Politically, West Indians were to stop feeling that they could not exert any influence (thus, they were registered so as to use a bloc vote as 'a bargaining counter' in close constituencies). Culturally, West Indians were to develop their sense of 'Negritude' in order to achieve 'cultural independence'.

The part of our culture which is English oriented cannot be wished away. . . . Rather the middle course lies in developing and consciously fostering what is best in our own sub-culture since our original African culture was ruthlessly suppressed and subordinated to the naked acquisitiveness of the Metropolitan country.[37]

Negritude would be the awareness, defence, and development of cultural values, a consciousness which would give the West Indian a sense of his own uniqueness, and a positive self-image that differentiated him from Englishmen. A positive programme for developing economic, political, and cultural strength was necessary. Further, discrimination in Britain was to be opposed by Conference. Three pamphlets published by Conference during 1965–7 —Maxwell, *Power of Negro Action*, F. N. Villier, *The Credit Union Explained*, and Joseph Hunte, *Nigger Hunting in London* (a critique of the police's handling of West Indian cases)—were a rough index of the central concerns of the 'new breed' of Standing Conference officers. Around the general problems of developing cohesion and fighting discrimination, ideas were to cluster and action for independence and ultimately for integration was to follow.

The structure of Standing Conference, with its reliance upon the constituent groups for strength, support, and active participation, was one constraint on decisive action. Groups were mixed in composition, having both black and white members. They were also mixed in their sorts of activity. Of the fifteen organizations affiliated to Standing Conference in the spring of 1967, six had multiracial membership. Four have been characterized as having mixed membership, between 'middle class' and 'working class'; one was characterized as 'middle class'; the rest as 'working class'. Three groups were involved in strictly economic activities; one in predominantly political activities (the British Caribbean Association); one in predominantly social activities (the West Indian Student Union); the rest in 'social and welfare' activities.[38] Of the eighteen organizations affiliated to Conference in 1959, only seven were still associated with Conference in 1967 (although, of these, three had slightly different names).[39] Of seventeen organizations affiliated to Conference at the end of 1962, after the passage of the Commonwealth Immigrants Act and the break-up of the Federation, eleven remained.[40] And of twenty-nine West Indian clubs and associations active in the London region, fifteen, as mentioned, had formal ties with Conference[41] in 1966.

The officers of Standing Conference, when looking at the West Indian community, discerned roughly five group types: 1. The multiracial, 'integrationist' groups, formed after the Notting Hill riots, that tried to bring white and black together in social activities. 2. A variety of religious groups.[42] 3. Social-welfare groups whose main activities were presenting debates, dances, guest speakers. Some of these clubs also performed informal welfare functions for their membership, established liaison with the police, or helped to explain and fill in forms. 4. Sports groups. 5. Economic development groups.[43] Conference had types 1, 3, and 5 affiliated, the social-welfare groups forming the predominant type, the integrationist groups dying off, and the economic development groups growing. Groups of type 3, social welfare, tended to have the longest history of relations with Standing Conference and one may infer that they were both the most durable and the most prevalent.

The book membership of the social-welfare groups varied between 300 and 500, membership being gained through the payment of a small dues. Their leadership tended to be static; the officers tended to be more affluent than the members and may have had more time to devote to the organization. They were often active in Church activities as well. The organization had a predominantly social orientation. Dances, beauty and sports contests, dinners, guest speakers filled a group's programme for any year. A bit of informal welfare work was also done: leaders made representations on behalf of individuals to the proper authorities, landlords, or employers.[44] Anti-discrimination activities did not occupy group members. Politics, although discussed, was not a subject on which much work was done: voter registration or canvassing were rarely attempted. 'There were few efforts made to get out into the communities and make contact with people and actively seek to find out what their problems were.'[45]

Despite the change in mood, attitudes, and goals among the most prominent Conference leaders, there was not a proportional change in the kinds of activity in which Conference was engaged by 1967. It was still to an extent a mirror image of one of the constituent social-welfare groups, sponsoring dances, outings, beauty contests, sporting contests, and special meetings for guest speakers. Policy was discussed at the monthly meetings. There was little community development or the welding together of organizations for co-operative action. The development of economic strengths proceeded only in three groups. Cohesion at a regional level had not been established through anti-discrimination work. There were no overt attempts to influence local council or parliamentary elections; few efforts to register voters; little lobbying of Parliament. In their attempt to press for extension of the Race Relations Act, they carried out only irregular testing for discrimination both within and outside the scope of the Act.

Individual casework (on police-migrant problems, landlord-tenant friction) was carried out by the officers of Standing Conference. Yet, there was no development of a strong organization with a building, money, and a secretariat. Internal development and anti-discrimination work were treated in a haphazard fashion (although the active officers of Conference spent a great deal of time—as much as 35 hours a week—on Conference business).

The most widely publicized activities of Conference during 1965–7 were ones which ignored the development of a unified West Indian community in London. First, in August 1965 there was an attempt to join the Birmingham Regional Standing Conference with the London Conference in a national organization for West Indians, a federation of federations, as it were. The publication of the White Paper, increased cross-burnings, letter threats, and the failure, as seen by Conference, of the police to protect West Indians from assaults by the British Ku-Klux-Klan, gave the impetus for the union. Vigilante groups were allegedly organized and there were to be patrols of neighbourhoods where threats had been received. A constitution for the union of the two Conferences was drafted and accepted in principle in late August 1965.[46] The problems of distance and lack of time made the union impossible to achieve. Moreover, the Birmingham Conference had in 1967 discontinued operations. It had not held a meeting since early in 1966.[47]

Second, a union of the Standing Conference in both Birmingham and London with the Indian Workers' Associations, Great Britain, and with the National Federation of Pakistani Associations was also planned.[48] Boycotts of the N.C.C.I. and an informal linking for common action were discussed, but again there was little concrete action behind the headlines. In both attempted alliances, a tone of suspicion and anger, the impulse towards self-development, a mood of bitterness shone through. A public stand was taken against the White Paper, the K.K.K., police ineptitude or brutality, the National Committee. But a posture was not supported by a programme.

The fundamental problems of developing cohesion and effectively fighting discrimination remained.[49] To discover why they were not confronted despite the wishes of some Conference officers, it is necessary to examine a question that has aroused both controversy within the West Indian community in London and the bitter resentment of any outside attempts to discuss it: the question of organization and leadership among West Indians. To some extent the problems of Conference, like those of C.A.R.D., were the problems of any voluntary organization: lack of time, money, and full-time personnel. But they seem also to have been the result of the ambivalent West Indian attitudes towards leadership, organization, and Britain.

## 3. PROBLEMS OF ORGANIZATION AND DEMANDS OF LEADERSHIP

To the leaders of Standing Conference, a number of specific organizational problems undermined the group. To a degree, these stemmed from the federal structure of the organization. The delegates from the constituent groups were less than constant in their attendance and commitment to advance Conference activities. As Neville Maxwell said at the 1966 annual general meeting:

These groups must back Conference more, to the hilt as it were, because without the groups there is no Conference. We must stop mouthing slogans if we don't believe them. All of us here want a strong Conference, but we need more delegate support.[50]

Too many of the groups were essentially social in nature and were not eager to participate in Conference activities and to move in the direction that Conference leaders favoured. The leaders of the constituent groups themselves were not fully committed to the idea of Standing Conferences: of the three delegates from the various affiliated organizations only one was usually a high-ranking officer. The top officials in the constituent groups gained status through their position in their own local community and to the leaders of Conference they often did not seem to want to reorient their leadership and their groups to the common problems of all West Indians in the London region (and ultimately Great Britain).[51] Yet these leaders were the ultimate authority for the officers of Conference. When Conference had to take important actions—such as propose the union with the Birmingham Conference or make public the organization of vigilante groups—special meetings were called so that the leaders of the constituent organizations and the leaders of Conference could consult.

Thus, because of the nature of the majority of the constituent groups—cultural organizations devoted to social activities—the constituent group leaders seemed, generally speaking, to have a different orientation from the leaders of Conference. As a result, on matters regarding action on discrimination or in the sphere of British politics, the leaders of Standing Conference, although more willing to become involved than the rest of the Executive Committee (comprised of leaders of the constituent groups), were unable to do so.[52] Moreover, many of the groups themselves were not strong enough or well enough developed in terms of active membership, resources, lines of communication into the communities, to give assistance.[53] The constituent organizations therefore made very limited contributions of personnel, money (affiliation fee was £2 per annum), ideas, or initiative.[54] Their involvement in the work of Conference and the broadening of Conference's base—through a constitutional amendment to allow Conference to have individual members—were major problems facing the organization. As Maxwell said at the annual general meeting: 'Is Conference just to be a "talking shop"? This image needs to be changed completely. We must stop being our biggest enemies.'[55]

Underlying the specific problems of developing and organizing the constituent organizations, was the more general problem of 'organizing' the West Indians in Great Britain. While the Conference leaders resented the facile assumption by anyone else that such a 'problem' did, in fact, exist, they were highly conscious of it themselves, being quite critical of various West Indian social and political patterns. Needless to say, the general phenomenon of the West Indians' failure to organize is extraordinarily complicated both to describe and to explain in depth, requiring tools from a multiplicity of disciplines—history, economics, sociology, psychology, anthropology, political science, and literature. A cross-cultural framework embracing the West Indies, Africa, and Britain is needed. Such a detailed and complicated discussion cannot be undertaken here. Yet, it is important to understand in general terms how the leaders of Standing Conference themselves defined the problem. Their responses and actions were in part explicable by their perceptions of the difficulties within their own communities. It may be helpful to suggest factors which could explain why the West Indians have had difficulty in establishing united, cohesive organizations to help develop their communities in Britain and to fight discrimination.[56] First, there is obvious heterogeneity in origin, class, and political organization among West Indians. This is one barrier to organizational efforts.[57] Second, as immigrants, the West Indians in Britain have concentrated largely on individual economic activity, have high residential mobility, and intend to return home within a few years after their arrival in Britain. That, too, could impede the growth of any stable social or political organizations.[58] Third, the slave and colonial past has fostered patterns of behaviour, for example, colour consciousness and discrimination, among West Indians themselves, which suggest a partial explanation for present difficulties.[59] Fourth, the pattern of discrimination against the Caribbean migrant in this country may have had deeply harmful effects on the capacity of the West Indian to develop his own communities and to take advantage of those limited opportunities offered by the receiving country. The deep and corroding effects of discrimination on the American Negro have been well documented. No one in Britain today is certain whether a similar experience awaits the West Indian immigrant and his children who choose to remain, whether the pattern of cumulative inequalities in housing, education, employment, and health care will become a vicious circle of disability which ensnares people, creates and perpetuates debilitating psychological conditions.[60] Fifth, the problem of West Indian 'cultural independence' and self-respect, the difficulties in evolving a viable group 'identity' for a people with British training and upbringing, a distant African past, and a history of slavery and national fragmentation, suggest themselves as another broad area one would examine in seeking the roots of West Indian disorganization.[61] Finally, the political experience of the West Indies, itself a product of some of the factors mentioned above, may condition the problems of association in Britain.

These general explanations for West Indian organizational difficulties could suggest that the patterns which frustrated the leaders of the Standing Conference were 'determined' by past experience and that these leaders were not 'responsible'. Yet, although the more political officers of Conference alluded to the roots of the problems, they were deeply concerned that the West Indians exercise will on their own behalf to counter the patterns. They saw a set of traits which they had encountered in their own experience that had to be combated. For example, the editorials in *Teamwork*, before it was discontinued, were a constant source of criticism and exhortation:

*Group Leadership*

Those of us who were here during the riots of 1958 will remember the hive of activity on the part of many West Indians. . . . Barely five years later we look on the result of all this activity and find . . . that [it] lasted for a while, and then began to taper off until we are left with only a handful of West Indians who are still imbued with the knowledge that the survival of one depends upon the survival of all. . . . For those who assumed the role of leadership during the riots, and then lost interest when it no longer provided the opportunity for self aggrandisement . . . we must apply different standards of judgment (than for members) in order to measure the extent of their disgrace of themselves and to the rest of the West Indian Community.[62]

### The Problems of Individualism

The complete anarchy which forms the pattern of West Indian Society is a direct result of our much vaunted individualism; but the continuation of a civilized existence necessitates the voluntary surrendering of a little part of one's freedom and resources for the preservation and progress of the whole. . . . The Standing Conference represents in an embryo the making of a truly great organization, but it needs the participation of the whole community.[63]

### Apathy and Leadership

Many West Indians take refuge in the practice of colour discrimination as a means of excusing their own failures. . . . We have to accept the fact that some West Indians know that their lives fall short of what they could become and are willing to accept second class status for themselves and the rest of us in exchange for 'a little peace and quiet'. . . . Nearly all of us at some time or the other have heard a West Indian say that he 'doesn't want to be a leader'. However, this supposedly modest rejection of leadership is very often allied with a refusal to support those who are willing to lead. This attitude—in particular—is the main brake on our efforts at social advancement, and we must all work harder to eradicate it.[64]

### The West Indies Federation and Leadership

Does the present disorganized condition of West Indians in Britain reflect the geographical and political order of things in the Caribbean? The fact that West Indians whatever their island origins live here quite harmoniously demonstrates the flimsiness of the geographical factor in explaining our lack of cohesion. Had the federation lived, Independence would have been achieved by now and the term 'West Indian' would have had a political significance quite apart from its cricketing significance. From this political independence, a sense of national dignity would have penetrated through to the man in the street who though concerned with bread and butter issues knows by intuition when his leaders through selfishness, shortsightedness or personal ambition have failed. We must unite here to better our united appeal to leaders in the Caribbean to do likewise for the good of the area.[65]

In the *Power of Negro Action*, Neville Maxwell referred to the 'general low level of organization among West Indians' and gave several reasons for 'this woeful disorganization'. First, people were concerned with 'bread-and-butter issues' and did not have time for the group work. Second, there was a 'lack of awareness of the benefits that can be derived from an organized community'. This came partly from narrow vision and from the complacent attitude that, despite the hardships in England, the standard of living might still be slightly higher than in the West Indies. However, a far more serious factor was the individualism or 'selfishness with which the West Indian is richly endowed'. Maxwell noted that this 'individual-ism' springs from cynicism about the value of leaders and groups, a disbelief that they can actually be established for other than selfish reasons. Third, there was a lack of national consciousness and the concomitant feelings that it would have inspired.[66] Individualism, cynicism, lack of national unity, complacency, these traits were used by the leaders of Conference to explain the lack of cohesion and organization in the West Indian community.

Another set of traits tended generally to explain the problems that the first-generation migrants had in uniting against discrimina-tion. Among newcomers there was a fear of taking positive and forthright action against discrimination. Similarly, there was a reluctance to protest publicly, partly because many were concerned that the news of a jailing or other results of civil disobedience might reach the West Indies.[67] And, as mentioned, many immigrants were not aware of the effects of discrimination and, because of the mechanisms at work, might not be aware of the discrimination being directed against them. There was also the sense that although they were relatively worse off than others in British society because of discrimination, they were none the less better off than they were back home. For all these reasons, it was difficult to get people to act in concert to combat discrimination. There was the further difficulty of making discrimination and injustice into a cause—even among their victims. Since the forms of discrimination are many, people felt them in an individual way and could be ashamed and humiliated by the experience. They did not know that other people were having similar problems and so did not want to make their humiliation public.

To help an oppressed people—beleaguered by a confused past, unsure of their place in a new society—to oppose discrimination, and to engage in the group politics of Britain was the role of the

West Indian leader. He had to overcome the sizable obstacles—
the particular problems of Standing Conference, the more general
factors that constrained his people, the traits of personality that
undermined his efforts. An escape from the past and the growth of
pride in self and in the West Indian people had to be encouraged.
Economic and social strengths had to be cultivated.

To perform these tasks, the West Indian leader, according to
Maxwell, had to have a number of qualities: 'foresight, enterprise,
tact, patience, the art of persuading others and *absolute dedication to
negritude*'.[68] Most importantly, leaders needed two special qualities
of mind. The West Indian had to be independent of whites: 'to
the extent that West Indian organizations or leaders are controlled by White Liberals to that extent is their independence and
effectiveness compromised'. Secondly, the leader had to avoid
'middle-class' attitudes and 'seek to identify himself at all times with
[the organization's] entire membership'.[69] To reverse the trends of
disorganization in the West Indian community was consistent with
the theme for independence that had been clear throughout Standing
Conference's history. Independence was always seen as a desirable
state and yet its implications had not so far been explored. There
was great ambiguity in the term. Was independence separation
from the white community, a purely internal development in West
Indian enclaves before emerging metamorphosed from the larva of
self-help to take over one's correct position as equal partner and
thus avoiding the perils of 'assimilation'? Or was it a form of
evolution which allowed contact with the host community and
indeed presupposed the help of that community, through passage of
laws and provision of services, in order to gain the goal of integration?

Integration posed severe problems of conceptualization for
Conference leaders as well. The desire for integration drew its
emotional strength from the spectre of 'assimilation' put forward by
Mrs. Patterson. Integration, depending on the state of equal
partnership for its realization, implied a rejection of British values
and norms and the development of one's own. Thus a difficult dual
process was suggested. Not only would West Indians as immigrants
have to adjust as strangers to a new society but at the same time
they would have to preserve their self-respect and develop a complex
configuration of attitudes, values, beliefs by which they could
preserve their own individuality. Yet the problem for Conference
leaders was not only to find a specific constellation of ideas, images,

and programmes that would give the West Indian the desired sense of pride and uniqueness, but to reach large numbers of West Indians with the message. 'Negritude' and 'Africanism' suggested a general orientation but not specific proposals for life in Britain.

The difficulty in defining and developing a new life-style for West Indians was manifested first on the level of rhetoric. Maxwell, while urging negritude and West Indian cultural independence, commended a programme which he called 'Operation Bootstrap', a phrase in the best self-help tradition of Victorian England. Similarly, the name of the news-letter, *Teamwork* (a name which current leaders wanted to retain if they could resume publication), had overtones of both fellowship and the co-operation of a British business organization or sports team. Moreover, the desire to develop internal economic strengths and to follow the Jews (who are an oft-cited example of a people who 'made it') into British society also reflected the residual values of the colonizing, now host, society. This is not to suggest that some Conference leaders were not critical of Britain: Maxwell castigated the social structure of Britain and vehemently (if vaguely) urged increased social equality.[70] It is, rather, to underline the obvious difficulties in achieving the 'cultural independence' desired.

In 1960, Ruth Glass wrote that a major factor which inhibited West Indian organizational development was the duality of West Indian attitudes: 'Should they take part in separate or "joint" integrated organizations?'[71]

There is the identification with coloured people and with it the view that they have to unite to achieve independence abroad and integration in this country. There is also identification with the 'British' and the wish to take part jointly with them in their activities.

By 1967, the emphasis among the most active leaders of Standing Conference was clearly on independence from Britain. Yet in a sense the problem facing Conference leaders was one that faced the dissidents on the C.A.R.D. Executive Committee. Standing Conference had no power. Given that fact, should it try to find a place in society by depending on and cultivating white goodwill? Or should it try to develop power independently in a way not clearly blue-printed. After the Commonwealth Immigrants Act, the White Paper, the Government's position on Rhodesia, the experience of the Negro in America, and recent developments in the Third World, the politically conscious leader in Standing Conference did not explicitly profess any desire for West Indians to emulate Englishmen. Still the central question of whether West Indians would gain an 'equal place in society' through independence or co-operation with British organizations was unresolved among the various parts of Conference.[72]

All members of the Standing Conference Executive, from the most active and political to the more conservative, wanted their organization to be recognized by Englishmen and they wanted to be proud and independent. All the difficulties bound up in the structural weakness of the West Indian community and the constraints of West Indian attitudes that the more active leaders had to confront undermined their confidence in their ability to bring about the change they wanted so badly. Thus, one may hypothesize that, even for them, closely tied to their desire for independence was a paradoxical desire for recognition by a host society about which they had serious criticisms. The fear of failing to gain recognition and independence did not induce Conference activists to identify with the British in the hope of gaining status and acceptance. It led them to be outspoken and angry about society. They could view the isolation and powerlessness which were part of daily life as being self-willed exile, not as a rejection from a society which they distrusted but which they would have liked to join. To others less active in Conference, the sense of powerlessness impelled them to ally with British organizations in the hope of gaining acceptance. Thus, the more active leaders of Conference would join with other immigrant groups to oppose the N.C.C.I. And yet both the Standing Conference Executive and the delegates' meeting would vote to recognize the National Committee. Powerlessness coupled with the search for power encouraged great pride and extreme sensitivity among Conference leaders—pride and sensitivity which made co-operation with other British groups difficult even under the best circumstances.


## 4. THE WITHDRAWAL OF STANDING CONFERENCE AND ITS IMPLICATIONS

Having discussed the history, problems, goals, failures, aims, and structure of Standing Conference, it is possible to return to the question of why it disaffiliated from C.A.R.D. For purposes of analysis, it is possible to distinguish three levels of reason that could explain the withdrawal: ostensible reasons, given by Standing Conference in public; justifying reasons, given by Standing Conference leaders in private; operative and determining reasons, which were probably the most influential in the decision.

As mentioned, the decision of the C.A.R.D. executives to join the National Committee for Commonwealth Immigrants was the ostensible reason for the disaffiliation of Standing Conference. This, coupled with the justifying reasons that followed from the demands made by Standing Conference executives at the initial session in David Pitt's surgery—the lack of C.A.R.D. militancy, the dominant influence of whites, the Labour party orientation—gave the impression of Conference as a separatist and militant organization dedicated to a strategy of confrontation, opposed to a white, middle-class organization, implacably hostile to the British Government.

To accept these reasons as an explanation gives a misleading view of both the nature of the split and Standing Conference. C.A.R.D.'s decision to join the National Committee was clearly a debatable question and one on which people of good faith could easily divide. C.A.R.D. members were hardly unanimous in their approval of the N.C.C.I. and the question was subsequently argued and re-argued within the organization. Both co-operation and boycott were positions that could be defended; but in the autumn of 1965, with the new Committee barely formed, its activities hardly adumbrated, one could not have escalated the decision into a question of final principle without attempting to change C.A.R.D.'s course. Or, if a final principle was being invoked, it would presumably have been expressed. The silence of Conference should be taken as an indication that the real problem C.A.R.D. posed was not clearly understood and was hard to articulate.

Even less substantial were the claims that C.A.R.D. was white-dominated and Labour-party oriented. The whites on the C.A.R.D. Executive, both before and after the founding convention, were eager to have immigrants control C.A.R.D. and build it into a strong organization. They did not want position for themselves; rather, they wanted to assist immigrant leadership as they could. The special activities in which they could be helpful, such as lobbying, need not have conflicted with the participation of Standing Conference. Similarly, C.A.R.D. had been publicly critical of the Labour party. It had strongly opposed the Race Relations Bill and criticized the Government for the White Paper.

David Pitt had resigned from the Executive of the London Labour party and from the Labour party affiliated British Overseas Socialist Fellowship.

Moreover, on the central question which Standing Conference wanted decided in the first meeting with David Pitt—the problem of representation on C.A.R.D. councils for existing organizations— the constitution that had been adopted satisfied Conference leaders. They never objected to the C.A.R.D. structure. Thus the ostensible and justifying reasons given by Conference were less than compelling and do not serve as a total explanation. They were no doubt important in some respect. The people in Standing Conference were predominantly of different occupational strata than those in C.A.R.D., being working class and lower middle class.[73] There were undoubtedly general suspicion and differences of vision. Certain aspects of C.A.R.D.—its active white members and the Labour party ties of both white and coloured—were seen from an unfavourable angle because of other factors which determined Standing Conference's perspective. But although it is too stark to say firmly that both the ostensible and the justifying reasons were solely rationalizations for other, less discernible ones, there is a substantial amount of truth to this. The incontrovertible fact is that Standing Conference did not ever participate in C.A.R.D. and the disaffiliation is not really a withdrawal so much as a turning away from a field on which there was never an engagement.

Thus, several other explanations arising from the foregoing discussion of Standing Conference cast light on the split.

DESIRE FOR INDEPENDENCE

Standing Conference leaders were clearly agreed on the need for the organization to have strength in its own right and to participate in British society as an equal partner. This desire, as suggested, arose from a variety of circumstances and is central to any understanding of Conference. Yet, as also suggested, there was ambivalence about whether independence would be developed in isolation or whether co-operation with individuals and institutions of the host society was necessary. To co-operate would mean that in a sense Conference had managed to achieve recognition and acceptance. The establishment of the National Committee in a sense posed this dilemma and the votes of Conference—to disaffiliate from C.A.R.D., ostensibly because of C.A.R.D.'s association with the N.C.C.I., and to co-operate with the National Committee—perfectly reflect the ambivalence.[74] They also suggest that a major reason for Standing Conference's decision to leave C.A.R.D. was due to:

## C.A.R.D.'S THREAT TO CONFERENCE AUTONOMY

During the spring and summer of 1965, C.A.R.D. had received much publicity about its success as a lobbying group and about its attempts to become spokesman for the three major immigrant communities. Little mention was made of Standing Conference in the national Press during the passage of the Race Relations Bill and C.A.R.D. had, at least for West Indian leaders, eclipsed Conference since the West Indian group had not been prepared for the lobbying work and had not actively participated in the attempt to amend the Bill.[75] C.A.R.D. had been better prepared, had more specialized knowledge and more contacts with members of the Labour party. C.A.R.D. was thus seen as 'the representative' of the immigrant community in Press reports and by others in London. Similarly, of the three immigrants who were asked to serve on the National Committee, two were C.A.R.D. officers. No members of Standing Conference were asked. Although Committee members were not chosen because they represented any particular group,[76] to prominent members of Standing Conference it seemed that C.A.R.D. was being viewed as *the* immigrant organization.[77] It was clearly necessary for Conference to distinguish itself from C.A.R.D. for fear of becoming a satellite of the larger, more broadly based organization.

## STANDING CONFERENCE WEAKNESSES

By participating actively in C.A.R.D., Standing Conference members would also have to reveal to others, both Asians and Englishmen, that there were real weaknesses in the organization. The complicated and often unsatisfactory relations between the Conference leadership and the local groups, the divisions within the Executive, the difficulties in carrying out specific programmes, the lack of 'militant' anti-discrimination activities: all these would have been lain bare before others. Unwillingness to lay oneself open to scrutiny and a defensive pride in Conference were important in the decision. The need for internal development was clear; the benefits of working with C.A.R.D. against discrimination and possibly having C.A.R.D. help in the development of Standing Conference were not.

## NEGRITUDE, MILITANCY, AND MULTIRACIALISM

The active leaders of Standing Conference, especially Crawford and Maxwell, were impressed with the experience of Negroes in America and Africa. They were convinced that West Indians needed to emphasize their own background and culture to develop a sense of pride in themselves. The reaction to the dangers of 'assimilation' suggests that Standing Conference leaders, in their concern about the development of a group identity, would be unwilling to lose themselves in a multiracial group. Questioning their past origins and current position, they would question multi-racialism in C.A.R.D., although advocating it for Britain as a society.

The emphasis on 'negritude' should not become 'black separatism', Maxwell was careful to point out in 1967. He said that the crux of the West Indian 'identity problem' was economic improvement. This should come first, accompanied by emphasis on West Indian nationhood, the richness of African culture, and colour consciousness.[78] Yet Conference warmly welcomed Malcolm X in London just before he was shot. And his emphasis on developing one's own strengths in strict isolation made a great impact on the delegates and Executive Committee members.[79]

For men like Maxwell and Crawford, negritude and a distrust of multiracialism were closely related to the development of a militant posture.[80] This is clearly a form of gaining recognition but it also reflects discontent with powerlessness. This militant posture—and it was only a posture in 1965–7—separated major Conference leaders from C.A.R.D., not because they were in fact more militant, but because to Conference leaders, as with dissidents, it was important to appear militant. Alliances with Indians against the White Paper or the announcement of the formation of vigilante groups gave Conference an importance that could not come through local development because of the great difficulties. In a sense, by opposing C.A.R.D. and appearing militant, Conference could define itself without the risk of action, just as C.A.R.D. could try to define itself through opposition to the National Committee for Commonwealth Immigrants (see Chapter Three).

DAVID PITT

In a sense the interpretation of the C.A.R.D.-Standing Conference split may be said to have rested with the personality and career of the C.A.R.D. chairman, Dr. David Pitt. He was key because of both his position and what he represented to the leaders of Standing Conference. His opponents gave special interpretation to certain important aspects of his life.

Pitt was regarded by many in Britain as one of the most prominent spokesmen for West Indians (Sir Learie Constantine being another). Yet Pitt had many times said that he thought of himself as an Englishman and regarded his place of birth as irrelevant. This apparent renunciation of the West Indies by Pitt and his willingness to accept English norms angered Conference leaders. They were also resentful that no one from the major West Indian organization, Standing Conference, was regarded as a spokesman for the Caribbean peoples in Britain. Pitt had succeeded in achieving position in Britain as a doctor, a Greater London councillor, and a Labour candidate for Parliament. He had conventional status in British terms that many members of the Conference leadership structure did not have. He was a well-educated professional man with middle-class origins. He was not familiar with nor identified with the rank-and-file West Indian who comprised the majority of the Caribbean population in this country. He was involved in a vast number of British organizations (medical societies, race relations bodies, political institutions). He had never taken any interest in working with Standing Conference and was at times positively contemptuous of its efforts. He was concerned about mobilizing white opinion in support of anti-discrimination work. To members of Standing Conference, he cared little about the hard task of organizing the West Indian community in Britain. He had connections with many people in British party politics. The members of the Standing Conference were not 'well-connected' and saw themselves outside the ambit of conventional power. He knew conventional political techniques from his experience in British politics and in the West Indies.[81] Members of Standing Conference were mistrustful of politicians—their easy rhetoric, their bright promises, their tendency (as Conference men saw it) to 'sell out' their followers. He had urged West Indians to join political parties—especially the Labour party. Yet the Labour party had continued and extended the discriminatory immigration policy of the Conservatives, and to Standing Conference it seemed highly unlikely that immigrants could affect the party structure by working within it. He had joined the National Committee without making any protest against the White Paper. He had seemed to accept the Government's immigration policy.

Some interpreted the C.A.R.D.-Standing Conference split in terms of a personal rivalry between Pitt and Jeff Crawford. If this implies that Crawford and Pitt were competing for the same position, it is wrong: Crawford never made any attempt to dislodge Pitt as the leader of C.A.R.D.

Yet Crawford (or Neville Maxwell) would have liked the recognition of being the (or 'a') spokesman for West Indians. This no doubt stemmed partly from a personal desire to have status, to be recognized by the knowledgeable and powerful as one who 'represents' the interests of a sizable and important group of people. Yet the personal dislikes and rivalries shaded into larger questions of attitude and policy. To members of Standing Conference Pitt could be seen as both an affront and a challenge: he was someone who had achieved a certain level of success partly because he was a West Indian and yet he did not seem to be as concerned with the West Indian community as he should be (that is, in the way that Conference members were).

The difficulties inherent in differences of policy, attitude, instincts, backgrounds, and career were further complicated by Pitt's personality. As chairman of both C.A.R.D. and the round table conferences at which members of the immigrant organizations came to formulate proposals about the directions in which C.A.R.D. should move, Pitt tended to invoke Cabinet procedures, listening to discussion and then 'gathering the sense of the meeting'. When this 'sense' did not correspond with the policy put forward by members of Conference, they became angry at what seemed an autocratic procedure. When opposed, Pitt also tended to lose his temper in an aggressive or heated way.[82] The personal factors clearly contributed to the disaffiliation.

The importance of personalities in understanding the causes of the split shows that it is difficult to establish precisely what the determinant factors were. Yet the thrust of the analysis above is that because of its history, its problems within the West Indian community, the challenges to West Indian leadership, Standing Conference would not join C.A.R.D. or any other multiracial coalition. Given the problems of Conference in mobilizing the West

Indians in London and uniting the West Indians in Britain, we may summarize the analysis by concluding that:

Standing Conference would not co-operate with C.A.R.D. or any similar multiracial federation, preferring to develop its own organization in the West Indian community before establishing a sustained working relationship with other nationalities. Nationality ties, not class or ideology, were the critical factors for the leaders of Conference.

The local organizations affiliated with Standing Conference, for a variety of reasons ranging from disagreement with Conference's stance to their own structural weaknesses and problems of leadership, would be extremely reluctant to participate in a coalition or in anti-discrimination work and community building.

Local West Indian groups elsewhere in Britain would not be joined in a national multiracial federation through the structure of some type of West Indian federation, which would, in fact, not exist for some years if present trends continued.

One could put the conclusions in a slightly different form by distinguishing between those West Indians who in 1967 were 'involved' in organizations (from 'paper' membership to active participation) and those who were not; between those who, if active in an organization, were involved in 'political' or anti-discrimination or 'welfare' work and those who were not.

In the London area (and presumably throughout Britain) there was a very small percentage of people who were active in some formal West Indian organization and who were involved in political, welfare, or anti-discrimination work. As seen by the leaders, the pattern of social cohesion stemmed from informal contact, not from organizational groupings.[83] And of those activists a larger percentage were involved (in the positive sense of participating) in social matters. Thus a very small minority were involved in and concerned with the areas of activity that concerned the C.A.R.D. leaders. Those who were in groups and not active in political, welfare, or anti-discrimination activities would have been difficult to mobilize for reasons suggested above.

Those who were in groups and were 'political' were likely to be concerned with the development of their own group. They resented whites or people of other nationalities. These activists, if Standing Conference was a prototype, were sensitive both to the problems of West Indians and the failure of British society to deal justly with its newcomers. They tended to be angry and prideful and therefore more likely to withdraw into isolation when rebuffed. In one sense, these activists questioned the whole multiracial idea. C.A.R.D.'s efforts to work through this small minority of active leadership did not offer a very promising pattern of involving West Indians in British group politics in the future. Coalitions of leadership structures not only seemed to be very difficult to sustain, but they would probably not direct their energies to the job of attracting members but rather to repelling each other.

C.A.R.D.—and national West Indian leaders—had to turn to the development of local organizations with a new orientation or to the task of transforming existing organizations. Speedy progress on this front seemed unlikely, given the host of problems plaguing the first-generation West Indian immigrant in Britain and the immigrant organizations as they existed in 1967.

## 5. THE NATIONAL FEDERATION OF PAKISTANI ASSOCIATIONS IN GREAT BRITAIN AND THE INDIAN WORKERS' ASSOCIATION, GREAT BRITAIN

C.A.R.D.'s efforts to co-ordinate effectively the work of the other main coloured immigrant groups—the Indians and the Pakistanis—were no more successful than the attempts to attract the West Indians. The Indian Workers' Association, Great Britain, was never formally affiliated to C.A.R.D., while the National Federation of Pakistani Associations in Great Britain was barely functioning in 1967 and had very little contact with C.A.R.D.[84]

Isolated from British society not only by their colour but by language, culture, and religion, the Indians and Pakistanis posed special problems for an organization trying to assure equal opportunities through anti-discrimination work in local communities and through attempts to pressure for change in public policy at both a national and local level. Just as with the West Indians, fragmented as a group by differences in place of origin and class, so the Indian and Pakistani nationality groups are subdivided by place of origin, language, and religion.[85] Not the least of the problems facing C.A.R.D. was the lack of solid information about the organizational life of either Asian group. This dearth of knowledge was one reason why the national approach was first tried. Presumably the national immigrant organizations would understand the structure of the local communities, the patterns of leadership, the needs of the working immigrant.

The relations of the major immigrant organizations with C.A.R.D. indicate again in very rough terms the kinds of problem that C.A.R.D. had in mobilizing immigrants and immigrant organizations. This discussion merely provides a view from one angle—and a distant view at that—into these communities and into the difficulties Indians and Pakistanis have in entering British life.

## THE NATIONAL FEDERATION OF PAKISTANI ASSOCIATIONS

The National Federation of Pakistani Associations, representing local Pakistani societies and welfare associations, agreed to affiliate with C.A.R.D. in March 1965. The impetus for joining C.A.R.D. had come from Tassaduq Ahmed, a London restaurateur and leader of London's Pakistani community, who had been central to the formation of the Federation itself in 1963. Ahmed had wanted to educate the Pakistani community about Britain, to orient it outwards towards full participation in British life, and to give it momentum to begin to seek for itself a place of equal respect and equal status. He had limited hopes that the Federation would prove to be the vehicle for such aims and looked upon C.A.R.D. as the lever by which Pakistanis might be thrust into British society. At first, the Federation leaders were reluctant to join the embryonic organization. They felt it was necessary for Pakistani immigrants to co-operate with sympathetic members of the host community to bring themselves out of isolation; C.A.R.D., in their view, might become an 'all coloured' organization, thus furthering immigrant isolation. Those present at the first meeting were discouraged by the militant, anti-white tone of some of the speakers, especially Marion Glean.[86] As Hamza Alavi said: 'To members of the Federation council a coloured people's organization would mean that there would have been further separation of the immigrant, rather than an attempt to draw him into British politics.'[87]

Within a few weeks, however, fears were calmed as the multiracial nature of C.A.R.D. became clear. As a symbol of its support and interest, the Federation decided to contribute £50 to the fledgling organization.[88] Tassaduq Ahmed asked Hamza Alavi to join C.A.R.D., and he did so in an 'unofficial capacity'. Alavi did not believe (nor did Ahmed) that the Federation, which drew its limited strength from organizations with a predominantly East

Pakistani membership, represented all the Pakistanis in Britain and he felt that his role was to 'build bridges' among the fragmented Pakistani community, and between that community and C.A.R.D.[89] Another member of the Federation, Zacharia Choudhury, chairman of its racial amity subcommittee, joined C.A.R.D.'s policy committee, and following the convention was elected to the Executive Committee.

Despite the early financial support, the Federation had limited contact with C.A.R.D. Alavi, as an independent member, communicated frequently with Ahmed and sought to involve other Pakistani organizations, suggesting that C.A.R.D. co-opt to the Executive Allam Ir Kabir, an officer of East Pakistan House, which was a political preserve for left-wing Pakistani students. Choudhury, both before and after the convention, associated with the dissidents and seldom reported back to the Federation Council or the Executive. During the late spring and summer of 1965, factional battles within the Federation resulted in the departure of Ahmed, the man who had been most pro-C.A.R.D. This led to a further diminution of the Federation's slight interest in C.A.R.D.'s development. With Ahmed no longer leader of the Federation, Choudhury and the Federation's general secretary, Nurul Islam, began to speak unhesitatingly for the Federation in C.A.R.D. A student involved in the socialist Pakistan Democratic Front, Choudhury had ideological leanings which put him in general sympathy with the dissidents' frustrations and with their critique of C.A.R.D. At the Round Table Conference held in October, he and Islam threatened Federation withdrawal because of C.A.R.D.'s decision to join the National Committee for Commonwealth Immigrants.[90] The older Federation leaders spoke with Choudhury during luncheon; and in the afternoon session at Africa Unity House, he and Islam were not as antagonistic to the C.A.R.D. leadership.[91] When Standing Conference announced their disaffiliation, Federation did not follow the lead. By the beginning of 1966, Choudhury attended C.A.R.D. Executive meetings only sporadically.[92] By spring 1967, there was hardly any communication between C.A.R.D. and the Federation (or, for that matter, between C.A.R.D. and any members of the Pakistani community in Britain). Although the C.A.R.D. office in Toynbee Hall was only several hundred yards from Stepney, one of Britain's largest Pakistani communities, there were, as of 1 June 1967, no Pakistanis on the C.A.R.D. Executive Committee. None of the places reserved for Pakistani organizations on the C.A.R.D. National Council were filled. Only one Pakistani, Tassaduq Ahmed, the original supporter of the C.A.R.D. 'idea', sat on the National Council, through co-option.

The National Federation of Pakistani Associations' lack of involvement in C.A.R.D. was due primarily to its lack of cohesion. It was founded in April 1963 by the leaders of the various Pakistani associations in Britain,[93] to deal with one specific problem: the need to get the best value for foreign currency (i.e. pounds) that the immigrants were remitting to their relatives in Pakistan.[94] The leaders were deeply concerned that it had become more profitable (and dangerous) for Pakistanis in Great Britain to have their earnings changed on the black market than to send them through the governmental channels. They wanted the Pakistani High Commission to pressure the Pakistani Government to alter the exchange rate, or provide bonuses for people sending money home. When this problem was effectively resolved, the Federation (a paper organization which had only been the ostensible base for an assiduous lobby of the High Commission) was plagued with a series of factional battles as various association leaders attempted to gain position through the Federation offices. The desire of Tassaduq Ahmed to turn the Federation towards community welfare work, anti-discrimination efforts, and Pakistani political activity in Britain, was frustrated. As he said: 'There wasn't really any attempt to make the Federation a race relations organization. It was impossible.'[95]

The associations which had brought the Federation to life had developed during the last fifteen years around activities that related to Pakistanis as a nationality group and not as coloured immigrants in a foreign country.[96] These groups tended to be oriented towards Pakistan and were concerned broadly with:

finding places of burial for Moslems;
giving dinners for visiting dignitaries from Pakistan;
making representations to the High Commission;
celebrating festival days;
providing cultural activities for immigrants;
providing a low, informal level of welfare advice to immigrants on such matters as immigration procedures or passports;
solving specific problems like the remission of funds.

Another major activity was fighting elections for positions in the associations. Generally, the leaders of the associations were not concerned with the kinds of problem that interested C.A.R.D. members. As Hamza Alavi said: 'Besides action on specific, Pakistan-oriented issues, the associations haven't felt a need to do other things, they haven't visualized a role for themselves in British politics.'

Again in very general terms, the Pakistan community in a given area in 1967 had three parts: students of middle-class origin who planned to return to academic, business, political, or professional life in Pakistan; workers (many of them single) who were in Britain temporarily, and who lived in dwellings with other Pakistanis; middle-class multi-occupational entrepreneurs who ran the internal economies of the communities, had families, and had been in Britain longer than many in the community. At the house or factory level, there would be leadership within the working class. But at a more communal level, those with higher economic status, gained through their ownership of groceries, restaurants, travel agencies, or property, had informal status within the community and sought to formalize it through the association. Workers, seeking a community out of loneliness and isolation, came into the association. Through links that went back to villages or regions in Pakistan, through help that they gave to the newly arrived migrant, and through the patronage they could distribute, the leaders gained the support of the workers. The associations were often marked with fierce contests for position. The battles conducted between rival sets of leaders were essentially for personal power and prestige. They mobilized people not on the basis of issues but because of the obligations and territorial alliances just mentioned. The workers did not generally participate in the leadership of the associations nor aspire to leadership positions. It was those with free time, the students and the successful businessmen, who vied for power and position either through a desire to fight Pakistani political battles in the English setting or to formalize status that accrues from an informal position of prominence in the community.

Given the tiered structure—from workers to the leaders of the associations to the Federation—and the hollow nature of the Federation itself, it became clear that C.A.R.D. could not utilize the Federation in co-ordinating the efforts of the local associations against discrimination. Moreover, given the failure of the Federation itself, new efforts at amalgamation, especially those initiated by a multiracial group, would be difficult; C.A.R.D. could not effectively conjoin the various associations for either concerted action or common statements. Still further, given the nature of the associations and the leadership structure suggested above, it was difficult for local C.A.R.D. efforts to gain the support of the various associations in local anti-discrimination work. If such work was to be undertaken, a difficult reorientation would have to take place both among the associations and among Pakistani workers who were isolated by attitudes, religion, language, and culture.

## INDIAN WORKERS' ASSOCIATION, GREAT BRITAIN

The politics and factional divisions that characterized the Indian Workers' Association during 1965–7 were complex and difficult to untangle.[97] The Indian Workers' Associations were founded in the 1930s to aid the Independence movement and to establish solidarity with British workers.[98] The waves of Indian immigrants that came from the Punjab in the 1950s altered the nature, function, and aims of the groups. The number of branches grew from eight to fifteen by the early 1960s and in 1958 a centralized Indian Workers' Association, Great Britain, was formed to co-ordinate the work of the branches. In the thirties, Indian intellectuals, businessmen, and professionals were concerned about helping the political efforts 'at home'. In the fifties, the groups broadened their membership base and became more concerned with welfare work—filling in forms for people, writing letters, working at the airports with immigration officers. In 1965, they claimed to be more concerned with anti-discrimination activities ranging from lobbying to demonstrations[99] and welfare work.

The two main leaders of the I.W.A., G.B., in 1967, were Rattan Singh, president, and Jagmahan Joshi, general secretary, both of whom were characterized by people involved in British race relations as pro-Peking Communists.[100] In 1961, as the Commonwealth Immigrants Act was being debated, Joshi helped found the Co-ordinating Committee Against Racial Discrimination (C.C.A.R.D., obviously not to be confused with C.A.R.D.), a federation of immigrant organizations and sympathetic British groups in Birmingham which was to oppose discrimination from a broader base.[101] At roughly the same time, strains were developing between the I.W.A., G.B., and the Southall Indian community. This story is extremely complex. For a number of reasons—i.e. different political approaches and ideologies; rivalry between Singh (president of the London I.W.A. branch) and H. S. Ruprah, a leader of the I.W.A. in Southall; a factional struggle for control of the Sikh temple in Shepherd's Bush—Southall broke away from the I.W.A., G.B., and established itself as an independent Indian Workers' Association.[102]

The I.W.A., G.B., did not have any formal contact with C.A.R.D. during its formative stage in the spring of 1965, and refused to affiliate. Southall I.W.A., on the other hand, agreed to support it. The reluctance of the national I.W.A. to work with C.A.R.D. was more clearly based on sharp differences in ideology than in the case of C.A.R.D. and Standing Conference or the Federation of Pakistani Associations. Ranjana Ash, whose political sympathies were close to Joshi's, tried unsuccessfully to persuade the I.W.A., G.B., to work in tandem with C.A.R.D. Distrust based on differences in fundamental political orientation was strong then and persisted. C.A.R.D. was characterized by I.W.A., G.B., leaders as a front organization for the Labour party, as a platform for careerists, as being dominated by the middle class.[103]

The leaders of the I.W.A., G.B., were genuinely committed to the development of a strong, exclusively working-class movement united on colour. They were not opposed to the concept of a multi-racial organization.[104] They felt that C.A.R.D. leadership did not have contact with the immigrant worker and therefore could not possibly lead the kind of organized effort against discrimination which they envisioned.[105] These ideological concerns were important enough to prevent any co-ordination or co-operation between C.A.R.D. and the I.W.A., G.B., from the outset.[106] Once the I.W.A., G.B., had failed to enter the C.A.R.D. organization and the Southall I.W.A. did, further co-operation from the I.W.A., G.B., was ruled out. Outside of its relations with the Southall I.W.A., C.A.R.D.'s contacts with local Indian Workers' Associations were rare and, where established, very slight.[107] In fact, the Southall Indian Workers' Association was the only immigrant group of a single nationality which had close relations with the national C.A.R.D. structure.

## 6. TOWARDS THE GRASS ROOTS

By June 1967, the organization of organizations idea was dead. C.A.R.D. did not really co-ordinate the efforts of other groups active in anti-discrimination work. It did not act as a clearing-house for information, nor did it help other interested organizations initiate further efforts against discrimination. Of the various forms for a 'movement' suggested in the typology in Chapter One, several had not been established. C.A.R.D. had not created a unity of interests among the national communities without establishing formal relations; had not stimulated a 'mass movement'; had not established an 'organization of organizations'.

Of the various types of group that were to be conjoined under the organization of organizations idea, C.A.R.D. had failed to enlist the support of the three major nationality groups—the Standing Conference of West Indian Organizations, London Region, the National Federation of Pakistani Associations in Great Britain, and the Indian Workers' Association, Great Britain. With the exception of the Indian Workers' Association, Southall (and a handful of other groups), no local immigrant organizations organized along strictly nationality lines were affiliated. Of the local groups affiliated to Standing Conference, only one—the multiracial, all-party British Caribbean Association—was formally tied to C.A.R.D. Of the local groups affiliated to the Federation of Pakistani Associations, none were affiliated to C.A.R.D. And none of the local branches of the Indian Workers' Association, Great Britain, had formal contact with C.A.R.D.

Of sympathetic British organizations, only the National Council for Civil Liberties was affiliated to C.A.R.D. Under the category of multiracial organizations already involved in race relations at the local level, there were two subcategories. First, of the voluntary liaison committees, which by June 1967 numbered thirty plus, only one, the Oxford Committee for Racial Integration, was affiliated to C.A.R.D. From local anti-discrimination groups that were multiracial, two were affiliated: the Cardiff Inter-racial Council and the Leicester Campaign for Racial Equality.

Of the various types of organization that could have affiliated to C.A.R.D., the multiracial organizations involved in anti-discrimination activities at the local level were considered by C.A.R.D. executives to be the most active. The majority of these were not 'affiliated' groups, but rather 'local C.A.R.D. groups' that had been started since the national founding convention under the vague provision in the constitution for area committees. By 1 June 1967 there were nine of these groups; and they, plus the Oxford Committee for Racial Integration, the Leicester Campaign for Racial Equality, and the Indian Workers' Association, Southall, were considered by C.A.R.D. executives to be the heart of the national organization. With the exception of the Indian Workers' Association, Southall, these groups were markedly similar.[108] Their primary characteristics were their multiracial character, their recent founding, and their fundamental purpose—to deal specifically with problems of discrimination among immigrants. There was variation in classification. O.C.R.I. was a voluntary liaison committee, and was 'affiliated'. The Leicester Campaign was founded before C.A.R.D. Of the other 'local groups', some had been founded at the suggestion of the C.A.R.D. Executive, others had begun operations at roughly the same time as C.A.R.D. in response to similar needs and, looking to C.A.R.D. for national leadership, had formally become C.A.R.D. 'locals'. Despite the slight variations, these groups were the dominant type of organization associated with C.A.R.D.

Clearly, C.A.R.D. failed to involve the existing immigrant organizations, or put another way, the existing immigrant organizations failed to involve themselves with C.A.R.D. Part of the problem was the inefficiency and weakness of the organization which stunted efforts at the very root. There were no regularized lines of communication, no intelligence about activities of the immigrant groups around Britain, no complete listing of immigrant organizations in British communities; regional or national organizers were not appointed until late in 1967. The reasons, recited as litany by those within C.A.R.D., involved the usual problems of a voluntary organization: time, money, and personnel were all scarce. Yet, although there was truth to this, the weaknesses of the C.A.R.D. organization were reinforcing: an organization cannot be built because there is no money; there is no money because there is no organization. Clearly, if there had been great support for C.A.R.D., there would have been a self-generating process by which a regularized, efficient, and financially strong organization would have developed. The lack of organization was both a cause and effect of C.A.R.D.'s failure to involve immigrants, either individually or in groups. And this failure must clearly be seen as part of a much larger problem than the lack of funds and an inefficient office.

In June 1967, C.A.R.D. had low concentration. The percentage of groups that could have affiliated and in fact did so was extremely small, no matter how one calculates 'immigrant' and 'sympathetic' organizations. The fact that no Pakistani organizations, only one Indian group, just two West Indian organizations, and no trade union locals had affiliated indicates the low order of magnitude.

In terms of amalgamation, C.A.R.D. faced three groups who ostensibly commanded a large number of local organizations. But, as we have seen, these groups did not affiliate with C.A.R.D. or if they did were simply paper organizations. Thus C.A.R.D. faced a universe with a low degree of unity; it had to gain the support of a host of immigrant and other organizations at a local level. Further, those organizations themselves may have had a low degree of 'representativeness'.

C.A.R.D. was faced with three 'federal' structures and was itself planned as a federal organization. Clearly the key cohesive force in such a situation was going to be consent, for only through consent would there come participation and real cohesion. Yet at least within Standing Conference and the National Federation of Pakistani Associations such cohesion simply did not exist. C.A.R.D. could not work effectively with the leadership of any of the umbrella organizations. Such co-operation between the leaderships might have been important. Ideally, C.A.R.D. could have helped build the various federal organizations and served as their spokesman. They were not powerful, they were not like unions, but they provided a way into the immigrant communities.

That the leaders of the federal structures established along nationality lines did not give consent and choose to participate is obvious. Why they did not is more difficult to explain. It is possible, however, to suggest several probable reasons. First, the leaders of the federal structures did not want to lose their own position of pre-eminence in another federal body of which they would only be a part. With Standing Conference, as we have seen, this consideration was undoubtedly crucial. Second, the relationship between the federal organization and C.A.R.D. was not clearly delineated. The benefits that would flow from association with C.A.R.D. were not sharply defined. And the 'immigrant interest' was not presented in a necessarily compelling way. Third, at least in the case of the Indian Workers' Association, Great Britain, there was genuine ideological distrust of C.A.R.D., compounded by the fact that an I.W.A. break-away group, the I.W.A. in Southall, was in the process, during the spring of 1965, of establishing working relations with C.A.R.D. Fourth, in the case of Standing Conference and the National Federation of Pakistani Associations, there was not clear similarity in function. The Federation was never very concerned about combating discrimination and promoting social equality. And Conference, although its most active leaders were deeply concerned about discrimination, was not engaged in actual anti-discrimination work. Fifth, the federal structures were weak, being dependent on the co-operation and participation of the local association leaders. Sixth, differences between nationality groups were still much stronger than the similarities that might bind all people with coloured skins in Britain.

As suggested, the local association leaders, at least in the case of the Standing Conference organizations in the London area and possibly with the Pakistani associations, tended not to be actively engaged in 'political' matters. Not only were they less than enthusiastic about supporting a national umbrella organization led by members of their own nationality, but because of the functions of the organizations and their founding purpose, they did not voluntarily give their support to national C.A.R.D. Thus there was no communication flow between these local groups and C.A.R.D. whereby, for example, C.A.R.D. could ask that a local branch of a national firm be tested for discrimination or the immigrant organization could ask national C.A.R.D. to intercede on its behalf with the Government in London. As Tassaduq Ahmed has said about the Pakistanis: 'To organize the individual Pakistani C.A.R.D. must go straight to people's door-steps and around the local associations. The association leaders are not interested in promoting the kind of work that C.A.R.D. wants to do.'[109]

By 1967, among those members of the C.A.R.D. Executive who were most interested in local organizing, there was a general wariness of the immigrant associations and a belief that, as Ahmed has suggested about the Pakistanis, it would be necessary to go directly to the individual immigrant to build up an organization. The vehicle for such organization building and community work would be the local C.A.R.D. organization, which would have immigrant association affiliates if individual nationality groups so desired, but which would attempt to work directly with the individual immigrant. And for a variety of reasons, some stemming from the immigrants' status as immigrants, some from their patterns of behaviour as conditioned by life in the homeland, some from their reasons for coming to Britain, they would not, it seems fair to generalize, be instinctively oriented towards a multiracial group (at either national or local level) engaged in British politics. C.A.R.D. would have to 'organize the communities' if it was to gain support.

How such organization would take place, what would be the nature of the support that individual immigrants would give were extraordinarily complex problems which C.A.R.D. was just beginning to confront.

Thus many of the assumptions held by the founders of C.A.R.D. in 1965 were proven wrong in two years. Individual immigrants did not come willingly into C.A.R.D., assuming that they were reached.[110] As a general proposition, immigrant organizations at both national and local levels were not strong enough to work against discrimination, nor could they involve large numbers of immigrants in such work. These organizations were not able to lead C.A.R.D. And C.A.R.D. efforts at the community level were no longer seen as a source of conflict between C.A.R.D. and the local groups, but as something absolutely necessary to the growth of the organization. C.A.R.D. did not develop as planned since the fundamental problems of motivating and uniting newcomers of three different nationalities proved more complicated and difficult than had been imagined. The enigma of how to develop political consciousness among immigrants and how to secure their involvement in an organization to oppose racial discrimination perplexed C.A.R.D. members after two years of the organization's existence.

## NOTES

1. The full name of the organization is the Standing Conference of West Indian Organizations in Great Britain, London Region. Standing Conference hereafter refers to the London regional organization. There is a Standing Conference for the Birmingham region.

2. Letter from Jeff Crawford, secretary of the Standing Conference, to David Pitt (12 October 1965).

3. *Guardian* (28 February 1966). Letter from Jeff Crawford to David Pitt (24 February 1966).

4. For discussion of these terms see Beer, op. cit., pp. 331-3; Finer, op. cit., pp. 1-5; Oliver Garceau, 'Interest Group Theory in Political Research', *Annals of the American Academy of Political and Social Science* (Vol. XIX, September 1958), pp. 106-9.

This discussion is for the moment not considering the strategic position in society of a group composed of immigrant and other organizations. It is not concerned with a fundamental problem: even if immigrants and their allies were organized in a unified body, were mobilized for effective decision-making that would move large numbers of immigrants and sympathetic British institutions, by virtue of what political relationship could they exercise influence on the Government? The term 'concentration' stems from descriptions of the characteristics of sectional pressure groups. But it is obvious that immigrants, although a section, are not a section in the sense of producer and consumer groups. Henry Ehrmann has discussed three broad factors which give pressure groups access to the institutions of government: factors relating to the group's strategic position in society; factors associated with the internal characteristics of the group; factors relating to the peculiar governmental institutions themselves. See Ehrmann (ed.), *Interest Groups on Four Continents* (Pittsburgh, University of Pittsburgh Press, 1958). The discussion will relate to the second factor. It should also be remembered that C.A.R.D. was not just interested in acting as a pressure group and in changing public policy. As the brief typology of functions above suggests, it was interested in performing other tasks for immigrants, including helping them to participate in British life through the organization. Thus, although pressure group terms form the frame of the discussion, they are not helpful if applied without remembering C.A.R.D.'s unique characteristics and the importance of the sociological perspective.

5. Beer, op. cit., p. 332.

6. To say that an organization 'represents' an immigrant community could have at least two meanings: a large number of immigrants in the area actually participate in the organization; the organization is the spokesman for the immigrant 'interests'. Its leaders when speaking to people outside the community are speaking for immigrants as representatives of the organization.

I am using 'representativeness' very loosely in the first sense to indicate whether immigrants are involved in any form of organizational life in the communities: that is, could C.A.R.D. reach individuals through the community organizations? In so doing, I am begging a host of questions. Yet as suggested above, the question of immigrant involvement in organization is tied up to part of the idea of an anti-discrimination organization. In many cases, discrimination is an individual problem and one which an organization can only meet at the individual level. Thus, in terms of helping people who actually suffer discrimination, the 'representativeness' of an organization in the first sense may be an important indicator of the ease with which C.A.R.D. could reach individuals.

7. Interview with Jeff Crawford (14 March 1967).

8. The Brockley International Friendship Association.

9. At the 20 February 1965 mass meeting held to launch C.A.R.D. publicly, Crawford spoke about the decision of Standing Conference: 'Although we were reluctant, the Standing Conference of West Indian Organizations has decided to affiliate with C.A.R.D. We have decided that now is the time to break down the barriers between groups. I appeal to the leaders and members of coloured organizations for close co-operation and tolerant compromise so that this movement can succeed. The alternative would be disaster.' (Transcribed from Hamza Alavi's tape of the meeting.)

10. See for example one article printed before the split, Brian Lapping, 'The Choice for Immigrants', *Guardian* (20 July 1965), and one after, 'West Indian Group Withdraws from Multi-racial Body', *Guardian* (28 February 1966).

11. Interview with Selma James (20 April 1967): 'They would not come in and say "Conference wants A, B, and C", and insist on getting it. I think they could have won.'

Interview with Anthony Lester (19 March 1967): 'Any large organization could have taken C.A.R.D. over. Standing Conference could have if it had wanted to, and Crawford could have become the leader.'

12. Letter from Jeff Crawford to David Pitt (24 February 1966). The letter was three paragraphs long, gave no specific reasons for the severance of the relationship, saying only: 'For some time now there have been differences—some of them very serious indeed—between Standing Conference and C.A.R.D. and efforts to eradicate or compromise these differences have failed.'

13. Source material for the early years of Conference is found basically in the minutes of monthly meetings (which were cyclostyled and distributed), in the

Annual Reports given by the chairman and secretary, and in the Standing Conference news-letter, *Teamwork*. The regular publication of minutes ceased at the end of 1962 and has occurred only irregularly since then. *Teamwork* was published from 1961 to 1964 when lack of funds caused publication to be suspended.

14. Interview with Jeff Crawford (8 November 1966). See also James Wickenden, *Colour in Britain* (London, Oxford University Press, for Institute of Race Relations, 1958) for a discussion of the racial violence in Nottingham and North Kensington.

15. Interview with R. E. K. Phillips, welfare officer, Jamaican High Commission (27 April 1967); chairman's Annual Report to Standing Conference, 1960.

16. Annual Report, 1960.

17. Chairman's Annual Report to Standing Conference, 1961. The debt owed to the High Commission is reflected in the following passage: 'Once again, it is possible to report that the assistance of the Commission, particularly through its Migrant Services Division, contributed tremendously towards the life and administration of Conference's affairs. . . . We look forward to years of mutual cooperation with the Commission.'

18. Glass, op. cit., pp. 208–9.

19. Interview with Clem Byfield, past president, West Indian Standing Conference (2 May 1967).

20. This function is shown in the original name of the organization: the Standing Conference of Leaders of Organizations Concerned with West Indians in Britain.

21. See chairman's Annual Reports, 1959, 1960. Also, minutes of the monthly meetings, 1960–1.

22. Interview with Jeff Crawford (8 November 1966). See also 'A Statement of Policy as Regards the Relationship Between the London Standing Conference and the Commission', presented by the High Commission to Standing Conference (22 September 1961). The ambivalence of the relationship is seen in the following passage: 'The Commission has permitted the Conference to meet on Commission premises. This postulates that on its part the Conference should pursue no policies which might be embarrassing to the Commission. That is not to say that the Commission wishes in any way to unduly control the scope of activities of the Conference.'

23. As Crawford has said in an interview (11 June 1967): 'Its break-up was a tremendous shock for us. We wanted a nation, we wanted a nation's economic unity and strength. We went on because we felt that West Indians should be pledged to working as one people. We are still dreaming of a united, federated West Indies.'

24. See *Teamwork*, 1963–4. Crawford at this time had become editor. For literature about the disillusionment of individual West Indians in Britain, see for example Wallace Collins, *Jamaican Migrant* (London, Routledge & Kegan Paul, 1965), and Henri Tajfel and John L. Dawson (eds.), *Disappointed Guests* (London, Oxford University Press, for Institute of Race Relations, 1965).

25. Minutes for this period are not available. Thus the conclusion about atmosphere is based on interviews with members of Standing Conference who were prominently placed on the Executive Committee. While it is true that they were in a sense trying to create such an atmosphere the conclusion has been generally corroborated by interviews with two British observers, Nadine Peppard and Felicity Bolton, both of whom were often present at Conference meetings during that period.

26. Interview with Jeff Crawford (8 November 1967).

27. *London Newsletter* of the West Indian Standing Conference (January 1961). The name of the *Newsletter* was changed to *Teamwork* in 1962.

28. Interview with Felicity Bolton (23 May 1967).

29. Revised constitution, 1962, Standing Conference of West Indian Organizations.

30. *Teamwork* (November 1963).

31. Patterson, *Dark Strangers*, pp. 352–3. Mrs. Patterson has defined assimilation: 'complete adaptation by the immigrants or more usually by the minority group or the individual members of it, to the values and patterns of the receiving society . . .'; and integration: 'the incoming group as a whole, through its own organizations, adapts itself to permanent membership of the receiving society in certain major spheres of association, notably economic and civic life. . . . To be satisfactory, integration on an equal basis requires a strong and adaptable minority group organization, which can negotiate successfully with the majority society . . .' (pp. 21–2).

32. Neville Maxwell, *The Power of Negro Action* (London, published by the author, 1965), p. 13.

33. Ibid., p. 12.

34. Interview with Clem Byfield (2 May 1967).

35. Maxwell, op. cit., p. 19. Emphasis added.

36. *Teamwork* (December 1963).

37. Maxwell, op. cit., p. 44.

38. The estimates and characterizations are based on the knowledge and experience of Jeff Crawford. Systematic material was not available. A list of organizations affiliated to Standing Conference in 1966 follows, and in parentheses the impressionistic material summarized in the text is given: British Caribbean Association (white-black ratio approximately 50:50, predominantly middle class [determined by either occupation or education], political and social activities); Brockley International Friendship Association (black, working class, social and welfare); Caribbean Co-operative League (black, middle and working class, economic); Clapham Inter-racial Club★ (white-black ratio approximately 50:50, middle and working class, social and welfare); Coloured People's Progressive Association★ (black, working class, social and welfare); Croydon Commonwealth Citizens Association (black, working class, social and welfare); Ferne Park International Association (white-black ratio approximately 50:50, middle and working class, social and welfare); Hornsey Co-operative Credit Union (black, working class, economic); North London West Indian Association★ (black, tiny percentage of whites, working class, social and welfare); Overseas Social Centre★ (black, working class, social and welfare); St. John's Inter-racial and Social Club★ (white-black ratio approximately 30:70, working class, social and welfare); West Indian Students Union★ (white-black ratio approximately 20:80, middle class, social); Willesden International Unity Association (black, tiny percentage of whites, working class, social and welfare); Caribbean United Nationals Association (black, working class, economic); Paddington Overseas Club★ (black, middle and working class, social and welfare). Those groups marked with a star (★) were in Standing Conference when it was first founded.

39. Groups affiliated in 1959 listed in 'Report of Meeting of West Indian Representatives of Groups and Others at a Conference on Community Development Work' (5 July 1959).

40. *Teamwork* (November 1962).

41. The list of London region organizations was compiled by the Jamaican High Commission in February 1967. The National Committee for Commonwealth Immigrants has since been in the process of compiling a similar list. Groups have very erratic life cycles and it is difficult to determine the precise number in the region at any one time.

42. See, among others, Clifford S. Hill, *West Indian Migrants and London Churches* (London, Oxford University Press, for Institute of Race Relations, 1963).

43. Maxwell, op. cit., p. 41.

44. Interview with Clem Byfield (2 May 1967).

45. Ibid. Two groups affiliated to Standing Conference, the Clapham Inter-

racial Club and the Coloured People's Progressive Association, are discussed by Donald Hinds, *Journey to an Illusion: the West Indians in Britain* (London, Heinemann, 1966), pp. 138–42. The Clapham Inter-racial Club fits Byfield's general description. Its aims are: To promote goodwill between people of all races. To foster and encourage a spirit of mutual understanding and respect between peoples of all nationalities (thus enabling smooth integration into the community) by study of their background, social, cultural, and historical. To arrange competitive games, discussions, debates; and to support activities which will create and maintain good relationships between people of all races.

Social functions and discussion groups are the predominant activities. 'The Club is very mild-tempered compared to American civil rights organizations', Hinds, op. cit., p. 139.

See Rex and Moore, op. cit., pp. 156 ff., for discussion of West Indian groups in Birmingham similar to those affiliated to Standing Conference in London. For example, the following conclusions seem to fit the pattern of the London social welfare group: '. . . [the] politically conscious complained bitterly that their community had failed to produce leaders capable of speaking on their behalf. When they made these criticisms they directed them towards the various welfare societies . . .' (p. 158). '[The Commonwealth Welfare Association] was uneasily balanced between being a protest organization and an organization to promote inter-racial goodwill . . . [its achievement] in checking discrimination must be negligible' (pp. 158–9). 'Clearly, voluntary organizations amongst West Indians had not got very far in making an effective West Indian protest against discrimination' (p. 160); 'organization beyond the limits of the family does not occur spontaneously. Their organizations, where they do exist, are formal and weakly supported' (p. 162).

46. See, for example, the *Observer* (15 August 1965); *The Times* and the *Guardian* (16 August 1965); *The Times* (27 August 1965); the *Guardian* (20 September 1965).

47. Interview with Keith Webster, secretary of the Birmingham and District Standing Conference (1 June 1967). The Birmingham Conference looked to London as being much better organized, much more aware of the problems in the communities, and better able to unite the disparate West Indian groups.

48. *Guardian* (22 November 1965); *Sunday Times* (27 February 1966).

49. The activities outlined for 1967 gave an indication of the kinds of ambitions that Standing Conference had. Six social events—dances or raffles—were listed specifically in the 'Programme 67'. There were other, more general listings: Information: the revival of *Teamwork*. Race relations: amendments to the Race Relations Act, recommendations about membership of the conciliation committees set up under the Act, more organized public relations, continued efforts to protect individual and collective rights. Apartheid: campaign to drive South Africa out of the Imperial Cricket Conference. Finance: continued encouragement and assistance in setting up credit unions. Education: greater efforts in assisting West Indian youths both during school life and after school in social and other activities, and in racial equality in employment. Membership: co-ordinated plans for mass membership either during late 1967 or early 1968. Promises: all-out determination to acquire a headquarters during 1967. New groups: encouragement to form new groups in those areas where they are badly needed.

50. Chairman's Annual Report, 1966.

51. Ibid. 'The major question is whether the affiliated groups can see themselves as part of a wider West Indian community with wider purposes.'

52. Within the Executive Committee, these tensions/conflicts of aim were apparent in the decision to withdraw from C.A.R.D. following the appointment of C.A.R.D.'s chairman and vice-chairman to membership on the National Committee for Commonwealth Immigrants and the Executive's subsequent agreement to support the National Committee. Further, the E.C. of Conference was apparently

very reluctant to take direct action—picketing, boycotts, marches—against discrimination, although a minority of Executive members supported such actions.
The Executive Committee was composed of ten officers and six Executive members.
The most active members and also the ones who were most 'political' tended to be
the ranking officers, but they could clearly be outvoted by the other members of
the E.C.

53. Maxwell, op. cit., p. 40: 'Are the existing groups in and out of Conference
organized so as to cater for the fundamental demands of the West Indian people?
Do they touch any real needs of people, by virtue of which they would be likely
to exert a magnetic pull towards the group?'

54. The budget of Standing Conference has been relatively stable during the
past five years at about £3,500 per year. Most of this is raised by dances and other
social functions.

55. Chairman's Annual Report, 1966.

56. Analyses of West Indian organization problems are found in Glass, op. cit.;
Patterson, *Dark Strangers*; Hinds, op. cit.; Rex and Moore, op. cit.; Banton, op. cit.;
Rose *et al.*, op. cit.

57. Glass, op. cit., p. 200; Banton, op. cit., Chapter 9; Patterson, *Dark Strangers*,
Chapters 16 and 17. Mrs. Patterson has written: ' "Principles of dissociation" in
Brixton are promoted by "the very evident social and cultural differences." '

58. Patterson, *Dark Strangers*, p. 316. See also Rex and Moore, op. cit., p. 114,
and Davison, op. cit., Chapter 7.

59. Patterson, *Dark Strangers*, p. 319. Skin colour is seen as both a principle of
association, since it unites West Indians generally, and a principle of dissociation,
since it divides West Indians by class.

60. For a discussion of the American Negro's difficulties in freeing himself from
patterns of discrimination and inequality in Northern urban centres, see Kenneth
B. Clark, *Dark Ghetto* (New York, Gollancz, 1965). For a general discussion of the
self-perpetuating nature of poverty, see P. Marris and M. Rein, *Dilemmas of Social
Reform* (London, Routledge & Kegan Paul, 1967), pp. 33–5. For a discussion of
reinforcing inequalities affecting British immigrants, see Peter Townsend, op. cit.

61. Consult a leading writer on identity, Erik Erikson, *Identity: Youth and Crisis*
(New York, Norton C. Norton, 1968).

62. *Teamwork* (May 1963).

63. Ibid. (July 1963).

64. Ibid. (June 1963).

65. Ibid. (April 1964).

66. Maxwell, op. cit., pp. 40–1.

67. Interview with Jeff Crawford (30 January 1967). 'People are very nervous
about any public activity. "If I were arrested," they say, "my mum would die of
heart break." We have had people tell us not to do anything because we would
embarrass the High Commission.'

68. Maxwell, op. cit., p. 37. Emphasis added.

69. Ibid., pp. 37–8.

70. Ibid., pp. 21–2.

71. Glass, op. cit., p. 200.

72. For a similar ambivalence, see Rex and Moore, op. cit., p. 163. Discussing
voluntary organizations, they write: '. . . precisely because the West Indian has
English aspirations, he experiences discrimination and it falls to his organizations
to try to remedy his grievances. The leaders of these organizations find themselves
in a dilemma. Are they to fight and possibly rupture the ties with the White community which do exist, or are they to use educational and goodwill activities to help
assimilation? They have failed and know they have failed because discrimination
still exists.'

73. The officers of Standing Conference for 1967 with positions and occupations were N. Maxwell, chairman, barrister; L. Dyke, vice-chairman, record shop owner; J. Crawford, secretary, Transport clerk; L. Chase, assistant secretary, clerk; S. Tait, treasurer, postman; J. Hunte, public relations officer, Civil Servant; A. Kelly, assistant P.R.O., Civil Servant; V. Laidlow, welfare officer, grocer; R. Riley, education officer, commercial artist; D. Dryden, membership officer, carpenter. Six were from Jamaica; three from Barbados; one from Trinidad. With the exception of Maxwell, none of the members had more than secondary education.

74. Joseph Hunte, a member of the National Committee's Legal and Welfare Advisory Panel, led the faction that voted to 'recognize' the National Committee. He was in favour of Standing Conference co-operation with C.A.R.D. and in fact worked with members of the C.A.R.D. Law and Order Committee on police cases (interview, 3 May 1967). Maxwell and Crawford were strongly opposed to the E.C. and delegates' meeting decision. See Chapter Four, section 6.

75. This was not a principled stand against the idea of lobbying or the use of contacts. They just did not have any. The lobbying success of C.A.R.D. was possibly the source of the charge of white domination. The fact that David Pitt and whites in C.A.R.D. like Lester were able to successfully lobby the back-benches could have easily caused resentment among the leaders of Conference.

76. Interview with Nadine Peppard (21 March 1967).

77. Interview with Jeff Crawford (14 March 1967): 'We were never asked and never will be. At the time, the people selecting the committee thought that C.A.R.D. represented all the immigrants and immigrant organizations and if we ask the chairman and vice-chairman of C.A.R.D. that will give adequate immigrant representation.' Crawford had been to see Miss Peppard before the committee was chosen to ask who was going to be on it and how the members were going to be chosen. (The quotation from Crawford does not represent what she told him.)

78. Interview with Neville Maxwell (5 June 1967).

79. Interview with Jeff Crawford (11 June 1967): 'I met with Malcolm X just before he died. He gave me his card—which I treasure. He said the black man should be aware of his blackness and of his own role. His visit had a great effect on people: it contributed to our renaissance, spiritually and emotionally.'

80. The ambivalence about independence from or co-operation with British society is seen in Jeff Crawford. He enjoyed being considered a militant and getting Press attention. And he enjoyed receiving an 'intimate letter' from the National Committee for Commonwealth Immigrants to participate in their employment conference (interview, 14 March 1967). Yet he also enjoyed being in the 'bad books' of the N.C.C.I. for his public opposition to them. He admired the American civil rights leaders and to an extent wished to see himself in that mould. 'I've never been arrested. I wanted to be chucked into a cell. For the first time I would feel what it's like.'

81. Born in Grenada and active in politics in Trinidad, Pitt was central to the founding of the West Indian National Party in Trinidad, a descendant of Dr. Eric Williams's People's National Movement. Several people knowledgeable about race relations in Britain have suggested that island rivalries were a possible source of the split. Presumably, the Jamaicans, who were a majority on the Standing Conference Executive, would reject the leadership of a 'small islander'. Yet I was not able to find that this factor was of importance. Maxwell and Crawford, two of Standing Conference's highest-ranking and most active officers, are from Barbados. And Conference members, as well as Pitt, were in favour of a united West Indies.

82. As one member of the C.A.R.D. Executive Committee, who was not distinctly on the side of Standing Conference, said: 'Pitt was more heavy handed than he should have been. When he sensed the opposition of Standing Conference he

wouldn't compromise on anything. He left them no alternative other than to knuckle under to his leadership or to leave. He would let them talk but then bang on the table and become angry.'

83. Actual figures are not available and one is left to the unsatisfactory device of common sense. See Glass, op. cit., Patterson, *Dark Strangers*, Rex and Moore, op. cit., for descriptions of low levels of organizational involvement in particular communities.

84. The Federation was still nominally affiliated to C.A.R.D., however.

85. Indian immigrants come from four distinct regions: the Jullandar and Hoshiarpur districts of Punjab in India; the central and southern parts of Gujarat in India; the Punjabi-speaking areas in West Pakistan and the Mirpur district of Kashmir now occupied by Pakistan; and the Sylhet district in East Pakistan. The immigrants are divided into three linguistic categories: Punjabi, a Kashmiri dialect similar to Punjabi, and Eastern Bengali. There is no mutual intelligibility among these categories and the immigrants must use a form of Hindu-Urdu as a lingua franca. The Indian immigrants are either Hindus or Sikhs. See Rashmi Desai, *Indian Immigrants in Britain* (London, Oxford University Press, for Institute of Race Relations, 1963), pp. 11–12. The Pakistanis come from the Punjabi-speaking areas in West Pakistan, the Mirpur district, and the Sylhet district. They speak either a dialect of Kashmiri, similar to Punjabi, or Eastern Bengali. They are of course Moslem. For a general discussion of the Indian and Pakistani populations in Britain, see Rose *et al.*, op. cit., Chapters 5–6, 23–5.

86. Interview with Tassaduq Ahmed (31 May 1967).

87. Interview with Hamza Alavi (14 May 1967). Suspicion of the new organization was also heightened by a story in the *Guardian* (12 December 1967) that an 'all black' organization was forming up. Members of the Council of the Federation had not been consulted and were angry that Pakistani participation seemed to be assumed although they had not given their consent.

88. Letter from Nuru Islam, general secretary of the Federation, to C.A.R.D. (25 March 1965).

89. Interview with Hamza Alavi (7 May 1967).

90. Dipak Nandy's notes from the Round Table Conference (24 October 1967).

91. Interview with Hamza Alavi (14 May 1967).

92. In November 1965, the Federation had joined with Standing Conference and the Indian Workers' Association, Great Britain, to oppose the Government's White Paper. A boycott was promised. *Sunday Times* (2 November 1965). In early October, a letter signed by Nurul Islam was sent on behalf of the Executive Committee of the Federation, asking for the resignations of Pitt and Alavi; Alavi, they said, did not in 'any capacity' represent the Pakistani community (undated letter from Nurul Islam to David Pitt). With the departure of Ahmed, the Federation Executive had become less sympathetic but the leaders of the associations who met in the Federation's Council were not as disposed to militant talk as members of the E.C., particularly Choudhury and Islam, and at the Round Table Conference in October they brought the Federation back into line with C.A.R.D. According to Hamza Alavi (interview, 14 May 1967), one factor in the refusal of the association leaders to support Choudhury was their fear of an increase in racial tension that the announcement by Standing Conference of vigilante patrols seemed to herald.

93. Twenty-three organizations formally launched the Federation on 14 April 1963. They represented twenty-one localities and an estimated 15,000 members. They were: Pakistan Welfare Associations from Bedford, Birmingham, Blackburn, London, Luton, Oxford, Scunthorpe, Sheffield; the Pakistan People's Association, Bradford and Haslingden; the Pakistan Associations in Bristol and Leicester; Pakistan Societies in Cambridge, Cardiff, Manchester, Oldham, and St. Albans;

Pak-Jubo-Shanga, Coventry; Pakistan Workers' Association, Coventry; Pakistan Muslim Association, Leeds; Pakistan Caterers' Association in Great Britain; Pakistan Muslim Welfare Association, Wolverhampton; Asiz Memorial Club, Birmingham. *Why a Federation* (London, National Federation, 1963), pp. 15–16.

94. In a speech given at the founding meeting, the chairman, Nasim Ahmed, listed the three main problems that Pakistani residents faced: security of life and property; jobs; and best value for the foreign currency they are earning. *Why a Federation*, p. 24. The aims and objects were:

The Federation shall try to inculcate the spirit of organized and disciplined life among the overseas Pakistani community in general and their organizations in particular.

The Federation shall provide a national platform for the Pakistani Associations in Great Britain, and in this regard the Federation shall be the national spokesman of all the affiliated associations. The Federation shall be responsible for directing and executing all measures aimed at prompting, on a national level, the social, cultural, economic, and religious interests of the overseas Pakistani community.

The Federation shall try to safeguard the interests of the Pakistanis in overseas countries and to guide them to discharge diligently their obligations to the host countries and to lead socially productive lives.

The Federation shall take measures to secure the co-operation of the Pakistan High Commission as well as the home Government in the efforts of organizing the Pakistani community, promoting a better social life, and in solving day-to-day problems of the overseas Pakistanis.

The Federation shall establish contact with the statutory authorities of the host country and fraternal organizations with the view to fostering understanding, good-will, and co-operation and to undertaking activities of mutual benefit.

95. Interview with Tassaduq Ahmed (31 May 1967).

96. The following very general and very brief portrait relies heavily on interviews with Hamza Alavi and on three of his papers: 'Pakistani Immigrants and the Labour Party', prepared for the British Overseas Socialist Fellowship (London, 1963); 'The Pakistanis in London' (London, B.O.S.F., 1964); 'Britain's Pakistanis Break out of their Isolation', *Peace News* (19 February 1965). The sketch presented here accords with the conclusions drawn by Rex and Moore, op. cit., pp. 164 ff., in their study of the Pakistani community in Birmingham: 'The most obvious association in Sparkbrook was the Pakistani Welfare Association. . . . Its current President was not at all clear on what precisely its present functions were, but said that it "helped Pakistanis with their personal problems and provided premises for functions" ' (p. 166).

'Few Pakistanis claimed membership of . . . any . . . associations. . . . What did seem to be the case was that amongst the more economically successful there were many who saw it as part of their duty to offer services to their fellow countrymen for reasons of charity or profit or a mixture of both' (p. 167).

97. For a detailed analysis see DeWitt John, *Indian Workers' Associations in Britain* (London, Oxford University Press, for Institute of Race Relations, 1969).

98. Interview with J. Joshi, general secretary of the I.W.A., G.B. (1 June 1967). See also Desai, op. cit., pp. 102–3: 'Its [the I.W.A.'s] objects were to further India's attempt to achieve independence, to promote social and cultural activities, and to foster greater understanding between the Indian and British people.'

99. The aims and objects of the central organization are reproduced in Desai, op. cit., p. 104. Even in 1958, the I.W.A. was explicitly in opposition to discrimination as it stated in aim (iv): 'to fight against all forms of discrimination based on colour, creed or sex, for equal human rights and social and economic opportunities and to co-operate with other organizations for the same ends'. This provides an interesting contrast with the vague aim of the Standing Conference, promulgated

at the same time, which called for understanding between the races and for integration.

100. Desai divided I.W.A. leaders in Birmingham into three categories: those who held prestige within their village-kin group; entrepreneurs who ran the internal economy of the community; the university-educated immigrants with experience of Indian national politics. 'Most members of the third group hold left-wing political views and some of them were members of left-wing parties in India' (p. 105).

101. The sponsoring organizations of C.A.R.D. were: the Birmingham I.W.A.; the Pakistani Workers' Association; the Birmingham University Socialists; the West Indian Workers' Association (now defunct). Joshi characterized the British organizations as 'radical-progressive'.

102. John, op. cit.

103. Interview with J. Joshi (1 June 1967). The dislike of C.A.R.D. as an organization associated with the Labour party was different for the I.W.A., G.B., than for Standing Conference. Conference disliked the Labour party because it had gone back on its word and had perpetuated discriminatory policies. The I.W.A., G.B., critique while including the Conference point of view, was also based on a broad conception of the proper nature of a 'labour' party. As Joshi said about C.A.R.D.: 'We knew from the United States that such a movement would only pacify people. We must do all that we can to make sure that the resentment among our people is not repressed. We must channel it into the proper forms of commitment.'

104. They were less concerned about the influence of 'whites' than the West Indians. In fact, they were quite clearly sensitive to the 'strategic' value of British citizens in their attempts to counter discrimination, as the formation of C.C.A.R.D. demonstrated.

105. As Joshi said (interview, 1 June 1967): 'C.A.R.D. is a political pressure group at the top, without having its feet on the earth. It has not reached the hearts of the people.'

106. This is not to suggest that the structure and activities of the I.W.A., G.B., were what they claimed, or what they would have liked them to be. A description of the I.W.A.'s success in carrying out its aims and its relation to the local communities is discussed by John, op. cit.

107. There were branches of the I.W.A. in Birmingham, Bradford, Coventry, Derby, Erith, Glasgow, Gravesend, Huddersfield, Leamington Spa, Leeds, Leicester, Nottingham, Southampton, Wolverhampton.

I.W.A.s in Bradford, Glasgow, Leamington Spa, and Leeds had been in touch with the local C.A.R.D. groups at various times.

108. In June 1967, there were local C.A.R.D. groups in Brent, Islington, West Middlesex, Croydon, Sheffield, Manchester, Leeds, Newcastle-upon-Tyne, and Glasgow.

109. Interview (31 May 1967).

110. Interview with Julia Gaitskell (24 February 1967): 'We are limited in our efforts because people have not identified the problems for themselves. The Manchester group canvassed Moss Side with the view of holding a neighbourhood meeting. I don't know how good the canvass was, but only three or four people came after about three visits to each house. One of the people said, "there are no problems in Moss Side", yet that's obviously not right. There's lots and lots of bitterness, but it seems to come out in verbal forms and is not canalized properly.'

# C.A.R.D. and the Formation of Public Policy: The Struggle for Anti-discrimination Laws

In the first years of its existence, C.A.R.D. had to face not only the splintered and fragmented 'structures' of the immigrant communities but also the political system, the structure of power. The main elements of the latter system—the political culture of Britain, the social and interest group configurations, the legislative and decision-making structures—were both a source of restraint on C.A.R.D.'s activities and a target area for its efforts. If C.A.R.D. was less than successful in its attempts to build a cohesive immigrant organization, it could none the less claim some notable victories in the area of public policy.

The C.A.R.D. proposals for anti-discrimination laws which were formulated in February 1965 served for two years as the basis for discussions about the proper shape of anti-discrimination legislation. Moreover, by a successful lobbying operation in the first months of its existence, C.A.R.D. was able, in conjunction with other forces, to alter significantly the Race Relations Bill of 1965. This alteration, together with the introduction of conciliation machinery as the primary means of enforcing anti-discrimination laws, and the establishment of the Race Relations Board to implement the Act, had a striking impact on discussions about the development of public policy and future governmental efforts in the race relations field.

C.A.R.D.'s attempts to secure anti-discrimination laws, of proper scope and enforced by the proper methods, monopolized the energies of its most active members through the autumn of 1967. As a pressure group, C.A.R.D. was concerned with directly influencing the decision-making process by its relations with the political parties, the Parliament, or the executive.[1] It wanted to affect indirectly the political culture of society through the Press, various forms of propaganda, or direct action. And it wanted to obtain the support of, or blunt the hostility of, other pressure groups. To understand C.A.R.D.'s efforts in shaping public policy, it is thus important to discover where C.A.R.D. chose to concentrate its efforts.

In theory there were a variety of means of exerting influence on the various elements of the political system. These ranged from threatening withdrawal of electoral support to bargaining directly with Government departments, from giving advice and counsel to the Government in private, to demonstrating publicly for particular policies. The type of influence C.A.R.D. was able to exercise and the kind its members would have liked to use are another aspect of C.A.R.D.'s policy role. Further, one may examine not only the target area for C.A.R.D.'s efforts and the nature of these efforts, but the determinants of the group's activities. Speaking generally, pressure group writers have distinguished four main determinants of an organization's activities: the structure of power in government; the structure of policy; the attitudes of those in government, in other interest groups, and in the public at large; and the nature of the resources of the group itself. In discussing the role of C.A.R.D. in shaping public policy, the last of the determinants has special relevance.

In the period under discussion, C.A.R.D. tried first to alter the provisions of the 1965 Race Relations Bill and, after its passage, to induce the Government to offer significant amendments to the Act. This period, 1965–7, was one of fluidity in policy-making. No official body took a firm lead in making policy about race relations within Britain (as opposed to immigration policy). An informal 'race relations constellation' developed including people in the Government, semi-official agencies, research institutions, and C.A.R.D. To assess C.A.R.D.'s effect on policy, several questions on how C.A.R.D. represented the immigrant interest will be answered. What was C.A.R.D.'s role in changing public policy? How did this role change? Did any theory about C.A.R.D.'s role develop among its members? What was C.A.R.D.'s position within the 'race relations constellation'? What would be the future of that constellation as the race relations field began to be marked out by official bodies and specialization of function developed? What was the nature of C.A.R.D.'s influence? With the passage of broad anti-discrimination legislation, how would the nature of this influence have to change? What organizational demands were implied if C.A.R.D. was to wield this different kind of influence?

## 1. C.A.R.D. AND THE RACE RELATIONS ACT 1965

On 7 February 1965, a membership meeting was held by the Campaign Against Racial Discrimination to discuss legislative proposals prepared by its Legal Committee. After a long meeting marked by strenuous debate, resolutions were passed committing C.A.R.D. to press for legislation against discrimination on the grounds of race, colour, religion, or national origin. They asked that such discrimination be made unlawful in housing, advertising, employment, insurance, public places, education, the granting of credit facilities, clubs offering largely public facilities, and all Government departments and bodies receiving Government grants, subsidies, and licences; that in the field of housing, legislation should attack refusal to sell or rent, or publication of discriminatory advertisements and should extend to all private estate agents, but exclude lodgings where the landlord shares private living facilities and resides on the same premises; that a statutory commission be created to oversee the enforcement of the law. [2]

These resolutions and the proposals that they reflected were markedly different from a whole range of proposed measures against discrimination which had been bruited about in Britain for over ten years. [3] The most prominent were those put forward yearly by Fenner Brockway, M.P. (now Lord Brockway), starting in 1956. Although Brockway's Bills varied in specific provisions, their general aim was to outlaw discrimination in public places and in firms that employed more than fifty people. Those who violated the law were to be fined. At the beginning of 1964 the Labour party National Executive Committee asked both the Shadow Cabinet and the Society of Labour Lawyers to draw up proposals for legislation. The three-man Shadow Cabinet, which included the future Home Secretary, Sir Frank Soskice, presented their proposals to the National Executive Study Group on Race Relations in June 1964. [4]

The Society of Labour Lawyers' Committee on Race Relations was headed by Andrew Martin, professor of Comparative Law at Southampton University, and included Cedric Thornberry, Peter Beneson, F. Ashe Lincoln, Q.C., Evi Underhill, and Anthony Lester (barristers); Michael Zander (lecturer in law at the London School of Economics and Legal Correspondent for the *Guardian*), and two co-opted members—E. J. B. Rose and Nicholas Deakin, then from the Institute's 'Survey of Race Relations in Britain'. Given a narrow brief by the National Executive Committee—they were only to consider questions of racial incitement and discrimination in public places—the Martin Committee ideas, presented to the N.E.C. in July 1964, were 'different from those of the Soskice group or the Brockway bills'.[5] On the question of discrimination in public places, the Martin Committee like Brockway and the Soskice group, recommended the use of criminal penalties. But the Committee did recommend that the areas covered by the law be extended from public houses, restaurants, hotels, and theatres to any premise used for public transport and to any place of public resort maintained by a public authority.

Yet, within the Martin Committee itself, there was sharp, often bitter disagreement. Those who held a minority opinion—Lester, Zander, Deakin, and Rose—were concerned about the form the Martin proposals were going to take. They thought that the brief given by the National Executive Committee was too narrow, that the Society of Labour Lawyers group ought to refer back to the N.E.C. for wider instructions, and that the law should be extended into other fields. Having some knowledge of discrimination laws in the United States, they were not in favour of criminal sanctions as the primary means of enforcement.[6] Their objections, expressed in a number of meetings, were overridden by other members.

Discouraged by the thinking of the Martin Committee majority, dismayed by the result of the Smethwick election, fearful that the Labour party might lose its nerve and not legislate, and concerned that if it did legislate, following the Martin proposals, the result would be clumsy, ineffectual, and more of a hindrance than a help in establishing a good legal framework for the development of race relations in Britain, Lester, Zander, and Deakin decided to draft their own legislative proposals. The 'Lester Group' (as Hindell characterized it) also included new members, who were friends of those representing the minority opinion on the Martin Committee. Three barristers, Jeffrey Jowell, Ian McDonald, and Roger Warren Evans, and a lecturer in political science at the London School of Economics, Bernard Donoghue, became involved.

In late November, they produced two sets of proposals, a 'white document' and a 'pink document'.[7] These proposals accepted the Government's intention to legislate only on the questions of racial incitement and discrimination in public places. They recommended, however, that the Government set up a Citizens' Council whose function would be to inquire into unequal treatment in housing and employment, conduct private negotiations between the involved parties, and publish findings, information, and recommendations on race relations. In the 'white document' a non-statutory Council was suggested. In the 'pink document' provision was made for a statutory body with powers of subpoena. These tentative and sketchy proposals were sent to the Attorney-General, the Lord Chancellor, and the Home Secretary, but in the busy days following the 1964 general election they received little attention.

At the same time as the 'Lester Group' was developing its ideas on ways to deal more adequately with discrimination, Lester was invited by Ted Roszak to come to the meetings of Multi-Racial Britain. Because of his experience there, his interest in the civil rights movement in the United States, and his knowledge of the proposed legislation, he was invited to the 10 January meeting of C.A.R.D., elected to the E.C., and made chairman of C.A.R.D.'s Legal Committee. This group consisted of members of the 'Lester Group'—Zander, Jowell, Warren Evans, McDonald—and the West Indian law students, Small and Bryant.

This committee, not the 'Lester Group', formulated the C.A.R.D. proposals, although there was of course overlapping membership. To an extent there was a marriage between C.A.R.D., which needed comprehensive and intelligent ideas about the form of legislation, and the white lawyers who needed a platform for their ideas. Yet, it is misleading to see the relationship so simply, since Lester and members of the Committee, especially Ian McDonald, were committed to the idea of a multiracial organization that would represent and organize immigrants. Also, Small and Bryant participated fully in the formation of the proposals. And changes in these proposals were made at the membership meeting in February.

The efforts of C.A.R.D.'s Legal Committee, strongly influenced by the researches of Jeffrey Jowell into the North American experience with anti-discrimination legislation,[8] were contained in the 'green document', which outlined a set of proposals that introduced a number of new ideas about anti-discrimination legislation into Britain. Modelled closely after the laws banning racial discrimination in Massachusetts and New York, passed following World War II, the 'green document' argued that legislation must deal with the worst problems and be enforceable.[9] Discrimination in housing and employment was singled out as the most severe problem, likely to grow worse during the following years as children of coloured immigrants 'attempt to obtain equal employment opportunities and improved housing facilities'. The authors went on to argue:

By regulating conduct and codifying national disapproval of racialism [anti-discrimination] laws can have . . . an indirect and salutary effect on prejudice. In Britain such laws do not exist. A public company or government department may refuse to employ coloured people, regardless of their qualifications. An estate agent or employment agency may enforce a colour bar. An insurance company may demand an automatically increased premium for a coloured person's car insurance cover. There is at present no remedy in the courts, no tribunal to which any appeal for help can be made, and no declaration in any statute of the equality of Her Majesty's subjects regardless of their race, colour, religion or national origin.[10]

While urging the need for legislation, the 'green document's' authors argued against criminal sanctions on the grounds that they would not be enforceable: first, because of the possible reluctance of authorities to prosecute; second, because of the heavy burden of proving the case beyond reasonable doubt; third, because there would usually be trial by jury, and juries might often be out of sympathy with such legislation. In any case, the authors noted, 'the main object of the law in this field should be to alter conduct, not to punish: and problems in employment and housing are too complex to be cured by criminal prosecutions'. The right approach, according to C.A.R.D., would be to create appropriate machinery which would rely upon education and private conciliation, and only in the last resort upon compulsory enforcement to reduce racial discrimination.

Thus, C.A.R.D. proposed that it be made unlawful to discriminate on the grounds of an individual's race, colour, religion, or national origin in the fields of employment, housing, public facilities, advertising, education, insurance, grant of credit facilities, and Government departments; and that a statutory commission be created to administer and enforce the law against discrimination by taking steps to eliminate instances of discrimination brought to its notice; to act as an authoritative source of information on discrimination; to take steps to inform the public on the aims of the law; and to attempt to obtain voluntary compliance with the law. And it suggested the procedures which the commission would follow in carrying out its functions.[11]

The document argued for this conciliation machinery in some detail, and asserted that experience in the United States and

Canada demonstrated that a vast number of cases could be settled voluntarily. C.A.R.D. also argued that the members of the new commission would become experts in race relations, have important information, dissemination, and research functions, and the perspective to understand the reinforcing aspect of discriminatory patterns.

At the 7 February C.A.R.D. meeting, there had been some argument over the exceptions for clubs (under public facilities), over exceptions for the small owner-occupier (popularly known as 'the Mrs. Murphy clause'), and over exceptions for those who employ workers in private houses. Lester and Richard Small argued for the exceptions on the grounds that the law could not be too intimate and still be effective and that it was politically expedient to make them. Although the exception for clubs was rejected, the other two were accepted and the C.A.R.D. organization was united on a comprehensive set of proposals for legislation.

These proposals were strikingly different from either the suggestions of the Soskice group, Fenner Brockway, or the Martin Committee. They were the first public and articulate presentation in Britain of the virtues of conciliation as a means of enforcement, and also one of the first strong and specific statements of the need for legislation in a number of fields, not just public places.[12] Commenting on the proposals, the *Guardian* noted that 'C.A.R.D. is slowly moving into action as the focus for rational opposition to racial discrimination'.[13]

In the next months, C.A.R.D. was to launch a lobbying campaign to educate Members of Parliament through letters and personal briefing and to arouse public opinion through the Press. In early March the Prime Minister announced his intention to introduce anti-discrimination legislation and by the long title of the Bill it was clear that the legislation would only deal with discrimination in public places (as well as with the problems of racial incitement). Although C.A.R.D.'s hopes for a broad Bill were frustrated from the outset (as the Legal Committee had expected), there could still be a battle for the kind of machinery that would enforce the proposed law. The proper conciliation machinery, as C.A.R.D. members were fond of saying, would provide the right vessel into which the problems of employment and housing could be poured when the present Bill, having been enacted, would be amended.

One stratagem for the lobbying efforts proposed by David Pitt was the petition campaign, but C.A.R.D. members—especially Pitt and Lester—were more concerned with quickly gaining support for the proposals among a wide range of people and groups and setting up general pressure against the Bill. They did send copies of the 'green document' to the Attorney-General, the Lord Chancellor, and the Home Secretary. But C.A.R.D., having little organization and hardly any membership, and being a new group that was likened to militant American civil rights organizations,[14] had to rely on more indirect methods. As Hindell has noted, Pitt, Lester, and the C.A.R.D. lawyers (aided also by Nicholas Deakin who was at this time on the C.A.R.D. Executive Committee) were able to gain favourable publicity for C.A.R.D. proposals in the *Guardian*, *New Society*, *Socialist Commentary*, *Venture* (the Fabian journal). A number of interested groups were either informally mobilized by C.A.R.D. members or worked directly in tandem with C.A.R.D. The British Caribbean Association, an all-party group, of which David Pitt was joint chairman, approved proposals like C.A.R.D.'s. The Institute of Race Relations sent information to Parliament showing the efficacy of conciliation machinery. Lester and his friends were able to reactivate the Society of Labour Lawyers' Race Relations Committee, under a new chairman, Philip Kimber. Not surprisingly, the proposals put forward by the committee were nearly identical to the 'green document's'. The Society of Labour Lawyers' 'Interim Report' appeared two days after the publication of the Home Secretary's Bill and was in sharp disagreement with it.[15]

After it was published, the Bill (which closely followed the Martin Committee proposals) drew sharp criticism. The *Observer* called it 'a botched job' and urged conciliation machinery.[16]

A number of newspapers echoed CARD in saying that the Bill did not really tackle the main problems, but none of them openly supported a full-scale statutory commission. Most of the critics not already immersed in the subject seized upon the simple notion that conciliation was more appropriate to deal with discrimination than the criminal law.[17]

Following the public criticism of the Bill, C.A.R.D. and the other sympathetic and informally linked groups circulated the 'green document' proposals to most Members of Parliament. C.A.R.D. lobbyists simply saw M.P.s whom they happened to know. It was a 'haphazard and spontaneous' process.[18] By the second reading of the Bill, the pressure which had begun with the formulation of

C.A.R.D.'s proposals in February had built up significantly. Maurice Foley, then Parliamentary Under-Secretary at the Department of Economic Affairs, had been made responsible in 'his personal capacity' for co-ordinating the Government's integration efforts and after intensive lobbying he was strongly in favour of conciliation. So was an all-party group of M.P.s established in the autumn of 1964 to oppose the extension of the Commonwealth Immigrants Act.[19] Significantly, the Shadow Home Secretary, Peter Thorneycroft, was also disposed to conciliation. In late April, he had invited David Pitt and members of the C.A.R.D. Legal Subcommittee to meet him at a flat near Westminster and, although he made it clear that he was basically against legislation, he indicated he might want to use the concept of conciliation as a switch with which to annoy Soskice. Four days before the second reading, he and Sir Alec Douglas-Home tabled an amendment which declined to give the Race Relations Bill a second reading because it would introduce penalties when a system of conciliation would be more effective, and because legislation on race would create more problems than it solved.[20]

By the second reading on 3 May, Soskice was prepared to retreat. In his speech at the start of the debate, he indicated that the Government was prepared to listen to the arguments of those who disagreed with the Bill.[21] Within a week, Donald Chapman, joint chairman of the British Caribbean Association with David Pitt and member of the all-party group on race which had opposed the extension of the Commonwealth Immigrants Act, proposed amendments to the Bill which suggested the establishment of a conciliation body. (Following the second reading, he had met with other members of C.A.R.D. Legal Committee and together they had drafted Chapman's proposals.)[22]

During May, Soskice drafted amendments to the proposed legislation. In the first part of the Bill dealing with discrimination in places of public resort, a civil remedy was substituted for the criminal sanctions. Provision was made for the establishment of a Race Relations Board which would act through regional conciliation committees. These committees would receive complaints, make inquiries, and where appropriate try to secure a settlement between the two parties. In the event that this was not possible, the committee would report to the Board which, if it decided that a pattern of discrimination did indeed exist, would in turn report to the Attorney-General. If he agreed with the evaluation of the Board, he could bring an action for injunction against the discriminating party. The penalty for defiance of such an injunction would be imprisonment for contempt of court.[23]

Soskice's retreat—in one sense a shrewd political move since it drew the fangs from the Opposition, blunted the criticisms of those pressing for a Race Relations Board with more power, and prevented a probable defeat in the Committee stage when Tories and back-benchers could have combined to defeat the Government position and introduce conciliation—was a significant victory for the 'conciliation' lobbyists.[24] A Minister had been forced to propose major alterations to a major Bill at a late stage.

The reasons for this shift are necessarily complicated. The Government was pressed for parliamentary time. It was probably not pleased at the outburst of criticism which greeted the publication of the Bill. With a slim majority, there were good tactical reasons for shifting before the combined pressure of the back-benchers and the Conservatives.

C.A.R.D.'s role, while it should not be over-estimated, was clearly crucial. C.A.R.D. had done more research into anti-discrimination legislation and experiences elsewhere than had the Government, the Press, or Members of Parliament. It was able to present a coherent set of proposals accompanied by cogent arguments and impressive precedents. Also, the situation was very fluid: the issue of race had burst suddenly on English politics, and Ministers were more concerned about the control of immigration than the promotion of anti-discrimination measures. As a result of Smethwick and Leyton, a good deal of emotional discussion about race and politics had surfaced. Understandably, C.A.R.D.'s relative expertise would be welcomed by journals, newspapers, sympathetic groups, Labour back-benchers, and Tories looking for a reasoned position.

C.A.R.D. literature, briefings, and the general dissemination of its ideas had a distinct cumulative effect. Some of the issues were imperfectly understood. The need for a statutory commission was not emphasized by all opponents of the Government's proposed legislation, but conciliation clearly had an appeal for people of all persuasions. Through informal links and personal connections, C.A.R.D. was able to help establish a climate and to present a clear position which proved to be of importance. Michael Zander could promote the C.A.R.D. proposals in the *Guardian*. David Ennals, M.P., could argue verbatim from the C.A.R.D. 'green document' in the second reading debate.[25] C.A.R.D. could brief Peter Thorneycroft at a crucial moment. Writers in the *Sunday Times* and in the *Observer* could argue for conciliation. The Society of Labour Lawyers' Race Relations Committee could be resuscitated by C.A.R.D. lawyers to argue against the very provisions it had originally suggested. Anthony Lester and David Pitt could brief M.P.s with whom they were friends. Groups like the British Caribbean Association and the Institute of Race Relations could weigh in with the proper arguments or information. Technical skill and knowledge combined with uncertainty and half-hearted support for the legislation from Ministers plus a desire among some back-benchers to improve the Government's record in race relations after the autumn retreat was enough to cause the shift.

To summarize, C.A.R.D. during the spring of 1965 was forced to operate as a promotional group. Although it was representing the immigrant interest it was forced to present this interest as a 'cause' and seek allies who would embrace it. The target structure at this time was very imperfectly understood and consisted of any interested groups, journalists, or back-benchers who were willing to listen to C.A.R.D.'s point of view and then put it as their own. C.A.R.D.'s assets were factual knowledge of North American experience and the ability to articulate it forcefully. That the proposals came from an 'immigrant group' seems to have been much less important than that they were reasonable proposals. Lack of time and C.A.R.D.'s own lack of resources and cohesion determined the type of influence that could be exerted. The direction in which the influence was wielded depended on the difficulty in gaining access to the Cabinet and the need to work indirectly through journalists and back-benchers favourable to C.A.R.D.'s position. In short, C.A.R.D. managed to plant seeds that could grow for others to harvest. It should be emphasized that the operation was done hurriedly and haphazardly. No campaign was mapped out; the points of influence were not analysed and evaluated. A rough coalition was quickly built up—many voices in a chorus intoning a roughly similar chant which, because of the special circumstances surrounding the Bill's publication, was partially heeded. C.A.R.D.'s particular strengths were operative in this instance because of others' weaknesses.

As a promotion group, C.A.R.D. depended on the goodwill of others. It could make no threats, exercise no sanctions. It could not claim the right to be consulted, it could not negotiate or bargain. It could not force people to act. The source of its 'power' was its ideas and information and it could only persuade and hope that the lessons were sympathetically received. Given the ambivalence about legislation at the time, this inevitably meant that the interest of the immigrants—the need for a strong statutory commission— would be compromised. C.A.R.D.'s inability to bring direct pressure to bear on any of the Cabinet Ministers—pressure which would stem from the organization of the immigrants as a sectional group with a role in society that was strategic and legitimized by the prevailing political culture—as well as the general confusion of the lobbying operation is seen in the Committee stage.

For, although in one sense the changes introduced by Soskice could be interpreted as a victory for the 'conciliation' lobbyists, in another it was of course a defeat. Although the principle of conciliation had been accepted and a new institution, the Race Relations Board, established, the scope of legislation was still too narrow. Moreover, the commission had no powers to subpoena, hold hearings, or take orders. During the hearings of Standing Committee B, C.A.R.D., through Shirley Williams and Donald Chapman, was able to put down amendments to the discrimination section of the already amended Bill.[26] But, although all the Labour back-benchers voted against the Government, the combination of Soskice and the Tories (now quiescent since the conciliation had been accepted) was impossible to overcome. C.A.R.D. had not been able to systematically lobby the members of Standing Committee B. With some of the dissatisfied Labour M.P.s there was extremely close contact. One of the Committee members remembers that there was continuous consultation, meetings were held twice a week, and Anthony Lester and his fellow lobbyists were very influential and effective. Another gave C.A.R.D. credit for the change to conciliation, by its passing helpful information to allies. A third mentioned the care with which C.A.R.D. prepared memoranda and cited its educational function as being crucial. A Conservative member of the Standing Committee remembers that C.A.R.D.'s views were 'of the greatest help' in developing his own position. They offered experience from other countries which was hard to obtain in England. With others, C.A.R.D. had less contact and could not do anything but provide written information.[27]

C.A.R.D.'s impact is thus difficult to measure precisely because of its indirect nature. One test is to ask whether, if the organizational efforts had been absent, the Act would have looked the same. The answer is no. Although the people active in C.A.R.D. might have used another vehicle, the fact is that they were active in C.A.R.D. (for reasons beyond the passage of legislation) and that they were of importance in shaping the debate on the Bill. The revised Race Relations Bill 1965 was not central to the problems of coloured immigrants in England, yet it provided a starting-point from which to move. Through a spontaneous gathering of forces in the midst of a situation that had been badly prepared by the Government, C.A.R.D. was able to establish a fund of goodwill and build a reputation for its lobbyists. C.A.R.D.'s point of view did not prevail during the spring of 1965, but it was a portent of the ultimate direction in which Government policy would develop.

## 2. FORCES FOR AMENDING THE ACT[28]

The passage of the Race Relations Act 1965 only pointed the way towards renewed C.A.R.D. efforts to change public policy. To C.A.R.D. members, the Act would have to be amended as swiftly as possible because it was deficient in scope and means of enforcement. The problem was: how to do it? In the summer of 1965, the Government was still thinking in terms of immigration control and the Home Secretary, who had never been deeply committed to the idea of anti-discrimination legislation, was not eager to subject himself to an ordeal similar to the one he had just endured. C.A.R.D. members were convinced that there would have to be either change at the top, in the Government, or pressure from below through flooding the new Race Relations Board with complaints outside the scope of the Act.

The quest for amended legislation was halted in August with the publication of the Government's White Paper. The immigration issue was again central and C.A.R.D. devoted its energies to countering the policy outlined by the Government. A pamphlet critical of the Government was written and 10,000 copies distributed.[29] In November, C.A.R.D. held a public lobby of the Commons, but the issue of whether C.A.R.D. members should join the National Committee for Commonwealth Immigrants divided the organization and C.A.R.D. was not clear about its own position on immigration policy.[30] The main attempt to counter the White Paper was made by the Action Committee for Rational Immigration Policy, a group in which C.A.R.D. members participated.[31]

## CHANGE AT THE TOP

In December 1965, a major change in the Cabinet signalled the beginning of a new period in C.A.R.D.'s efforts for adequate anti-discrimination legislation. Sir Frank Soskice, bothered by ill health, resigned as Home Secretary and was replaced by Roy Jenkins, then Minister of Aviation. Familiar with developments in the American civil rights struggle through friends in the Kennedy-Johnson administration, Jenkins was disposed to extend the law if it was politically possible.[32] Where Soskice had been reluctant, Jenkins was willing, in fact eager, to legislate on discrimination in employment and housing if cause could be shown and the climate changed. He began carefully preparing the ground for such a move shortly after he assumed office.[33]

In a series of speeches given during his first year and a half in office, Jenkins began step by step to commit the Government to the initiation of new legislation. In May 1966, speaking before a meeting of the voluntary liaison committees in his first major address on race, the Home Secretary noted: 'My mind is far from closed about future changes in the Act.' He also said that many felt there was need for legislation in employment and housing, but 'For the moment I reserve judgement on the legislation point but I am in no doubt that the employment aspect of the matter in particular is rapidly becoming central to the whole future success of our integration policy.' And he affirmed: 'A strong lead is essential, and there will be no question of the Government avoiding its responsibility for giving such a lead.'[34] By October, in a speech to the Institute of Race Relations, he could report on the progress of the Race Relations Board and note that the process of conciliation 'is hindered by the lack of powers to compel alleged discriminators even to talk to local committees'. He mentioned again the possibility of widening the scope of the Bill.[35] By February 1967, addressing a National Committee for Commonwealth Immigrants Conference on Racial Equality in Employment, Jenkins could warn that, although he did not want to anticipate the Government's decision on the subject of further legislation, none the less, industrial relations in Britain had not been built on a purely voluntary basis and state action had often been necessary.[36] By May, he could tell the London Labour Party Conference:

If further legislation is necessary to deal with this issue, we should not be frightened of it . . . the correct legislative framework can make it much more difficult for men's minds and hearts to move in the wrong direction and much easier for them to move in the right direction. American experience provides overwhelming evidence that this is so. For us to fall behind America in the leadership the Government offers towards racial tolerance would be an intolerable situation.[37]

Jenkins's speeches were delivered to increasingly 'political' audiences and were characterized by their increasingly sharp focus on the need for new laws. Another indication of Jenkins's intention to take positive action in the broad area of integration was the transference of Maurice Foley from the Department of Economic Affairs and a position as part-time co-ordinator of Government efforts for integration, to the Home Office as a full-time Minister with responsibility for all aspects of the Government's policy towards coloured immigrants—integration *and* immigration.[38] In early 1966, Jenkins appointed Mark Bonham Carter as chairman of the Race Relations Board, demonstrating still further his desire for diligent enforcement of the Act and his receptivity to extending the scope of legislation if possible. Bonham Carter, grandson of Asquith and friend of Jenkins since college days at Balliol, agreed to take the position on the condition that after a year he could recommend an extension of its powers.[39] Bonham Carter was to be assisted by John Lyttle, a former member of the Labour Party Research Department at Transport House who was also broadly sympathetic to the need for extending the Act.[40] Besides the changes and additions in personnel in the Government and the emergence of Jenkins, Bonham Carter, Foley, and Lyttle, all of whom in the spring of 1966 were in principle in favour of extending legislation, there were several obvious institutional changes which affected lobbying in the new period. First, the Race Relations Board began operations under Bonham Carter and its two other members, Sir Learie Constantine, former High Commissioner for Trinidad and Tobago, and Alderman Bernard S. Langton, former Lord Mayor of Manchester. As a Government-financed body it was charged with implementing the first sections of the Race Relations Act. The officers of the Board in London would not only oversee the formal activities of their organization but, as experience in the United States and Canada suggested, gain insight and experience into race relations by setting up local conciliation committees and dealing with complaints. Both their expertise and a natural bureaucratic tendency for increasing the area of jurisdiction of one's activities would work in favour of the Board pressing for wider legislation and broader powers.

Second, the National Committee for Commonwealth Immigrants, set up under the White Paper in the autumn of 1965, would also act as a form of lobby group. Its functions were not clearly outlined in the White Paper, but they fell into two broad categories: giving advice to the Government, and building up the network of local voluntary liaison committees.[41] As will be discussed in this chapter, the nature of the 'advice' that the National Committee would give to the Government was as unclear as the role of the Committee itself. However, both through its members and certain of its special advisory panels, the National Committee would be a semi-official force for the extension of legislation.

Thus, in the stages when legislation must be initiated, C.A.R.D. and other groups would naturally try to affect the relevant Minister. But in this case, given Jenkins's attitude and the development of official and semi-official bodies favouring further legislation, they would consider not so much how to influence him, but how to influence the general climate of opinion and affect both Westminster and the Cabinet so as to allow Jenkins to act.

### FAMILY RELATIONS

Besides the changes in personnel and the growth of institutions with specific responsibilities for formulating and implementing public policy concerning immigrants, a more informal, less easy to describe configuration also began to evolve after the 1965 Act. Because the racial problem came to Britain with relative swiftness, the number of people actively concerned about shaping public policy to aid immigrants was relatively small at the time. Those involved, whether academics, members of official or semi-official organizations, or activists in 'immigrant groups', tended to know others with similar predilections and concerns. A 'race relations constellation' developed, comprising a number of organizations linked informally by common concerns and common attitudes, and a group of 'race relations professionals' who worked both within and outside the Government. As Eric Silver said in February 1967:

At the centre of the race relations effort in Britain today is a 'family relationship'. All these people are in one way or another connected. They all have a sense of their role. They are committed to ameliorating race relations. But they hardly work along strict civil service lines; they have little sense of protocol. They often communicate, let their hair down together, discuss each other's problems and projects.[42]

To understand C.A.R.D.'s role in the period after passage of the Act, it is necessary to have at least a rough idea of the form that this *ad hoc* configuration took since C.A.R.D. members were influential in its evolution and since they could, because of the weaknesses of their own organization, choose to work through the variety of organizations of which the 'race professionals' were members.

The main cohesive element among these 'professionals' was general agreement on the need for improving the conditions of life of the coloured immigrant in Britain. There was also specific agreement on the need for legislation similar to that outlined in the C.A.R.D. proposals of February 1965. This shared attitude was necessarily important as a force which made people work closely together. Yet the 'professionals' were hardly a closed group (just as the 'constellation' was hardly a formal alliance). They did not necessarily devote full time to race relations, nor did they operate self-consciously in tandem. Through constant contact with one another they were able to know what others in the field were doing and to complement rather than duplicate their efforts. In the campaign for extension of laws, this informal planning could produce multiple activities giving an impression of strength. The 'professionals' often joked about their similarity to a stage army with the actor-soldiers disappearing through one trap-door to re-emerge from another. They were all conscious that through overlapping membership they wore 'different hats' in the same enterprise.

The 'constellation' can be broadly described by noting the organizations with a rough similarity of views regarding new legislation, by indicating certain individuals who were in close and continual, if informal, contact, and by examining the interlocking memberships some of them shared. As of 1 June 1967 a number of organizations had made public statements in favour of amending the Race Relations Act. Among these were the Race Relations Board, the National Committee for Commonwealth Immigrants, a number of the voluntary liaison committees, C.A.R.D., the National Council for Civil Liberties, the British Caribbean Association, the United Nations Association, the Society of Labour Lawyers, the Indian Workers' Association, Great Britain, the Indian Workers' Association, Southall, the Standing Conference of West Indian Organizations, London Region.

The Institute of Race Relations and its 'Survey of Race Relations in Britain' while technically restricted in their charter from making corporate statements about public policy were in the persons of their highest officers in support of extending legislation. Similarly, several junior Ministers who were back-benchers during the Race Relations Act debates in 1965 were sympathetic to extension. These were Shirley Williams at the Department of Education and Science; Reginald Freeson, at the Ministry of Power; Maurice Foley, at the Ministry of Defence, formerly Minister with special responsibility for immigrants at the Home Office; and David Ennals, his successor at the Home Office. Several journalists had a special interest in race relations and were in favour of wider laws: Eric Silver of the *Guardian*, Colin McGlashan of the *Observer*, Malcolm Southan of the *Sunday Times*. These organizations and individuals comprised the 'race relations constellation' at the time.[43]

Of all the people in these organizations, the most active and in most continuous contact were Mark Bonham Carter; John Lyttle; Nadine Peppard, general secretary of the National Committee for Commonwealth Immigrants; Martin Ennals, Information Officer of the National Committee; his brother, David Ennals; Nicholas Deakin and E. J. B. Rose of the 'Survey of Race Relations'; Anthony Lester, Dipak Nandy, and David Pitt of C.A.R.D. These one might identify as the 'race professionals'. Some were active full time in race relations, others were not, but all were distinctly concerned with changing public policy.[44]

As seen from the C.A.R.D. perspective, contacts with the other 'professionals' had developed over the years but were moulded during the initial period of lobbying against the Race Relations Bill. Nadine Peppard was then general secretary of the undernourished National Committee (on which David Pitt served) and was connected with the London Council of Social Service. She gave evidence to the Society of Labour Lawyers' race relations subcommittee (reconstituted in 1967). So did Lyttle, who as research assistant in the Overseas Department at Transport House, was in touch with C.A.R.D. about its legislative proposals. Lyttle and David Ennals were both members of the British Overseas Socialist Fellowship. As an M.P. on Standing Committee B, Ennals was briefed by C.A.R.D. Deakin was on the C.A.R.D. Executive Committee and he and Rose were involved in passing information about laws on to interested M.P.s. By accident then, many of the people with whom C.A.R.D. members had been in close contact in the spring of 1965 were to become prominent in the main organizations in the 'race relations interest'. The need for wider legislation was thus carried into the new period by individuals who had either been briefed by C.A.R.D. or who were sympathetic with its legislative position.[45]

A crucial element in the family relations configuration was the relationship between Jenkins and Bonham Carter. C.A.R.D. managed to have access to both men. Hugh Gaitskell's daughter, Julia, had become a member of C.A.R.D. Executive Committee in July 1965. Through her father she had grown close to both Roy Jenkins and Mark Bonham Carter. Anthony Lester during the autumn of 1965 had been in contact with Bonham Carter about the possibility of establishing a new organization, to be funded by a trust, which would be a source of information in the race relations field and which could be used as a consulting agency by local government unions, or other local groups. When Bonham Carter became chairman of the Race Relations Board, he was in contact with Lester and through Bonham Carter C.A.R.D.'s position was transmitted to Jenkins.

To summarize: in contrast to the period before the introduction of the Race Relations Bill, during the months following Jenkins's appointment and the establishment of the Race Relations Board and the National Committee for Commonwealth Immigrants, the race professionals and the race relations constellation that they represented were able to exercise considerable influence. This was partly because of the sympathetic lead of the Home Secretary, partly because policy was being formed concurrently with the evolution of the professionals and the constellation, partly because there was developing acceptance of a fairly specific set of proposals first presented by C.A.R.D.

## 3. INITIATING LEGISLATION: C.A.R.D.'S EFFORTS

In early 1966 the C.A.R.D. members who were deeply concerned about amending the Race Relations Act saw the organization's role as 'providing straw with which the Home Secretary could make his bricks'. Specifically, there was a distinct need to provide proof that discrimination was in fact widespread in Britain, to show that the Race Relations Board as constituted and empowered could not deal with the problem, and to shift the public debate from immigration control to the needs of the second generation and the problems of integration. C.A.R.D.'s strategy had three strains. First, there was the tactic testing to prove discrimination. Second, there were a series of 'brain-trusting' tasks like submitting evidence, writing articles, drafting model legislation, which were performed by C.A.R.D. members (most often Anthony Lester). Third, because of C.A.R.D.'s weaknesses, there were attempts to win over as many organizations as possible to the C.A.R.D. point of view and to encourage them to state the need for legislation publicly.

C.A.R.D.'s efforts must be seen in the broader context not only of the institutional and personal developments in the 'race relations interest' suggested above, but within the context of the decision-making structure. Although the Home Secretary had been from the first generally in favour of extending the law, the final decision to initiate legislation obviously rested with the Cabinet. Jenkins's tasks were to persuade his fellow Ministers that discrimination was a serious social problem; that legislation in the sensitive areas of employment and housing was the right way to confront the problem; that the Government should defy the organized resistance of the trade unions, employers, and other segments of the public if necessary. The Trades Union Congress and the Confederation of British Industries were not going to look favourably on a law dealing with hiring and firing, promotion, and training. After the imposition of the prices and wages freeze in July 1966, the industrial pressure groups tended to view anti-discrimination legislation as but another attempt by the Government to regulate vital aspects of industrial relations.[46] Speaking broadly, the industrial and economic Ministers would be reluctant to further exacerbate the relations between the governmental departments and their main constituents. In housing, the Government risked the antagonism of many middle-class voters.

A basic problem of power in race relations was raised. Could the reformers in the 'race relations interest' overcome the veto power of industrial institutions like the T.U.C. and the C.B.I. or the potential negative of a large voting bloc? In January 1967, the T.U.C. and the C.B.I. reacted negatively to a Government proposal that an anti-discrimination clause—similar to the Fair Wages Resolution of 1946—be inserted in Government contracts.[47] In the field of legislation, both the T.U.C. and C.B.I. had made it clear to Ray Gunter, Minister of Labour, that although they wanted to end discrimination, they favoured voluntary methods, that is negotiations, not sanctions imposed by legislation.[48]

Even after the quiescent general election of 1966, when race did not figure as prominently as in the election of 1964, the question of immigrants' role in Britain still loomed as a potentially destructive issue for any party that was not circumspect. It seemed to the 'race professionals' in 1966 that the Government would have to legislate early in 1968 to avoid taking an electoral risk at the next general election and that the intention would have to be announced before the Queen's speech in the autumn of 1967. Those who were politically acute within the 'race relations constellation' felt it necessary to allay the doubts of the Cabinet—political doubts (could a Labour Government afford to legislate in such a sensitive area?), practical ones (would legislation as outlined work?), and moral ones (was legislation the right way to deal with the manifestation of personal prejudice?).

One of the main obstacles to further legislation was the lack of proof of discrimination, proof that could be used to convince the indifferent and the antagonistic that the 'problem' was based on white attitudes and actions, not the immigrants' failure to adjust to the host society. Missing from Britain were the institutionalized discrimination of the American South and the stark patterns of massive deprivation in the American North which had led to explosive riots. Absent too were the drama and tragedy which had done so much to heighten America's consciousness of its racial problem. Discrimination took more muted forms in the twilight areas of Leeds, Birmingham, or North Kensington.

Discrimination in Britain would have to be made dramatic and it would have to be documented. The idea for testing discrimination had come from the United States via Anthony Lester. Lester had visited America during the summer of 1965 and through his contacts in the Congress of Racial Equality had become convinced of the need for efforts in the local communities to uncover cases of discrimination and to make these cases public.[49] Testing was originally conceived as a strategy for pressing for legislation. The scope of the Race Relations Act was narrow and did not include the main problems of discrimination that affected immigrants. By testing in these areas and forwarding the complaints to the Race Relations Board, C.A.R.D. could both publicize discrimination and give the Board evidence from which it could argue for an extension of its powers. The organization could also gain insight into the variety of mechanisms and evasions that characterize patterns of discrimination. As the strategy was first conceived in the autumn of 1965, there was to be little effort made to actually solve cases because of C.A.R.D.'s limited resources. Final solution was a long and difficult process and, without the support of law, difficult to achieve. The strategy was not to bring immediate relief (although immediate action would of course be taken where possible) but to push for a legal framework which would then make subsequent casework meaningful.

In the autumn of 1965, C.A.R.D. printed a pamphlet on 'How to Expose Discrimination', and distributed 10,000 copies to affiliated organizations. C.A.R.D. members were urged to report cases of discrimination and to test for discriminatory practices if people did not come forward. For a variety of reasons the organizations did not respond with alacrity. Some local groups understood the legislative strategy imperfectly. Others were reluctant to spend time simply collecting cases without trying to solve individual ones.[50] Most were probably lacking in personnel willing to carry on the difficult job of testing.

Two efforts to test emanated from the Executive Committee of C.A.R.D. A Complaints Subcommittee was established in June 1966. Originally headed by Julia Gaitskell it was to be a clearing-house for cases of discrimination sent to C.A.R.D., but it soon moved into a testing role and developed special techniques. One method was simply to write pairs of letters to firms, employment agencies, or estate agents—one from a white, another from a slightly more qualified coloured immigrant. A second method was role-playing. The principle of proving discrimination was the same as in letter-testing, through comparison of the experiences of a slightly more qualified immigrant and a white. By November 1966, Robert Souhami, a white physician, was formally selected as head of the Complaints Committee and potential testers were contacted in various parts of London. Complaints were uncovered on entry to jobs in public corporations and private enterprise; on interest rates and car-hire facilities; and on flat-finding agencies.

The second testing effort which emanated from the Executive Committee was the summer project of 1966. Directed by Dipak Nandy, this was modelled on the famous summer project that the Student Non-violent Coordinating Committee held in Mississippi during the summer of 1964. It had a series of aims relating to 'community development' and the strengthening of local groups, but one of its goals was to collect and uncover cases of discrimination. Twenty-four students and coloured school leavers worked in three communities—Leeds (Hyde Park), Manchester (Moss Side), and Southall—for four weeks. During that time fifty-two cases of discrimination were sent to the Race Relations Board. The results underlined the fact that second-generation coloured immigrants were also victims of discrimination and, therefore, that the problem of discrimination was not simply one of newcomers having a difficult time adjusting to a strange country. The project also discovered in Southall that of 1,000 qualified Indian graduates, a large majority were able to obtain only unskilled or semi-skilled jobs. These people who had been given priority vouchers to enter Britain were unable to take advantage of their skills.[51] The results of the project were given a wide coverage by the Press.[52]

By March 1967, C.A.R.D. had managed to send over 150 complaints to the Race Relations Board, one-third from the summer project testing, the rest from the London-based Complaints Committee. Over 90 per cent of these 150 were outside the scope of the Race Relations Act 1965. The impact of the C.A.R.D. campaign was revealed in the Annual Report of the Race Relations Board which appeared in April 1967. In its first fifteen months of operation (from 8 December 1965 to 16 March 1967), the Board had received 309 complaints of alleged unlawful discrimination.[53] Of these, only 85 cases—27.5 per cent—came within the scope of the Act. The remaining 224 cases—97 in employment, 37 in housing, the rest in a variety of areas—could not be dealt with by the Board. Most of these cases, especially those in employment and housing, were the result of C.A.R.D. testing. In the Report, the Board recommended extension of the Act so that it could have powers to deal with the crucial areas of discrimination, citing the evidence accumulated in its own work and contained within the P.E.P. report as demonstration of sufficient need. Through testing, C.A.R.D. had been able to help substantially in showing the existence of discrimination, had given needed evidence to the Race Relations Board, and in the process had increased public awareness of the problem of discrimination.[54] Moreover, testing had demonstrated to C.A.R.D. members the intricacies of discriminatory patterns and in areas like employment agencies or private housing given members of the legal committee ideas for tightening the legislative proposals. C.A.R.D. members, already sensitive to the harsh effects of discrimination, were struck by the hardships and anguish that these patterns caused and as a result produced a report on discrimination presenting outstanding cases.

It emphasized the 'lack of any kind of assistance for the victims [of discrimination], not to mention the absence of any possibility of redress'.[55] The report reiterated the need for legislation, noting that victims of discrimination had nobody except the Race Relations Board to help them and that the Board was often unable to do so.

If the testing tactic depended largely on C.A.R.D. organization, C.A.R.D.'s brain-trusting activities in the area of legislation depended primarily on one person, Anthony Lester. Between January 1966 and June 1967, Lester wrote a number of articles putting a case for legislation similar to the one outlined in the February 1965 proposals.[56] He was able to brief Bonham Carter. And he was asked to draft legislation. On 16 December 1966, Maurice Orbach, M.P., introduced a Private Members Bill in Parliament amending the Race Relations Act 1965. The Bill had been written by Lester and Roger Warren Evans and was in essence a transformation of the C.A.R.D. 'green document' proposals into legal language.[57] Orbach did not push the Bill to a vote because the Home Secretary did not think that the time was propitious; none the less the Bill would serve as a guide to M.P.s when the time came for specific debates about legislative proposals from the Government.[58]

Lester also wrote evidence on discrimination in employment which was presented in January to the Royal Commission on Trade Unions and Employers' Associations. After discussing the incidence of discrimination, the C.A.R.D. document again put forward its legislative proposals.[59] The *Guardian* called the evidence 'the most cogent case for extending the Race Relations Act' yet presented.[60]

Lester was also able to get two other organizations to support C.A.R.D. legislative proposals. In his capacity as a member of the Society of Labour Lawyers, he and Cedric Thornberry wrote a 'Third Report of the Race Relations Committee' which followed the original Martin Committee Report and the Interim Report published on 9 April 1965 (opposing the Martin Committee proposals as embodied in the Race Relations Bill). The Third Report, which was released on 15 November 1966, warned that the cultural and colour discrimination which was practised against the first-generation coloured immigrant would become simply and blatantly colour discrimination with the second. It did not attempt to show the extent of discrimination, except through Press cuttings, but argued that 'the right type of legislation can break habits of discrimination and prevent them from spreading further'.[61] The right type of legislation was outlined and was strikingly similar to the original C.A.R.D. proposals (and of course to the subsequent Orbach Bill).

In November, at the suggestion of Lester, the International and Commonwealth Bureau of the Fabian Society convened a conference on racial policies in Britain. Papers by academics and race professionals were given, including one on the 'Need for Legislation' by C.A.R.D.'s legal expert.[62] In November, the National Committee for Commonwealth Immigrants endorsed in principle the need to extend the power of the Race Relations Board and the areas covered by the Act. This decision followed similar statements by the National Committee's Special Advisory Panels on Housing and Employment. Although it is not possible to claim that C.A.R.D. members were solely responsible, it is also true that Lester as vice-chairman was influential on the Employment Panel; Roger Warren Evans and Nicholas Deakin were active on the Housing Panel; and Pitt, Hamza Alavi, and V. D. Sharma were vocal members of the National Committee. Pitt, Alavi, Deakin, Warren Evans, and of course Lester had all been deeply involved in the original C.A.R.D. lobby and were among the first in Britain to be familiar with foreign legislative experience.

Besides the mobilization of the Fabian Society and the Society of Labour Lawyers, Lester, earlier in the year, had been able to convince the Employment Panel of the National Committee to convene a national conference on racial equality in employment. Lester had originally hoped that C.A.R.D. could mount the conference but it was soon clear that the organization's resources were inadequate, and he presented the idea to the Advisory Panel. It was quickly accepted both by the Panel and by the National Committee. Lester was given money to go to the United States and make contact with experts in American civil rights. In February 1967 the conference was held.

American speakers stressed the need for legislation in the United States and the importance it had in changing behaviour and insuring equality of opportunity.[63] Speakers from industry and the trade unions warned that legislation might not be the answer and that the voluntary handling of discrimination in industry would be best.[64] Bonham Carter urged that British leaders should heed the experience of other countries and should admit that severe problems did in fact exist in Britain. Representatives from the upper levels of the T.U.C. and the C.B.I. were not present,[65] and there was little Press coverage. Yet it was another step in the preparations for the introduction of legislation.

Lester was also able to get David Marquand and Ben Whitaker, M.P.s, to put questions on the subject of discrimination in insurance, exchanges, and local authority housing. Thus, C.A.R.D. by testing, by utilizing the resources of others, by working with the 'race professionals' had been able to put forward the case for legislation in a number of different settings.

## 4. INITIATING LEGISLATION: C.A.R.D.'S IMPACT

Following the National Committee's conference, the pressure for legislation began to build significantly. In March, a community study of Sparkbrook, Birmingham, by John Rex and Robert Moore was published. The deprivation of the immigrants in Sparkbrook and their problems in struggling against the barriers of discrimination in housing provided concrete and poignant evidence of the hardships of living in England's immigrant areas and evoked a spate of editorial comments about the dangers of allowing enclaves of 'second-class' citizens to develop.[66]

In April, further sociological evidence was published, corroborating claims from the 'race professionals' and others that discrimination was widespread. The Political and Economic Planning report on *Racial Discrimination*, the results of a sample of six areas throughout England, demonstrated clearly that discrimination was not a defensive fantasy in the minds of interested parties—the immigrants and those who claimed to speak for them—but was a harsh reality scarring British life. By interviewing immigrants and those who were in a position to discriminate, as well as by conducting 'situation tests' where the conditions of potential discrimination were reproduced, the report gathered evidence to show that there was substantial discrimination in employment, housing (including private rental, purchase, and public rental), credit facilities, insurance, and personal services. Two main trends were discerned:

As immigrants become more accustomed to English ways of life, as they acquire higher expectations and higher qualifications, so they experience more personal direct discrimination. This is apparent in the local differences between areas with established communities as opposed to new communities. It is reflected in the experience of school leavers who are the children of immigrants.

Awareness of discrimination, prejudice and hostility, tends to make immigrants withdraw into their own communities.[67]

The idea for the report had originated with Bonham Carter and was strongly supported by Jenkins. Clearly, if legislation was to be initiated, hard evidence of need should be produced. The report had been sponsored jointly by the Race Relations Board and the National Committee for Commonwealth Immigrants, and financed by the Joseph Rowntree Memorial Trust.[68] Speaking at a press conference releasing the report to the public, Mark Bonham Carter noted that the report 'disperses the mythology which surrounds so much discussion about race relations'. Discrimination must be seen as the responsibility of the employer and the estate agent. Laws were clearly needed.[69] Press reactions were quick and pointed. Editorials in *The Times*, the *Guardian*, the *Observer*, the *Sunday Times*, *The Economist*, plus articles sympathetic to legislation in the *New Statesman* (written by Dipak Nandy), *New Society*, and the *Spectator* established a new tenor to the debate. The need for legislation, after months of building and preparation by the 'race relations constellation', was suddenly assumed by the Press. The discussion could turn to the form that legislation would take, the problems of mollifying the T.U.C. and the C.B.I., handling the housing interests, and blunting the possible efforts of the opposition party.

Also appearing at the end of April were the Annual Report of the Race Relations Board (which argued strenuously for the extension of laws from American experience and the evidence in the P.E.P. report), the C.A.R.D. report on discrimination, and a Bow Group report which supported further legislation. In late May the report of a special committee headed by Harry Street, Professor of Law at the University of Manchester, was sent to Roy Jenkins by the Race Relations Board. This committee, sponsored by the R.R.B. and the N.C.C.I., had examined anti-discrimination legislation experience in other countries. The way had been prepared for the Home Secretary's speech in May and for the declaration of intent by the Government during the summer.

In late July 1967, Roy Jenkins announced that the Government would extend the Race Relations Act 1965 into the fields of housing, employment, credit facilities, and insurance. The Home

Secretary also announced that the powers of the Race Relations Board to deal with complaints would be enlarged. Within C.A.R.D. there was a buoyant round of congratulations. The range of C.A.R.D. proposals published more than two years before were now being voiced by the Government's Home Secretary and put forward as potential amendments to the existing law. As the representative of a powerless and disorganized section of society, C.A.R.D. had from one perspective skilfully manoeuvred to obtain general acceptance for its proposals. Yet, although there is some truth to this, one must look at the nature of C.A.R.D.'s efforts and the influence it exercised in order to understand the impact of the organization.

In the months following the publication of the White Paper, C.A.R.D. had been dependent primarily on the goodwill and idealism of the Home Secretary.[70] It had also been dependent on personal contacts with the 'race relations constellation' and more particularly with a smaller group which I have called 'race professionals'. C.A.R.D., acting as a promotional group, thus had to rely on the support of people with power and the ability of its members to create alliances with others who broadly shared the values and agreed with the programmes that C.A.R.D. advocated. The ability to form alliances and to take advantage effectively of the idealism and concern of potential allies was the source of whatever strength C.A.R.D. had. This ability was also an indication of C.A.R.D.'s weakness.

If Roy Jenkins had not become Home Secretary and had not appointed Mark Bonham Carter to head the Race Relations Board, it is doubtful whether the Government would have introduced legislation when it did. If Sir Frank Soskice had stayed at the Home Office and his attitudes had not changed, then he would have been either a passive actor or a negative influence in the struggle to get legislation initiated. Jenkins clearly encouraged efforts for extended anti-discrimination. His speeches, his appointment of Bonham Carter, his warm support of the P.E.P. report reflect his importance in stimulating the move for new laws.

If Jenkins's role was clearly central, how did C.A.R.D. influence the attainment of the three general goals that the Home Secretary had to achieve in order to legislate? He had to do the following:

*Persuade his fellow Ministers that discrimination was a serious social problem.* The P.E.P. report takes precedence here undeniably. It was conducted by an impartial research group. It was thorough. It received a great deal of Press coverage.[71] C.A.R.D.'s testing efforts, publication of a report on discrimination, and presentation of evidence to the Royal Commission inquiry into trade unions had much less impact. As a piece of evidence the P.E.P. report carried much more weight than any of the C.A.R.D. evidence of discrimination or even than the report of the Race Relations Board. The report was important. It gave Bonham Carter ammunition in both his official and personal attempts to gain wider powers for the Board. C.A.R.D. testing efforts were therefore necessary but not sufficient. They could have been especially necessary since before the P.E.P. report was published members of the 'race relations constellation' were not sure how convincingly it was going to demonstrate the incidence of discrimination in Britain. C.A.R.D.'s efforts were thus to an extent a safety measure. And, although the P.E.P. report was the major work in that area, C.A.R.D.'s testing work contributed both to the body of evidence and, through the Press reports of its efforts, to a more general public awareness of the problem.

*Show that legislation was the right way to deal with the problem.* Here C.A.R.D. had significant impact. It argued directly through its report on discrimination and evidence to the Royal Commission on Trade Unions (and both activities received publicity in the national Press). Through Maurice Orbach, it formally introduced its ideas into Parliament. It exerted direct influence over the Society of Labour Lawyers and the British Caribbean Association, and through these groups and the Fabian Conference, drew further attention to its legislative proposals. And, either through direct participation or through provision of evidence, it helped the National Committee for Commonwealth Immigrants and the Race Relations Board put forward their own demands for extension of the law. Further, the National Committee's employment conference gave American and Canadian speakers an opportunity to argue from their own experience, and the Press began to echo the cumulative demands. In short, although C.A.R.D. as an organization did not have great impact on the public and was probably not widely associated with the idea of extending the law outside the 'race relations constellation', C.A.R.D. members developed a reputation as experts on legislation which meant that they were consulted by a number of groups as a matter of course.

The Cabinet was probably influenced most directly by the report presented to the Home Secretary by the Street Committee.[72] It was an impartial group, staffed by distinguished lawyers. It was called in to make a determination about the effectiveness of legislation without any indication from the outset of a particular bias for or against the introduction of laws. Yet, in broad terms, in a comprehensive document produced between glossy covers, the Committee followed the lead taken by C.A.R.D. two years before. C.A.R.D. members were called before the Committee to give evidence. They were in close contact with Geoffrey Bindman, one of the Committee's three members who was legal adviser to the Race Relations Board. The report examined the history of anti-discrimination laws in North America, made proposals for broadening the scope of the Race Relations Act 1965 and for giving the Race Relations Board more muscle in the enforcement of a new act, and in dry legal language generally espoused the political cause C.A.R.D. and other organizations had been insistently advocating. The purpose of the Street report, like the P.E.P. report, was to put the weight of authority and objectivity behind the partisan claims of the 'race relations constellation'.

*Convince the Cabinet to defy the organized resistance of the T.U.C. and C.B.I. and the diffused discontent of home-owners to take a decision that might not be politically popular.* To a degree, a group makes the introduction of legislation politically possible by showing the extent of discrimination and demonstrating the efficacy of legislation. However, in terms of direct contact with the Cabinet or either the T.U.C. or C.B.I., C.A.R.D.'s influence was negligible. There was some lobbying at the Labour party and T.U.C. annual conferences. But in the period leading up to the introduction of new legislation, C.A.R.D. did not establish working relations with the industrial Ministers or with officials in industry or with any important section of the trade union movement. Lacking influence and being seen as a committed group representing a special interest, C.A.R.D. had to defer to the skills of Jenkins and Bonham Carter for direct negotiations with important groups who were potential antagonists. Moreover, C.A.R.D. was not able to organize counter-pressure by arousing demonstrations of public support for the legislative cause by any large voting or producing bloc.

In the period leading up to the introduction of legislation, C.A.R.D. was not as prominent as it was during the fight to amend the Race Relations Bill in 1965. Then the Government's lack of careful preparation and C.A.R.D.'s relative expertise combined with other factors to allow C.A.R.D. to play a central role. That its role was no longer so central was partly due to the different nature of the task at hand—getting legislation initiated is different from getting it amended. It was also due to the institutionalization of a race relations structure with the formation of the National Committee for Commonwealth Immigrants and the Race Relations Board. C.A.R.D.'s strengths in 1965 were relative knowledge, experience, and contacts. By 1967, C.A.R.D. no longer had a monopoly on these. As discrimination came increasingly to be viewed as a serious problem, those in Britain who were concerned made their voyage across the Atlantic to Canada and the United States to observe the workings of anti-discrimination legislation and to gain insight into the problems of race relations in both the American South and in the complicated urban areas of the North. Access to relevant literature also increased. Others in the race relations field thus developed expertise once possessed solely by C.A.R.D. members. Politically, the whole lobbying operation became much more sophisticated under the leadership of Jenkins and Bonham Carter.

Given its own weaknesses, C.A.R.D. was forced to act as a promotional group and thus part of its strategy was to establish a set of alliances, a coalition based on the idealism, goodwill, and general similarity of function of allied groups and individuals. C.A.R.D. worked through the 'race relations constellation' given cohesion by the group of 'race professionals'. These relationships developed in a period when there was a certain unanimity of interest, a common desire to press for legislation behind the Home Secretary. But the ships would not always sail on a single course. The personal relationships and interlocking memberships would become less important as differentiation of institutional function developed.

The period that ended in mid-1967 was in a sense anomalous because C.A.R.D. had gone along with and helped develop a consensus about new legislation. Once the point was reached where one could assume that legislation in some form was going to be introduced, the form became of central importance. C.A.R.D. would find itself more clearly defined from the other members of the wide-ranging coalition that had formed to promote new legislation. C.A.R.D. members in 1967 felt that by the time the Street report proposals had been referred back to the Race Relations

Board, then passed on to an intra-departmental group of Civil Servants, and finally put before the Cabinet, they would probably differ in significant ways from proposals C.A.R.D. would like to see enacted.[73] The limits of being a group promoting a cause and the imperatives for developing a movement would be felt again.


## 5. AN INDEPENDENT FORCE?

C.A.R.D. members who were active in promoting the legislative amendments to the Race Relations Act 1965 felt in mid-1967 that the role of C.A.R.D. was about to change markedly. The clouds of consensus which seemed to obscure differences between the main groups in the 'race relations constellation' would to an extent be dispersed by the winds of controversy and conflict. Differentiation in function and orientation would separate groups that were joined in the campaign for new laws. C.A.R.D., it was felt, would have three main tasks once the Government submitted its Bill:

Press for amendments if the proposals did not accord with C.A.R.D.'s.
Oversee and promote successful enforcement of the Act, once it was amended.
Make recommendations to the Government on, and propagandize for, a range of social, economic, and immigration policies which affected immigrants but which had been slighted during the legislative campaign.

To perform these tasks, C.A.R.D. would have to develop internal strengths and change its relationships with the two governmental organizations responsible for insuring integration of the immigrants and their children into society.


### C.A.R.D. AND THE RACE RELATIONS BOARD

As of the spring 1967, the relations between the officers of the Race Relations Board and members of C.A.R.D., particularly Anthony Lester, were close. Mark Bonham Carter, John Lyttle, and Lester were often in consultation about general strategy and tactics in pressing for legislation.[74] C.A.R.D. complaints gave the Board a strong ground from which to argue for the extension of the Act and broadening of its powers. And the Board members, in conjunction with Jenkins, were informally lobbying members of the T.U.C., C.B.I., and the Press. The Board also made representations to the relevant Ministers about problems of discrimination, sometimes at the suggestion of C.A.R.D. officers.[75] The close relationship depended both on personal contacts and the strong similarity of interests and functions. Both organizations wanted extension of legislation, broadening of the Board's powers, and the swift end of discrimination. In its Annual Report, the Board cited C.A.R.D. and acknowledged its importance in making legislation effective:

Most people who suffer the humiliation of being discriminated against prefer to forget it, and groups such as the Campaign Against Racial Discrimination . . . play an important role in informing those discriminated against of their rights and of the public interest at stake. The Board is satisfied that such independent groups concerned with the interest of minorities are essential if the individual complaint procedure is to work satisfactorily.[76]

In a period when the scope of legislation was narrowly circumscribed, C.A.R.D. and the Board could work together, through informal contact, to change the law. But when legislation of a broader nature was passed, C.A.R.D. as an organization would be forced more directly and publicly to oppose the Board. Personal relationships between members of each group could remain close but, in bald terms, it was C.A.R.D.'s interest to make sure that those who suffer discrimination receive redress—it would be the advocate for individual immigrants (and coloured school-leavers). The function of the Board would be more judicial, mediating or arbitrating between the claims of two different sets of people. C.A.R.D., acting as a partisan for immigrants, would not always be satisfied with the Board's action, thus creating a certain degree of tension and conflict.

As an organization for immigrants C.A.R.D. would have a number of functions relating to the Board and its network of regional conciliation committees. It would:

1. Supervise the general enforcement of the amended Act from the perspective of the 'immigrant' and the coloured school-leaver.
2. Get out into the local communities and encourage victims of discrimination to make complaints.
3. Test areas to uncover discrimination.

4. Test areas falling outside the amended law.
5. Test areas which had been dealt with by the Board and/or its committees to insure that discrimination had stopped.
6. Test cases which had not been dealt with by the Board because of inadequate evidence.
7. Help to prepare cases to be presented to the committees and/or the Board.
8. Check people selected to sit on the regional committees.
9. Try to settle cases of discrimination that could not be handled by the Board and its committees.

To an extent the Board would depend on C.A.R.D. and similar groups for the successful administration of its mandate. To root out discriminatory cases often requires the aid of a group with contacts in the local immigrant communities. Yet, even if the officers of the Board were to remain as sympathetic to C.A.R.D. as they were in 1967, there were areas of C.A.R.D. activity with relation to the Act—especially 1, 5, 7, 8 above—in which C.A.R.D. and the Board understandably had different perspectives. Further, C.A.R.D.'s general role as persistent advocate for immigrants would mean that it would argue strenuously for individuals, against those who discriminate or who are alleged to discriminate, to allow the Board to perform its conciliatory, or quasi-judicial, or judicial function.

The obvious differences between the functions of the Board and of C.A.R.D. in the new period were seen by C.A.R.D. members to have implications not only for the relationship between the Board and C.A.R.D. but for C.A.R.D. itself. No longer would C.A.R.D. be able to rely on the good offices of the Board and the skill (in both a political and technical sense) of the Board's officers. To perform adequately the different functions that would be attendant on the new legislation and to carry out effectively its role as the Board's critic, C.A.R.D. would need greatly expanded resources. They would be needed for the provision of legal services and for the establishment of an effective network of organizations in immigrant localities for the difficult, tedious, and necessary work of making contact with immigrants and convincing them to overcome their reluctance to press for the alleviation of the problems caused by discrimination. If C.A.R.D. was to oversee effectively the implementation of the amended Act, there was an obvious organizational imperative for independence and for strength. As one chairman of a conciliation committee said: 'You [referring to C.A.R.D.] and I are going to do battle in public on many bitter occasions. But it is important that you be strong enough so there is general equality between us.'

## C.A.R.D. AND THE NATIONAL COMMITTEE FOR COMMONWEALTH IMMIGRANTS

C.A.R.D.'s relationship with the National Committee by mid-1967 was both more complicated and more difficult to describe precisely than its relationship with the Race Relations Board. Members of C.A.R.D. Executive Committee, subcommittees, and National Council sat on the National Committee and its advisory panels. Drawing lines between C.A.R.D. members acting on C.A.R.D.'s behalf or on behalf of the National Committee was at times a difficult task. None the less, although the relationship was complex and fluid, important characteristics emerged.

C.A.R.D. from the first was, in terms of personnel, deeply committed to the National Committee. Of twenty people on C.A.R.D. Executive Committee elected after the national founding convention (and who served until October 1966), seven—David Pitt, Hamza Alavi, Jocelyn Barrow, Anthony Lester, Gurmukh Singh, V. D. Sharma, and Dipak Nandy—were on either the National Committee or its specialist advisory panels.[77] These people were the heart of C.A.R.D., being among its most active members. Of the sixteen on the C.A.R.D. Executive elected in the autumn of 1966, nine served on the Committee or the advisory panels.[78]

As outlined in the White Paper, the functions of the National Committee were:

To promote and co-ordinate the activities of the voluntary liaison committees and advise them in their work; recruit and train liaison officers to serve with these committees; provide a central information service; organize conferences, arrange training courses, and stimulate research; advise on questions referred to them by the Government or which they consider should be brought to the attention of the Government.[79]

These tasks were essentially to establish the V.L.C. network throughout the country; to give the Government advice; to educate the general public (construed both as individuals and groups) about policies for integration. As outlined in the Committee's Annual Report, its central task was to 'promote integration'. This was to be effected primarily by 'education'. As the Committee said in the Report:

If it were necessary to sum up in one word the complicated task in hand, that word would undoubtedly be education in its widest sense. Education in school and out of school, education of adults as well as children, education of newcomers as well as the indigenous population, education through conferences, through committee work, through the Press . . . and, not least, education through legislation.[80]

But the promotion of integration through education 'in its widest sense' could be a constructive policy or a platitude. It was a broad delineation of function—and an ambiguous one. And ambiguity was the hallmark of the Committee's function and role. Even in the circumstances of the Committee's reconstitution and in its name were elements of confusion. The National Committee drew its terms of reference from the White Paper: thus its function of promoting integration was enunciated in a document which also contained a policy of discrimination against coloured immigrants. The proposition 'for' was double-edged: was the Committee to speak 'for immigrants', putting their point of view, or was it to do things for immigrants, suggesting to some condescension towards a helpless and backward people.[81] Similarly, the phrase 'Commonwealth Immigrants' was confusing and oblique: it referred in genteel fashion to 'coloured' immigrants. And it did not include the second generation of coloured citizens in Britain although many of the Committee's policies were naturally directed towards the children of the newcomers.

The confusions went deeper than the level of symbols. First, the Committee was set up after the shock of 1964 to serve two rough purposes: first, implicitly, to calm the fears of the majority in Britain about the immigrant presence; second, explicitly, to press for the integration of immigrants and counter discrimination. But as Philip Mason has noted, 'The committee has always been conscious of the extreme difficulty of reconciling these ends and in all our work there is the conflict between the two ideals of representing the whole community and championing the minority.'[82]

Second, the nature of advice itself was not at all clear. Was the advice to be given from the perspective solely of the immigrant community and speak of their needs, or was it to try to balance other considerations in its presentation? Put another way, was it to give advice as a Government body or as the representatives of the immigrants? These were radically different perspectives and could yield quite different types of statement and policy. Further, was advice equivalent to pressure? Should the National Committee not only make public recommendations through its panels and secretariat but also try to press these proposals on the Government, not only through recommendations and statements but through obtaining allies and other techniques of a lobby? In short, was the National Committee to be an informal equivalent of a Royal Commission or a pressure group?

Third, what strata of British society was the Committee to educate and for what purpose? Assuming that it was aiming at people with influence—officials, executives, union leaders, leaders at local and national levels—was the goal to educate them so that they would co-operate in the 'integration' of immigrants? Or was the Committee's job to educate immigrants, make them aware of their right to an equal place in British society, and help them press for legitimate demands? There was further ambiguity about educating 'people with influence': would polite representations asking for tolerance be the most effective means or would some form of pressure—critics on C.A.R.D. were to say confrontation—be necessary to create an atmosphere in which change was possible?

Fourth, the Committee was concerned about dealing with the problems of immigrants, but these problems are often general ones in Britain: bad housing, overcrowded schools, etc. Immigrants, as the Board recognized in its Annual Report, are especially susceptible to the effects of these problems because they are strangers and because they suffer from discrimination.

The Committee has to steer a somewhat complex course. It is engaged in the work of community relations . . . and must take care never to build up a separate structure of services and therefore a separate position for the immigrant. At the same time it must do everything possible to reverse the undoubtedly negative trends of today.[83]

There was severe confusion about the nature of the Committee's functions and structure, and about leadership. With its Committee, panels, voluntary liaison committee structure, and permanent administrative staff, the N.C.C.I. was plagued by divided responsibilities. In terms of pressuring for policies and using the Committee to change attitudes, no strong leader had emerged by spring 1967. The Archbishop of Canterbury, as chairman of the Committee, had not developed into a forceful spokesman, defining the Committee's interests. And there was no clear acceptance by a single person of formal and informal responsibilities for strongly defining the Committee's public policy posture as there was with the Race Relations Board under Bonham Carter. Nadine Peppard, the Committee's general secretary, was fundamentally concerned with the administration of the voluntary liaison committee complex and did not see her role as a political one.[84] Martin Ennals, however, at the time thought that the National Committee should act as an interest group but should not be seen to do this.[85]

The National Committee when it was first reconstituted in the autumn of 1965 seemed to C.A.R.D. members to be of use as a 'platform'—offering C.A.R.D. a chance to 'lobby by proxy'. The Committee's resources and the prestige of its members could be utilized primarily to press for legislation. C.A.R.D. members could try to influence the Government departments in other areas, especially immigration, through the Committee structure. The presence of the Committee and its large supply of money[86] seemed to offer the chance to press the Government on legislation and other policy matters. There was a necessary ambivalence in C.A.R.D. itself about the National Committee. On the one hand, it would not speak with as unadulterated a tone as C.A.R.D. about immigrant problems, but its money and the prestige of its members might compensate for this by getting the 'right people' to listen to reasonable policies regarding coloured people in Britain. Yet the very ambiguities of the N.C.C.I.'s objectives, functions, and leadership fed the initial uncertainty of C.A.R.D. members.

By June 1967, a number of C.A.R.D. Executive Committee members had grown increasingly dissatisfied with the organization's close connection with the National Committee.[87] They saw several specific problems with the association. The decision of David Pitt and Hamza Alavi to join the Committee in 1965 set off rancorous debates within the organization and continued to cause strains. C.A.R.D. members questioned the advisability of using their ideas in the N.C.C.I. panel structure rather than publishing them as C.A.R.D.'s own policies. To these members, their ideas had to voyage uneasily through the panels and the Committee before being presented as 'recommendations' and since the Committee had, in their view, failed to press for its policy recommendations but only presented them in the form of public statements, there was the sense that C.A.R.D. could be just as effective in making its own public declarations of policy. There was also the fact that

C.A.R.D. members, who worked on a voluntary basis anyway, gave time to the N.C.C.I. that they should not withdraw from C.A.R.D.

Besides the difficulties within the C.A.R.D. organization that participation within the Committee structure had caused, a number of specific criticisms of particular actions by the National Committee caused an exacerbation of initial scepticism. For example: a proposal to the Employment Panel by Anthony Lester that the local V.L.C.s be used to gather information on discrimination was rejected. Also, the Employment Conference, although suggested by Lester, was deficient in several respects. The Press planning and coverage was not adequate. The top leaders of the T.U.C. and C.B.I. were not persuaded to come. The report of the Conference was not released until early June, with little publicity, thus, by its tardiness, not adding to the impact and momentum created by the P.E.P. report. In May, Michael Dummett, a prominent member of the Oxford Committee for Racial Integration (a voluntary liaison committee and an affiliated C.A.R.D. group), was arrested in Oxford for picketing a hairdressing salon that allegedly practised a colour bar. Officers of the Race Relations Board called immediately to ask if they could be of any help. The Information Officer of the National Committee offered to help as well and suggested a lawyer. But the Committee itself made no public statement. It called a meeting to decide whether it was proper for a voluntary liaison committee to hold demonstrations. In the end, no statement was made.[88]

Thus, a mood of suspicion and distrust developed between the two groups. Some C.A.R.D. Executive Committee members were restive and highly critical. Members of the permanent staff of the National Committee sensed this and resented C.A.R.D.'s critique of the Committee's lack of purposefulness and C.A.R.D.'s claims that it had 'infiltrated' the National Committee and tried to 'radicalize' it.

These specific problems related back to a general assessment of the purpose of the National Committee and C.A.R.D.'s relation to it. This was the source of a major argument within C.A.R.D. in 1965, and in 1967 it became the first major political issue that the C.A.R.D. Executive Committee debated since the early bitter days of 1965.

At one pole was David Pitt, who had always seen the National Committee as a means by which C.A.R.D. could make its point

of view known to Ministers and Civil Servants. He said that he
did not expect too much from the National Committee, that he
was disappointed not to have been able to push it as hard as he
would have liked, that it had taken some good steps, and that
C.A.R.D. should wait until legislation was introduced and passed
before making any decision to withdraw members from the Committee.[89] The Committee was seen as a means for pushing the
Government towards more 'reasonable and intelligent' policies
regarding immigrants.

In deferring a decision about the National Committee, Pitt was
supported by the Executive Committee. At a meeting on 8 June
1967 to discuss the National Committee 'issue', the decision about
firm action was postponed until late autumn. None the less a strong
position paper written by Dipak Nandy argued strenuously against
the National Committee, not only in terms of C.A.R.D.'s specific
problems with the N.C.C.I. but with regard to its general position
in the 'race relations constellation'. In his more general critique,
Nandy was continuing the debate begun nearly two years ago.[90]

Nandy evaluated the performance of the Committee in the
three major areas of work—advising, establishment of the V.L.C.s,
education—and found it wanting.[91] Aside from the problems of a
new organization and the administrative difficulties to be expected,
Nandy felt that the confusion about the Committee's functions and
role had led to its uncertain performance. The National Committee
could never claim to 'speak for immigrants in the way that the
I.W.A. or Standing Conference or C.A.R.D. did. But it could
do one or two things.'

It could either declare itself a welfare agency specially constituted
for the benefit of immigrants.
Or it could declare itself as an agency committed to those changes
in white attitudes, native institutions, and bureaucracies needed to
ensure the achievement of racial equality.

Nandy started from the premise that there was the need in race
relations for a 'respectable' body, but that the National Committee
had failed even by that (vague) standard. He argued:

It is neither a good 'paternalist' welfare body (for which a good case could
be made out), nor is it an intelligently radical 'respectable' body, which is
what we need. Its characteristic style is paralysis and non-statement,
covered by a frenzied involvement in social work and 'leadership training'.
. . . It has, moreover, built up a complicated national structure which

could easily become an immovable obstacle to any other agency in the field.[92]

Nandy was concerned that the Committee, through its work, generated 'an atmosphere of superficial liberalism, of generalized good will, attitudes which are of little use in the struggle to change attitudes'.[93] He was supported strongly in the June Executive Committee meeting by Michael Dummett who argued that the existence of the National Committee meant that, even if C.A.R.D. members were not so deeply involved in the Committee's work, the C.A.R.D. point of view would be obscured by the presence of a semi-official body with an ambiguous role. He feared too that the National Committee might be viewed by the Government as indeed the 'spokesman' for the immigrant communities, that the Government would not heed the proposals and criticism of other groups, and that by its unsure actions, from C.A.R.D.'s point of view, the Committee by creating the impression of purposeful action did more harm than good.[94]

Nandy's evaluation was not an exhaustive critique of the National Committee, although he described major difficulties in definition and orientation. Assessing the National Committee is not attempted here.[95] From our point of view, the attacks on the National Committee should be seen as the formulation of a fundamental problem for C.A.R.D.: should it co-operate with the National Committee and try to strengthen it, or should C.A.R.D. withdraw personnel from the Committee structure and state openly that the N.C.C.I. should not be viewed as 'representing the immigrant interest'. In the autumn of 1965, when the amendment of legislation was still a glimmer on the horizon, it seemed reasonable to a majority of the C.A.R.D. Executive Committee to try to use the National Committee to press for the first priority: the establishment by the Government of a basic legal framework which would demonstrate the intention of the Government and the host society not to tolerate discrimination.

Yet the Committee had always posed the threat of being not a conduit to the Government but a buffer between the Ministers and C.A.R.D. Consultation from the Government's point of view would naturally occur with the Committee, less easily with 'immigrant groups'. Lacking resources, C.A.R.D. had turned to the National Committee; with legislation in sight, the problem of power was raised again. C.A.R.D. members, still uncertain about the conception of organization, were seeking in some sense to define it through a critique of the National Committee.

It is here that the curious ambiguity about C.A.R.D. as a pressure group came into play. As suggested in Chapter One, C.A.R.D. had to be both a group promoting a cause and one which represented a section. It shared with the National Committee the job of promoting a cause; but it was fundamentally different because its terms of reference were in a sense narrow and clear. It was to put the immigrants' case as intelligently and forcefully as it could, with effectiveness as the only criterion of success. For the National Committee, as we have seen, things were not so simple. Because of its weakness, C.A.R.D. was forced to represent an interest, not as an interest group with formal recognition by the Government of its claim to have a voice on Government councils, but as a promotional group. As a promotional group, C.A.R.D. needed allies, one of them being the N.C.C.I. The danger posed by the National Committee was that it was in a sense a competitor for the position of 'promoter of the immigrants' cause'. It would be listened to by authorities. And yet it would not be as outspoken for immigrants as C.A.R.D.

Despite the relationship of its members to the N.C.C.I., C.A.R.D. sent deputations to see Ministers and issued public statements on a variety of policy questions. But the organization had not by mid-1967 been able to establish regularized channels of consultation with the Home Office or other departments whose policies had important ramifications for immigrants. (C.A.R.D.'s contact with Roy Jenkins was a notable exception, arising from rather unique personal contacts, not from institutional recognition.) One is thrown back to the phrase, 'building strengths'. C.A.R.D. members realized that this was what they would have to do if they were to receive the recognition that would come from speaking for large numbers of immigrants. If C.A.R.D. could build a strong organization, it was thought, then perhaps the National Committee would not be a governmental advisory body, but a meeting place for high Government officials and representatives of the immigrant interest.

Power. That remained the puzzle. In mid-1967, C.A.R.D. members believed that the organization had five actual or potential sources of influence.

The expertise of its members on racial questions.
Personal contacts of its members with key people.

Voting strength of potential C.A.R.D. members in key constituencies.

Alliances with sympathetic groups, not only with other immigrant organizations, promotional groups, and groups directly involved in race relations, but with producer groups, especially trade unions. Strong, tightly knit C.A.R.D. locals, commanding the support of a substantial number of immigrants out of the total immigrant population in the area. The local groups would pressure local government, establish alliances at the community level, engage in voter registration or direct political activity, actively boycott or demonstrate in support of C.A.R.D. policy or in opposition to discriminatory or harmful public or private practices.

Strikingly, little thought was given to developing independent economic power for the immigrants—in contrast to the position developed, though never really implemented, by the leaders of Standing Conference. In 1967, what strength C.A.R.D. had, came primarily from expertise and personal contacts. The organization still had a top but no foundation.

Voter registration was tried in London, but a strategy for wielding electoral power was only in the most speculative stage.[96] Alliances with major immigrant organizations had failed. Attempts to gain the support of even the more sympathetic trade unions failed too.[97] Unions had not affiliated or given money to C.A.R.D., nor had they spoken out in support of immigrant interests. To many C.A.R.D. members at the 1967 turning-point, the most promising route of development lay with local organizing. If the organization was going to influence public policy, local development was thought by an important group in C.A.R.D. to be the stratagem which would make the powerless strong.

In late May 1967, C.A.R.D. held a 24-hour vigil in Whitehall near Downing Street to urge new legislation. C.A.R.D. leaders made clear that the event was not a demonstration of protest, but rather an effort to show that immigrants supported those in the Government who were in favour of extending the anti-discrimination laws. Because C.A.R.D. could not draw in many people, the number standing silently on the pavement was purposely kept to twenty an hour so that it would not seem that C.A.R.D. had tried to hold a mass rally and failed. But the vigil was a demonstration—a demonstration that C.A.R.D. could not bring immigrants to Whitehall to support legislation. The Press gave it scant attention. No one from the Government met with the coloured people. The incident aptly underscored the point that C.A.R.D. could not mobilize immigrants to affect public policy. Whether the vigil was a harbinger of a larger, more powerful organization or the portent of continued powerlessness and lack of support was the critical if unanswered question.

## NOTES

1. A general description of the fundamental relationships between pressure groups and the elements of the political system is given by Gabriel Almond, 'A Comparative Study of Interest Groups and the Political Process', *American Political Science Review* (March 1958), pp. 270 ff. See also Samuel H. Beer, 'Group Representation in Britain and the United States', *Annals of the American Academy of Political and Social Science* (Vol. XIX), p. 136.

2. C.A.R.D. press release incorporating the resolutions (8 February 1965). There was also a resolution about racial incitement, an area with which the legislation soon to be proposed by the Government was to deal. (See Sections 6 and 7 of the Race Relations Act 1965). For our purposes, the questions of racial incitement and public order will not be discussed since the main thrust of C.A.R.D.'s efforts was directed towards the anti-discrimination provisions of the forthcoming Bill.

3. Keith Hindell, 'The Genesis of the Race Relations Bill', *Political Quarterly* (October-December 1965), pp. 390-405, deals in some detail with the origins, stages of evolution, and enactment of the Bill. This discussion is intended to examine C.A.R.D.'s role for purposes of comparison with the group's later efforts and not to cover the same material as Hindell. Although I have some corrections and slight modifications of his interpretation, I am indebted to his researches.

4. For detailed discussion of their proposals, see ibid., pp. 392-3.

5. Ibid., p. 393.

6. Interview with Anthony Lester (13 May 1967). There were also sharp disagreements over civil libertarian questions concerning problems of reconciling the desire to outlaw racial incitement propaganda and the need for free speech.

7. 'Memorandum on a Citizens' Council' and 'A Citizens' Council: Memorandum II, Draft Bill'.

8. Jeffrey Jowell, 'The Administrative Enforcement of Laws Against Discrimination', *Public Law* (summer 1965).

9. *Proposals for Legislation* (London, C.A.R.D., February 1965), p. 1.

10. Ibid., p. 2. For confirmation of the suppositions about discrimination, see P.E.P. report, op. cit.

11. These were in outline: (a) any person considering himself aggrieved could initiate a complaint to the commission; (b) the complaint would be investigated by members of the commission's conciliation staff which would attempt by mediation, persuasion, and conciliation to achieve compliance with the law; (c) failing mediation, the commission would have the power, if necessary, to hold a formal inquiry, with powers to subpoena witnesses and authority to take evidence on oath; (d) the formal inquiry would take the form of a hearing before officers of the commission at which the commission representatives might dismiss the complaint or make an appropriate order (including compensation or injunctive relief to the individual complainant); (e) in the event of non-compliance with its order the commission would bring proceedings in the County Court to enforce it; (f) appeal on a point of law would lie from the County Court to the Court of Appeal.

12. Brockway had suggested outlawing discrimination in employment in some of his Bills. Dr. Kenneth Little, author of *Negroes in Britain* (London, Kegan Paul, 1947), had in 1952 suggested conciliation machinery in a report to the Commonwealth Sub-committee of the N.E.C. But both were put forward before the possibility of actual legislation in Britain was a real one. C.A.R.D.'s proposals were thus unique in terms of both scope and enforcement. Hindell, op. cit., p. 390.

13. 11 February 1965.

14. For summary of early Press comment which viewed C.A.R.D. as a militant and angry organization in the mould of an (imagined) American civil rights organization, see Theodore Roszak, 'New Campaign to Attack Colour Bar', *Peace News* (19 February 1965). Also C.A.R.D. secretary's report (July 1965).

15. *Guardian* (10 April 1965).

16. *Observer* (11 April 1965).

17. Hindell, op. cit., p. 397.

18. Interview with Anthony Lester (13 May 1967).

19. Interview with Mrs. Shirley Williams, M.P. (24 May 1967).

20. *Guardian* (29 April 1965).

21. As he noted during the debate: 'I need hardly say that while the Bill was in course of preparation, we gave careful consideration to possible alternatives, including conciliation, but on examining them we felt that there were serious difficulties in the way of their adoption. However, we are quite ready to try again.' 711 H.C. Parl. Deb., col. 929, 3 May 1965.

22. *Guardian* (8 May 1965); interview with Anthony Lester (13 May 1967); letter from the C.A.R.D. Legal Committee to members of Standing Committee (May 1965). The last asked for support of the Chapman amendments as 'they attempt to translate the best foreign experience into an English context'. It ended: 'C.A.R.D.'s Legal Committee is at your disposal should you wish to obtain any further information about foreign experience with legislation, or to make use of its drafting services.'

23. Race Relations Act 1965, Sections 2 and 3.

24. Besides Hindell, see Finer, op. cit., pp. 75–7, for a description of the C.A.R.D. victory.

25. 711 H.C. Parl. Deb., cols. 988–93, 3 May 1965.

26. Hindell, op. cit., p. 403. C.A.R.D. had prepared a list of amendments which were sent to all members of Standing Committee B. C.A.R.D. lobbyists were in close personal touch with Mrs. Williams and Chapman to draft amendments that they wanted to propose. Interview with Anthony Lester (13 May 1967). Minutes of C.A.R.D. membership meeting (23 May 1965).

27. For the interview information cited above I am grateful to Mr. Louis Kushnick of the University of Manchester who is currently working on a thesis detailing the implementation of the Race Relations Act.

28. The material that appears here was written before drafting or publication of Rose *et al.*, op cit. Material from *The Politics of the Powerless*, then in unpublished form, was used in Part VI of *Colour and Citizenship*, 'Roy Jenkins and Legislation Against Discrimination: A Case Study'. As suggested in the Preface, I used C.A.R.D. as the focal point for research. The presentation of events is from C.A.R.D.'s point of view in order to illustrate the functioning of the organization in Britain's system of group politics. The perspective of the narrative in Rose *et al.*, is of those at the centre of Government, especially Jenkins. The two accounts are, none the less, complementary. The material that follows, while not seriously modified by the analysis in Rose *et al.*, is not as complete from the perspective of Government and other interest groups. However, material appearing here has not been rewritten to take account of the presentation in Rose *et al.*, and should thus be read in conjunction with the analysis in *Colour and Citizenship*.

29. Hamza Alavi, *The White Paper: A Spur to Racialism* (London, C.A.R.D.,

1965). The pamphlet castigated the continuation of the Government's discriminatory immigration policy as outlined in Part II of the White Paper and also the integration proposals put forward in Part III: 'This section of the White Paper is a contradictory bundle of prejudice and pious hopes. No positive proposals are offered. . . . And the Government has totally ignored the pre-conditions of integration: a national leadership which is committed in words and actions to the idea of racial equality; and above all, the participation of the immigrant communities themselves in the formulation of policies which affect them.'

30. The lobby, held on 16 November 1965, consisted primarily of people from the Oxford Committee for Racial Integration, the Leicester Campaign for Racial Equality, and the Indian Workers' Association, Southall. Approximately 75 to 100 participated, and Press coverage was poor.

31. The Action Committee for a Rational Immigration Policy was formed in the autumn of 1965 and comprised Labour M.P.s, members of the Fabian Society, the Bow Group, Young Liberals, the National Council for Civil Liberties, C.A.R.D., and the Society of Labour Lawyers. Its chairman was Reginald Freeson, who had been on the all-party group which opposed the extension of the Commonwealth Immigrants Act in 1964. He also had been a member of Standing Committee who voted against the Government position.

32. Jenkins's reforming tendencies were evident in 1959 when he published *The Labour Case* (Harmondsworth, Penguin, 1959), which advocated reform in a number of areas including immigration laws. For Jenkins's background, see Rose *et al.*, op. cit., pp. 513–14.

33. Interview with John Lyttle, Chief Conciliation Officer, Race Relations Board (25 April 1967): 'I have no doubt at all that the principal factor in the shift of atmosphere is Roy Jenkins. Without him the campaign for the extension of the law would not have got anywhere. He has taken the Government step by step into a place where the Government will probably not be able to refuse to legislate.'

34. Address to a meeting of Voluntary Liaison Committees (23 May 1966). In this address the Home Secretary also expressed his much-quoted definition of integration: 'I define integration . . . not as a flattening process of assimilation but equal opportunity, accompanied by cultural diversity, in an atmosphere of mutual tolerance' (London, N.C.C.I., 1966).

35. 10 October 1966.

36. Roy Jenkins, *Racial Equality in Employment* (London, N.C.C.I., 1967), p. 10.

37. The *Observer* (14 May 1967).

38. Mr. Foley's title was Minister with Special Responsibility for Immigrants. He was replaced in early 1967 by Mr. David Ennals.

39. *Observer* (20 February 1966).

40. See below. Also for the actual recommendations, Race Relations Board, *Report for 1966–7* (London, H.M.S.O., 1967).

41. N.C.C.I., *Report for 1966* (London, N.C.C.I., 1967).

42. Interview (21 February 1967).

43. Members of the Standing Conference and I.W.A., G.B., did not have frequent contact, formally or informally, with other members—either organizations or individuals—of the 'race relations constellation'. There was no official backbench group in Parliament in favour of legislation. The Action Committee for Rational Immigration Policy had become inactive. There were of course a number of M.P.s who favoured the extension of laws, but I did not do research on the attitudes in the House and so did not include a discussion of how M.P.s fit into the family relations model. As will be discussed, certain M.P.s have been in close contact with C.A.R.D. For discussion of the attitudes of the Labour and Conservative parties towards immigration and general divisions within each party, see Foot, op. cit.

44. There was then no equivalent of the Civil Rights Leadership Conference in

the United States, a coalition of civil rights and other organizations which acts in concert on issues.

45. Viewed from a different perspective C.A.R.D.'s participation in the 'family relations configuration' could be hinted at by listing the organizations to which its two main lobbyists, David Pitt and Anthony Lester, belonged. Pitt: C.A.R.D. (chairman), British Caribbean Association (joint chairman), the National Committee for Commonwealth Immigrants, Socialist Medical Association (member of National Council), Fabian Society, Greater London Council. Lester: C.A.R.D. (chairman of Legal Committee), Society of Labour Lawyers, Fabian Society, Council of the Institute of Race Relations, British Overseas Socialist Fellowship, National Committee for Commonwealth Immigrants (vice-chairman, Employment Panel).

From a different perspective, the nature of the family relations structure could be suggested by the number of people associated with C.A.R.D. who were also members of some part of the National Committee structure. Of C.A.R.D. members on the Executive, the National Council, or one of the C.A.R.D. subcommittees, thirteen belonged to some part of the National Committee. Committee: Pitt; V. D. Sharma (C.A.R.D. Executive Committee; Indian Workers' Association, Southall, general secretary); Tassaduq Ahmed (National Council; former president National Federation of Pakistani Associations); Felicity Bolton (National Council; British Caribbean Association, secretary). Administrative Staff: Martin Ennals (E.C.). Panels: Education—Jocelyn Barrow (C.A.R.D. Executive Committee; vice-chairman, Camden Community Relations Council). Employment—Lester, H. S. Dhillon (C.A.R.D. Executive Committee, treasurer; Indian Workers' Association, Southall), L. T. Squire (National Council). Housing—Roger Warren Evans (Legal Committee). Information—Dipak Nandy (E.C., director summer project; former chairman Leicester Campaign for Racial Equality; Council of the Institute of Race Relations). Legal and Civil Affairs—Michael Dummett (E.C., chairman Law and Order Committee; chairman Oxford Committee for Racial Integration); Gurmukh Singh (E.C.; Camden Community Relations Council).

46. Eric Silver, 'Prejudice Against the Race Bill', *Guardian* (13 January 1967).

47. *Sunday Times* (8 January 1967).

48. *Sunday Times* (29 January 1967).

49. 'Notes for C.A.R.D. from the American Civil Rights Movement' (18 September 1965).

50. Interview with Dipak Nandy (20 March 1967). Nandy came to the organization from the Leicester Campaign for Racial Equality. Talking about the experience of testing at the local level he said: 'Until National C.A.R.D. persuaded us, the Leicester Campaign thought it was silly to struggle for legislation. It was stupid to test a lot of cases without giving help to individuals. Legislation has always lacked a reality factor for local groups, even though members strongly feel discrimination. I don't think we have succeeded in translating the campaign at the centre into propaganda for our own troops.'

51. *Summer Project 1966, Report* (London, C.A.R.D., 1966).

52. Articles appeared in the *Guardian* (29 August 1966), the *Daily Mirror* (29 August 1966), *The Times* (29 August 1966), the *Sun* (29 August 1966), the *Daily Telegraph* (29 August 1966), *New Society* (1 September 1966).

53. Race Relations Board, *Report for 1966–7*, op. cit.

54. How much public awareness was increased is of course difficult to quantify. Martin Ennals, Information Officer of the National Committee for Commonwealth Immigrants, believed that C.A.R.D.'s role in testing, especially during the summer project, had a significant impact: 'C.A.R.D. had done an enormous amount to shape public opinion into a position where it accepts the fact of discrimination. People don't necessarily agree with C.A.R.D.'s proposals, but they recognize that what C.A.R.D. was saying was justifiable.'

55. *Report on Racial Discrimination* (London, C.A.R.D., April 1967).

56. He had articles in the *Spectator, Socialist Commentary,* the *Observer,* and a Fabian Research Series pamphlet.

57. These proposals, it should be remembered, were closely modelled on the Massachusetts and New York laws against racial discrimination.

58. See *Race Relations Act 1965 (Amendment Bill)* (London, C.A.R.D., 1966). For Orbach's speech, much of it similar to arguments advanced by C.A.R.D. since early 1965, see 738 H.C. Parl. Deb., cols. 897–905, 16 December 1966. At the same time as Orbach introduced his Bill, Lord Brockway introduced a similar version in the Lords: see 278 H.L. Parl. Deb., col. 1834.

59. *Memorandum of Evidence* presented to the Royal Commission on Trade Unions and Employers' Associations (London, C.A.R.D., 1966).

60. *Guardian* (13 January 1967).

61. Race Relations Committee, Society of Labour Lawyers, *Third Report* (London, S.L.L., 1966), p. 4.

62. This paper and the others are collected in *Policies for Racial Equality* (London, Fabian Research Series, No. 262, 1967).

63. For a full report of conference speeches, see *Racial Equality in Employment.*

64. For example the speech of Sir Kenneth Allen, ibid., pp. 1–3.

65. The exception was Frank Cousins of the Transport and General Workers Union who pledged his union's support for legislation 'if there was no other way' to deal with the problem. See *Racial Equality in Employment,* pp. 97–100, for his speech. But as Colin McGlashan wrote in the *Observer* (26 February 1967): 'The major union leaders and employers virtually boycotted the Conference.' It took 600 invitations before fifty places for industry could be filled. Only eighteen union representatives came, ten from professional and white-collar unions that are least involved in race relations problems.

66. See, for example, the leader in *The Times* (16 March 1967).

67. P.E.P. report, p. 13. The survey was conducted by Research Services Ltd.

68. The Director of the Rowntree Trust was L. E. Waddilove, chairman of the Housing Panel of the National Committee for Commonwealth Immigrants, and a member of the Advisory Committee of Political and Economic Planning. Other members of the Committee were: Mark Bonham Carter; Nicholas Deakin; C. S. Moser, Professor of Social Statistics, University of London; Dipak Nandy, Lecturer, University of Kent and member of the C.A.R.D. E.C.; Nadine Peppard; John Rex, Professor of Social Theory and Institutions, Durham University; E. J. B. Rose; R. M. Titmuss, Professor of Social Administration, University of London; and D. H. deTrafford, chairman, Employment Panel, N.C.C.I.

69. Speech at the Waldorf Hotel (17 April 1967). Bonham Carter concluded: 'The Race Relations Board has been in existence for a little more than a year. When I was appointed as chairman, the Home Secretary agreed that we could recommend changes in the Act if we saw fit. Up to now we have taken care not to make any statement about extending the present Act. In view of our experience in the last year, of the complaints we have received formally and informally, of the evidence brought to our attention in the course of carrying out responsibilities, and in the light of the P.E.P. report, it is the unanimous view of the Race Relations Board that the Race Relations Act should be amended and extended. . . .'

70. For purposes of analysis it will be assumed that these characteristics have shaped his actions. Clearly, however, his support of anti-discrimination legislation may be seen as part of a complex of motives: desire to write a good record as Home Secretary, desire to appeal to the left wing of the party as a means of moving upwards in the Labour Government, desire to define himself in contrast to Harold Wilson.

71. Typical of the leaders written at the time of the P.E.P. report's publication

and of the skill of the race professionals was the one in the *Sunday Times* (23 April 1967). Spread eight columns across the top of the editorial page, the leader argued sharply against the reluctance of the C.B.I. and T.U.C. to accept legislation and said the 'change in the law should be quick and decisive'. 'The major fault' in Britain, it suggested, 'is still one of recognition. If there was a sufficiently urgent sense that a racial problem existed, Britain would have a mass civil rights movement. . . . At least there would be more community associations—tough minded, politically alert, and able to confront local authorities who now get away with discrimination by stealth . . . a coloured community has no other lobby but itself, and to be effective it needs the help of committed whites. But where is the commitment?' Harry Evans, *Sunday Times* editor, was a member of the National Committee for Commonwealth Immigrants Information Panel.

72. Harry Street, Geoffrey Howe, and Geoffrey Bindman, *Anti-discrimination Legislation: The Street Report* (London, P.E.P., 1967).

73. The powers of enforcement that the Race Relations Board would be given were a central source of concern. C.A.R.D. members wanted the Board to have powers of subpoena and be able to establish independent conciliation tribunals that would have some judicial powers if their mediating efforts were unsuccessful. It was feared that the T.U.C. and C.B.I. would strenuously protest against the inclusion of such a provision in any new legislation. See Chapter Four.

74. Interview with John Lyttle (25 April 1967).

75. Ibid.

76. Race Relations Board, *Annual Report for 1966–7*, p. 9.

77. An eighth C.A.R.D. Executive Committee member, Martin Ennals, who was co-opted in March 1966, became Information Officer of the National Committee in May 1966. However, he was never an active member of the E.C. and spent most of his time on National Committee business.

78. Alavi had resigned from both C.A.R.D. and the National Committee. The other six who had been on the Committee remained. Len Squire, H. S. Dhillon, and Michael Dummett were new members of the C.A.R.D. Executive who also served on the National Committee or its panels. A number of other people with mixed allegiances also served on the Committee and its panels, and C.A.R.D. As National Council members or members of C.A.R.D. subcommittees these were not as active in the actual activities of C.A.R.D. itself.

79. N.C.C.I., *Report for 1966*, p. 24.

80. Ibid., p. 8.

81. Dipak Nandy, 'The National Committee for Commonwealth Immigrants: An Assessment', presented to the Executive Committee of C.A.R.D. (June 1967).

82. Philip Mason, 'Race Relations in Britain', presented to the National Committee for Commonwealth Immigrants (June 1967).

83. N.C.C.I., *Report for 1966*, p. 8.

84. Interview (23 March 1967). Miss Peppard said that 'politics is not my line'.

85. Interview with Martin Ennals (18 October 1966): 'I'd like to think of the National Committee as a pressure group. If we aren't, we aren't doing the job. If we seem to be a pressure group on the other hand then we are not doing the job. The art of this sort of work is not to seem to be applying the pressure.'

86. The National Committee budget was roughly £150,000 per year. Half of this was reserved for the funding of liaison officers to work with the voluntary liaison committees. The rest went for the work of the national structure. Interview with Nadine Peppard (May 1967). A further £50,000 had been given to the N.C.C.I. by the Gulbenkian Foundation for the establishment of Fair Housing Groups in communities. *The Times* (April 1967). See also, *The Housing of Commonwealth Immigrants* (London, N.C.C.I., 1967). The N.C.C.I. budget should be contrasted with C.A.R.D.'s annual expenditures of roughly £3,500.

87. C.A.R.D.'s relationship with the National Committee must be seen on two levels: the national policy-making and advising level, and the local plane, with the development of the voluntary liaison committee structure. In discussing C.A.R.D. difficulties with the National Committee, I am referring primarily to the problems arising from C.A.R.D.'s contact with the N.C.C.I. at the national level. The C.A.R.D. critique of the V.L.C.s, although mentioned here, will be discussed in the next chapter.

88. Interview with Michael Dummett (5 June 1967).

89. Interview with David Pitt (29 May 1967).

90. The debate continued was about the first issue, whether C.A.R.D. should join the National Committee: not the second, about whether Pitt and Alavi should have consulted the C.A.R.D. National Council. After several acrimonious meetings of the Executive and the National Council, no decision was taken in 1965. Plans were then in progress for the publication of a C.A.R.D. news-letter. The first issue was to include a debate on the National Committee. Ian McDonald, a member of the Legal Committee and leader of the Islington C.A.R.D. group, and Selma James prepared papers which were not printed. McDonald argued that C.A.R.D. members should not join because C.A.R.D. would lose its identity and not be consulted by the Government; because C.A.R.D. should try to pressure the Government, to try conciliatory measures though the National Committee was to accept the terms of reference of the Government; because joining the National Committee was dividing the 'anti-racialist movement'. Mrs. James's argument was similar to McDonald's.

91. 'The National Committee: An Assessment', pp. 1–5.

92. Ibid., p. 6.

93. He had argued in a similar vein in his critique of the V.L.C. structure, 'An Illusion of Competence', in Lester and Deakin (eds.), op. cit., pp. 35–40.

94. Interview with Michael Dummett (5 June 1967).

95. See Rose *et al.*, op. cit., pp. 522–5, for an evaluation of the N.C.C.I. before it was transformed into the Community Relations Commission.

96. The strongest advocate of voter registration within C.A.R.D. was David Pitt. Interview (29 May 1967). He believed on the basis of the 1961 Census and the results of the 1964 general election that immigrants, if politically organized, could be the swing votes in a number of constituencies since they represented more votes than the difference between the two candidates. Pitt pushed for the allocation of C.A.R.D. funds in the autumn of 1965 and 1966 for voter registration in London's Hackney Borough (his own) in preparation for the general election and the Greater London Council election. In 1966 funds were allocated for voter registration before the electoral rolls closed in December. According to the director of the project, Johnny James, about 4,000 immigrants were visited in a door-to-door survey. The number actually registered was not determined and there were no efforts by C.A.R.D. to organize voters during the G.L.C. campaign. Besides the slight attempts at voter registration by C.A.R.D. in London and by some of the local C.A.R.D. groups in the North, and a survey distributed through local and affiliated groups before the general election asking how the local candidates treated 'race questions', C.A.R.D. paid little attention to electoral politics through mid-1967.

97. C.A.R.D. in 1967 approached Jack Jones of the Transport and General Workers Union to ask if the T.G.W.U. would put out a pamphlet in conjunction with C.A.R.D. on discrimination in employment and affiliate formally with C.A.R.D. The reply to both questions was negative.

# CHAPTER FIVE

# The Politics of Faction:
# The Model-makers Overthrown

By the spring of 1967, C.A.R.D. was in a state of limbo, detached from the political structure and from the immigrant communities. Although individual C.A.R.D. members did have access to people with political influence, the organization was not recognized as being able to command the allegiance of thousands of Indians, Pakistanis, and West Indians. Ministers and M.P.s might listen to C.A.R.D. because the organization's members had illuminating ideas or because of personal friendship or because certain C.A.R.D. members were individual immigrants, influential in their own right. Such contact was limited to polite exchanges. C.A.R.D. members had no bargaining strength with which to impress their points upon officialdom,[1] no real sanctions save the dire spectacle of a racially rent society engulfed by riot. C.A.R.D. had also failed to sink organizational roots deeply into Britain's coloured communities or to mount any substantial attacks on discrimination or other substandard conditions at the local level.

Many members of the Executive and National Council were acutely aware of C.A.R.D.'s limitations. At the National Council meeting following the 1966 annual convention, a number of C.A.R.D. members expressed disappointment with the development of the organization. Michael Dummett argued that 'C.A.R.D. had lost faith in itself: Locals say that nothing good is being done by the national group; why should we join? Members of the national Executive have more loyalty to other groups of which they are members.' Dipak Nandy observed that 'C.A.R.D. is not projecting the image of an ongoing organization. The convention should be seen as the culmination of the initial phase in C.A.R.D.'s development. We must now begin to work with positive programmes in the communities.' Other members likened C.A.R.D. to the Fabian Society and to the Trades Union Congress, 'before it had any local organizations'.[2] There was general agreement that C.A.R.D. should continue to have a policy role and that it should devote more time to local organizing. But the lineaments of the organization were still only seen in broadest outline, almost as a caricature of models which had preceded C.A.R.D. in America. With the introduction of legislation imminent and a crisis in attitudes towards the National Committee for Commonwealth Immigrants developing, some C.A.R.D. executives—especially Dipak Nandy, V. D. Sharma, and Anthony Lester—began to think systematically about the direction in which C.A.R.D. should evolve.

The efforts of the model-makers were soon to be frustrated. Led by Johnny James, the West Indian assistant general secretary, new forces emerged at C.A.R.D.'s annual general meeting in November 1967. Controversy raged over resolutions as to whether coloured persons should exclusively lead C.A.R.D., and that linked attacks against racism in Britain with the 'struggle against imperialism' around the globe. When a challenge to the credentials of James's cohorts was rebuffed by Dr. David Pitt, prominent members of the Executive Committee walked out. Among these were V. D. Sharma, Dipak Nandy, Anthony Lester, and Julia Gaitskell, who had been at the centre of C.A.R.D.'s lobbying activities during the past two years and who had been preparing for a community-oriented future. Outnumbered at the convention's first session, these leaders could not outflank their opponents at a reconvened second session because the C.A.R.D. local structure—so often discussed, so seldom shorn up—was embarrassingly under-developed. As C.A.R.D. was taken over and splintered, the course that had been charted by those who walked out (who shall be described as the Nandyites) was blocked.[3]

## 1. A MODEL ORGANIZATION: DELIVERING THE GOODS

To the Nandyites in the spring of 1967, the multiracial coalition of intellectuals called C.A.R.D. was equipped solely to develop policies for racial equality and to take advantage of contacts on Fleet Street, in Whitehall, and at Westminster, and to press these policies upon the public and the Government. Strong local growth was necessary to give weight and strength to C.A.R.D.'s policy voice. Local development was demanded too by those who wanted

C.A.R.D. to oversee implementation of an amended Race Relations Act.

But the functions of C.A.R.D. community groups stemmed fundamentally from a triple bureaucratic failure at the local level. It was on the streets and in the neighbourhoods of Britain's industrial cities that C.A.R.D., in words often used by Nandy, 'had to deliver the goods'. The need for C.A.R.D. local groups was seen as the response to the inability of local authorities, voluntary liaison committees, and immigrant associations to deal adequately with the needs of immigrants and their children. The critique as it was developed was couched in general terms but it implied a crucial role for C.A.R.D. As Nandy said in June 1967: 'The question facing us now is whether C.A.R.D. will be another national pressure group or whether we can go back to the grass roots for some other model of political conduct. We must develop a theory of local groups and local politics.'

First, the local authorities would not act positively for the welfare of immigrants. In a paper presented to the Information Panel of the National Committee for Commonwealth Immigrants, Nandy argued that 'with a very few exceptions, the attitude of local authorities in areas of immigrant settlement towards race relations has been a combination of resentment and bewilderment'. Nandy contended further that local authorities, if asked to deal with race relations problems, would respond in four unsatisfactory ways.

Firstly, they would define problems of race relations as 'immigrant problems', implying that society had a set of norms to which immigrants had failed to conform and that as 'deviants' they needed the help of 'remedial measures'. Secondly, they would evade problems of discrimination by arguing that they had to treat all citizens equally and could not treat immigrants specially, or that it was not the right time to confront such problems. Thirdly, they would be guilty of 'tokenism'. That is, local authorities if forced to act would adopt minimum measures, tardily. Fourthly, they would see immigrants themselves as a source of social problems and thus attempt to 'contain' immigrants and those problems. Problems that afflict immigrants, for example illness or multi-occupation, would be viewed as something that should be isolated and contained from the perspective of the society at large, not for the harmful effects that they might have on individual immigrants.

Because of these attitudes and reactions, Nandy argued that local authorities would not be likely to take necessary initiatives in solving problems of race relations.[4] Although he acknowledged that the treatment was hardly complete, given efforts that some authorities had made, his analysis presupposed that a large number held such attitudes.

It was this structure of attitudes that the voluntary liaison committees in each area would attempt to alter. Yet Nandy also argued: 'I am not convinced that they have even recognized the need for it; nor am I convinced even if they had that they possess the appropriate equipment for undertaking the task.'[5] As with the National Committee for Commonwealth Immigrants, Nandy saw that there were grave confusions in the concept of the voluntary liaison committee's role. Would it interpret the demands for equal opportunities of the minority to the dominant white society, or act as spokesmen of that society to the minority group? Nandy believed that the second pattern was most prevalent. This stemmed from two sources. First, the history of the voluntary liaison committees went back to the 1950s and the initiative for the establishment of local friendship councils had often come from local Councils of Social Service.[6] To Nandy, the fact that the V.L.C.s often had a social work base or sought social workers to be their paid 'liaison officers', indicated that they were concerned with immigrant problems both as individual problems and as welfare problems. He argued that 'there is a persistent tendency to shy away from the problems of *discrimination*', to forget that the 'problem is not a person . . . but the denial of rights to a person and to a whole group'.[7] Structural sources of inequality were not carefully examined. Further, the voluntary liaison committee would be composed of people from all sections of society, including representatives nominated by the Borough Council and 'representatives of every organization and society . . . which is concerned with the well-being of the citizens of a particular borough'.[8] Thus it was argued that the V.L.C.s, seeking to gain the co-operation of the main interests in the society and the local authority, could not press for immigrant demands. They would be more disposed to create 'harmonious' relations than to fight discrimination and possibly cause conflict. Nandy's unstated assumption was that it was in the interest of the 'community' to reconcile and dampen conflict and that the V.L.C., being composed of representatives from all parts of the community, would tend to share this view.[9]

A third bureaucracy which would prove inadequate in trying to meet immigrant demands was that of the various immigrant organizations. These often did not deal directly with the basic social problems that affected the lives of individual immigrants.[10] To Nandy:

Established immigrant organizations are often the only organizations which confer status and esteem to the immigrant in the eyes of his compatriots. (Moreover, it is rare to find such an organization which is centrally concerned with the problems of life here and is not either a social club, as are most West Indian organizations, or homeland oriented, as are most Indian and Pakistani organizations.) Because of its status-conferring function, the established immigrant organization will guard power and control jealously. One result is that younger immigrants, who are often more involved in life in Britain, and still more the second generation, have few opportunities for participating in a meaningful way in organized activity both in defence of their rights and in furtherance of their place in the wider society.[11]

Not only were these organizations inadequately equipped to cope with problems of discrimination but their leaders were seen by the voluntary liaison committees as representatives of the immigrant community. Yet many of these leaders, according to Nandy, were not eager to press for immigrant demands but instead were willing to pay deference to the institutions and values of the wider society. Immigrant participation on the V.L.C.s was thus often an illusion.[12]

Out of these general tendencies and problems emerged a role for local C.A.R.D. groups. A group with a clearly defined role of combating discrimination would be needed in a situation where organizations' functions and leaders' roles were ambiguous. C.A.R.D. in theory hoped to represent the unrepresented through multiracial organizations that would stimulate immigrant organizations or circumvent them. It would press hard for policy against recalcitrant public authorities. It would force the voluntary liaison committees to take firmer stands and to mediate between a strong pressure group and the local authority. In outline, C.A.R.D. local groups would theoretically have at least five main functions:

1. Police the Race Relations Board's Conciliation Committee in the area.
2. Press the local authorities for better policies regarding immigrants. Try to change the climate of opinion in the community.
3. Insure that immigrants had access to welfare services and could take advantage of them. Oversee implementation of social reform legislation, for example, the 1965 Rent Act, which is administered at the local level. The welfare function would in theory be performed by the voluntary liaison committee in a particular city, but

given a broad analysis of its function and membership, C.A.R.D. members felt that there would not be 'proper' immigrant participation on these committees, and that in any event, the committees would not go into the communities and seek to specify immigrants' problems: this job would be C.A.R.D.'s.

4. Involve individual immigrants in the work of the local C.A.R.D. group. Give people who may feel isolated from the larger urban community an opportunity to seek a place in a group oriented towards the community (albeit towards changing it).

5. Devise and implement strategies for gaining power and working change at the local level. This would be as general as evaluating the dynamics of the city's government, economy, and social system, detailing desirable changes, and pin-pointing pressure points where efforts should be concentrated.[13] It could be as specific as trying to win over (or take over) locals in trade unions or developing tactics of education and/or civil disobedience to bring the cause of the immigrant before the public, either to engage the sympathy and arouse the conscience of the average citizen or to present the general public, in the form of local government, with a situation that demanded action heretofore not granted to such problems.

As always, the grave obstacle to the performance of all functions was the involvement of the immigrant and his children. At a national level, C.A.R.D. needed the strong support of local organizations to carry out more effectively its pressure group role. At the local level, the community C.A.R.D. group needed the support of individual immigrants if it were to influence effectively the local authorities, the V.L.C.s, and the regional conciliation committees. To gain this support, some members of the C.A.R.D. Executive in 1967 believed that the local organization must simply 'deliver the goods'. This phrase was crucial to their thinking about building an organization. C.A.R.D., following American civil rights groups and certain developments in the U.S. Government's anti-poverty programme, should take 'direct community action' to alter significantly conditions that affected the individual immigrant.

'Community action' has come to be associated with developments in American civil rights and anti-poverty activities. The words connote a multiplicity of objectives based in turn on numerous assumptions. To oversimplify and foreshorten, the aim of 'community action' is to go directly to those disadvantaged citizens who are not touched (or are positively harmed) by the various bureaucratic structures, both public and private, of the Welfare

State. The goals are not only to gain power, make the existing institutions more responsive, give services, and define problems, but to raise consciousness and stimulate involvement. Often, at least in private, radical community efforts in the United States, such raising of consciousness and stimulation of involvement come through explicit strategies of conflict.[14]

Along with the twin goals of change and involvement, an implicit objective in community action programmes was the active participation of citizens in determining matters that affected their lives. This hopeful platitude was based on at least two assumptions: Negroes and other poor people after decades of discrimination and impoverishment needed an opportunity to regain their own self-respect; the community action group, itself a symbol of revolt against modern bureaucracies which 'dehumanized' their clients, would be more free-form, less centralized, and more responsive to its constituents than the more established institutions. Conflict between the goals of developing power and leadership, and encouraging individual participation and broad-based decision-making have long been hallmarks of community action practised by some radical groups in the United States (as opposed to the action programmes instituted by the federal government in which organized blocs of residents often compete bitterly with City Hall for control of the federal funds).

By the spring of 1967, these subtleties (which were glaring conflicts in the United States) had not begun to surface with much force. Dipak Nandy believed that immigrants of all three nationality groups were apathetic for reasons as various as the groups themselves. Despite the variation, he assumed that this apathy, the reluctance to participate in organizations, and collectively to seek a better life in British cities, was not the same inertia that characterized the other welfare poor. The immigrants' immobility, thought Nandy, stemmed from their ignorance of the welfare system and from an inability to visualize an organization that could offer them specific rewards and the promise of meaningful change. If an organization operating at a neighbourhood level could 'deliver the goods'—could solve a case of discrimination, help find a job, negotiate with landlords, argue against local authorities with some visibility and some success, or perform other adaptive services for immigrants—then immigrants in the particular locality would join the organization, give it strength (in terms of numbers, if not money), and provide the momentum for enlarging it. Experimentation at the local level was needed to sharpen the concepts of community organization and community action. In the performance of these unique functions lay C.A.R.D.'s value and the source of its future strength.[15]

If the 'theory' of local group development was still at the informal stage, the image of what C.A.R.D. would look like if local organization was successful was also only faintly seen. The Nandyites held a vision of national C.A.R.D. acting as the spokesman for a number of strong local C.A.R.D. groups; initiative would come from below, not above. Local groups, active in combating discrimination at the community level, would ask national C.A.R.D. for money, for help with particular Ministers on specific problems, for information about the activities and techniques used by other groups, for usable research material. National C.A.R.D., taking information gathered at the local level, would formulate policy recommendations for the Government, and with the force of a local network behind it, press for the adoption of these general policies. An experiment in multi-racial co-operation, C.A.R.D. would be a force for social reform on a variety of problems—not just race—within British society. It would be part of a larger coalition of reforming groups in Britain which would in turn develop into a potent force in electoral politics. Young coloured Englishmen would press for more than equal opportunities, seeking not just to compete for a place in the social structure, but to make that structure more just and more egalitarian.

## 2. PROSPECTS FOR C.A.R.D. IN THE SPRING OF 1967

Discouragement and anger marked members of the C.A.R.D. Executive during the spring of 1967 because the vision of the model organization remained so distant and insubstantial. The Campaign Against Racial Discrimination was a name which stood for a small coalition of weak organizations and for the efforts of the C.A.R.D. Executive Committee. Individual members numbered approximately 3,000. Of these, roughly one-half to three-fifths came from the London area: the bias that was present at the very first C.A.R.D. meetings in 1964 and which the authors of the constitution wanted to counter still prevailed.[16] If one used the December 1966 list of local C.A.R.D. groups and affiliated organizations as a guide and added the estimated membership of these groups to the individual membership, C.A.R.D. at the time could be said to 'represent' anywhere from 8,000 to 15,000 people. But such a proposition was essentially meaningless. The crucial question with an organization like C.A.R.D. was whether members gave money or time to it.[17] Aside from the nine local C.A.R.D. groups,[18] the Oxford Committee for Racial Integration, the Leicester Campaign for Racial Equality, the Leeds Campaign Against Discrimination, the Indian Workers' Association, Southall, and its own subcommittees, C.A.R.D. received little time or money from individual members of affiliated organizations.

One major obstacle to C.A.R.D. development was lack of funds. The organization's expenditures were approximately £3,000 a year. During 1966 and 1967, more than £1,000 had been given by trusts to mount summer projects. Another trust gift had been given to provide the salary for a C.A.R.D. national organizer. Most expenses were for the minimal requirements of any organization: printing, typing, office help. Most of the revenue came from individual subscriptions. A concert or two had been held and there was an occasional £100 donation, but the organization was desperately in need of money. Funds were required, at the very least, to hire part-time regional secretaries to complement the national and regional organizers; to print C.A.R.D. literature professionally; to finance projects carried out by local C.A.R.D. groups; to float large-scale summer projects to establish C.A.R.D. organizations where they did not exist; to hire office staff to deal adequately with correspondence and record-keeping; and to establish a legal defence subsection of C.A.R.D. that would handle the legal problems of immigrants under an amended Race Relations Act.

C.A.R.D. could tap a number of potential sources: other minority groups in Britain like the Jews; other immigrant organizations (especially Pakistani and Indian business groups); trade unions; foundations (for specific projects); local businesses; interested citizens (through a national appeal). Yet there was little optimism among members of the C.A.R.D. Executive that money would be forthcoming. Britain had not reached a stage where the efforts of immigrants to gain equal opportunities aroused anything like the sympathy generated for the civil rights movement in the United States in the first half of the sixties. The problems were not seen to be as dramatic as those in Alabama and Mississippi. C.A.R.D. members believed that they were caught between a cross-fire. It was not respectable to give to an organization that had 'campaign' in its name because of the militant connotation. But there had not yet been the kind of protest, friction, or tension which would arouse emotions. Unless the example of American citizens proved a stimulant, C.A.R.D. members felt that the racial situation would probably have to worsen in Britain before they could obtain the money that they needed. C.A.R.D. only needed about £8,000 more a year to begin to initiate some of its projects, but there was a feeling of sadness and even desperation that 'a racist will have to burn down Brixton' before it would be possible to get donations of that size. As a member of the C.A.R.D. Executive Committee said:

We are not at the stage where the problem is regarded as serious enough. There is no group to our left to make us sufficiently respectable to tap business pockets. Nor is there enough trouble around so that it is in the interest of the community to support a group like ours. Nor is there a long tradition of injustice, as in the States, which makes the Liberal community feel guilty and arouses them to give money.

A second obstacle to growth was tension between C.A.R.D.'s national and local structures. David Pitt had always wanted tight Executive control over local developments so 'that the same sort of problems which bother the Labour party don't bother us'.[19] By the spring of 1967, he had begun to accept the likelihood that local groups would, of necessity, have a large measure of autonomy, but he was not pleased with the prospect since he felt it would create difficulties for a leadership that might be moving in a different direction. With his belief that policy should emanate from the centre of the organization, he was not in sympathy with important parts of the community action idea outlined by other C.A.R.D. members. In any event, he was not the person to support strongly such developments. He would go along. But with little enthusiasm.[20]

Further, C.A.R.D. had become an organization in which decisions were often taken outside the Executive Committee or the National Council. People acted on their ideas and the E.C. was rarely a forum for debate. Pitt accentuated this tendency by trying to avoid discussion and referring matters back to the committees. Thus there was not much enthusiasm generated about actual participation in the organization. People tended to work on their own specific projects. This was in keeping with the fact that many currently on the Executive also had obligations to other groups, ranging from the National Committee for Commonwealth Immigrants through voluntary liaison committees to local immigrant groups. Those not involved in specific projects were not stimulated to become active in C.A.R.D.

In addition, a lack of communication between local and national structures bedeviled C.A.R.D. By June 1967, the original goals set forth in the constitution were within reach. National C.A.R.D. could co-ordinate the efforts of its local groups, act as a clearing-house for information, and participate with organizations in initiating efforts against discrimination. But generally speaking, these tasks were not done. For example, in testing for discrimina-tion, the C.A.R.D. cases came primarily from the summer project work and from the London-based Complaints Committee; both efforts had been stimulated by Executive members. National C.A.R.D. could not translate the need for getting cases to leaders at the local level. It was felt that unless organizations could get results that were palpable, they could not win the support of those in the local communities. Without this support they could not help national C.A.R.D. with the implementation of its testing strategy. As Dipak Nandy said:

Unless local groups could make gains that could be seen, it would be difficult for C.A.R.D. to organize outside London. People outside London are just not willing to spend time or money on projects that simply dovetail with policy established by National Council.[21]

But the need for interchange was none the less great:

When I was working with a local organization there was the overwhelming feeling that problems were being dealt with without knowing what other people were doing. Every problem seems unique and solutions have to be worked out from the start. To come to the national organization was an absolute revelation. One discovers that people are talking about the same things and that the parochial problems are part of a larger system of injustice. The national organization could lift the sights of the local and the local must give the national a sense of particularity; what it's like to actually suffer discrimination.[22]

And as an indication of C.A.R.D.'s new resolve to move towards the grass roots, V. D. Sharma was chosen as national organizer after he expressed willingness to leave his job with London Trans-port and to resign his post with the I.W.A., Southall. Regional organizers were appointed in the North (operating out of Leeds) and the South (operating out of West Middlesex).

## 3. THE EMERGENCE OF LOCAL C.A.R.D.: PROBLEMS

The greatest constraints on the implementation of the cloudy but evolving C.A.R.D. idea of 'community action', arose obviously enough in the neighbourhoods of British cities. There the future of C.A.R.D. would be decided. National C.A.R.D. could help. But the hard work of implementing the strategies suggested by Nandy and others had to come from local initiative, taken by local leaders with direct lines to immigrants. Producing results would be extraordinarily difficult if C.A.R.D.'s limited experience through 1967 was an indication. At that point, C.A.R.D. local groups were still in embryo and this makes a full discussion difficult. Also, generalizations are fraught with danger because of wide variation in experience and locality.

None the less, some basic observations are possible. C.A.R.D. local groups, with the exception of the Leicester Campaign, were founded after C.A.R.D. itself, from early in 1965 through 1967. Membership ranged from 25 to 250. Some members paid dues, most often they did not. Annual expenditures never exceeded more than £500. Most of that was raised through subscriptions, public meetings, or jumble sales. Depending on locality, there tended to be roughly equivalent numbers of white and coloured in the organizations. Similarly, about half the officers were white and half coloured, although of the nine C.A.R.D. groups existing in June 1967, six had white chairmen.

Activities included: general reconnaissance of the areas, e.g. surveys, canvassing; testing public places, employers and employment offices, and housing for discrimination; direct action against such discriminatory practices as posting 'No Coloured' advertising on tobacconists' walls or providing information about poor housing conditions; countering anti-immigrant propaganda in the Press; setting up advice centres and handling individual welfare problems; holding meetings to exhort and enlist the newly found faithful. Some groups co-operated with the voluntary liaison committees, some felt hostility towards them. Some had alliances with local immigrant groups and saw that their role was in fact to stimulate them into action. Others felt that the immigrant groups were weak and oriented towards the wrong goals and should be circumvented.

Contacts with employers and trade unions were established irregularly.

The local groups had severe difficulties in determining at what points pressure could be applied and then doing it successfully. The external constraints were legion: the political culture generally; opposition from local authorities, the Press, the welfare bureaucracies; entrenched prejudice among members of the community; and the great complexity of problems like housing or employment. Internal obstacles stemmed from inadequate resources and also from the more subtle and delicate problems of bringing individual West Indian, Pakistani, or Indian immigrants into the organization and getting them to work together. Three brief descriptions of local organizing efforts undertaken by C.A.R.D. during the first years of its existence will indicate, by example, some basic problems at the local level.

## C.A.R.D. SUMMER PROJECTS

During the summer of 1966, the tentative ideas about community action were to be tried out in three British localities. C.A.R.D. was to commit one-third of its yearly budget to support volunteers for four weeks in Leeds, Manchester, and Southall. It was an experiment in community action to gain support among immigrants. C.A.R.D. also wanted to test for cases of discrimination and to train 'a core of young people in civil rights work'.[23]

Although the last two goals were achieved to an extent, the 'community action' aim was not attained. Members of national C.A.R.D. had wanted to go around bureaucratic structures and to reach the individual immigrant who had no group to defend his interest. The local C.A.R.D. groups proved to be an obstacle to this goal since they had their own interests and projects in the areas and because they did not want the summer volunteers to disrupt their position in the community either through militancy or ineptitude. At the end of the summer, the local organizations were not any stronger than before nor had they been able to sustain any developments instituted by the volunteers. When the students departed, community action ended.

In the summer of 1967, C.A.R.D. again committed large sums of money to a summer project. This time an attempt was made to establish an organization in an area where no C.A.R.D. group existed, namely, Soho Ward, Birmingham.

The central objective of Project '67 should be: first, to establish community organizations amongst immigrants and, second, to win these organizations for C.A.R.D.[24]

The project attempted to organize labouring West Indians and leave behind an ongoing immigrant organization, hopefully staffed by second-generation coloured citizens. The project also was courting trouble. Provocative action was not planned, but the decision to go into one of Britain's most 'difficult areas in terms of race relations' stemmed from the ambiguous desire that 'trouble' accompanied by publicity might focus Britain's attention on the problems of community work and give C.A.R.D. the publicity needed to attract more widespread financial and immigrant support.

According to Nandy, people in the area were dissatisfied with the West Indian Federation. The leaders of this organization at first wanted to be given a place within the C.A.R.D. group but when they were turned away a mood of hostility towards the experiment developed. As a first step, C.A.R.D. volunteers sought men and women within the area who, although holding no official position, might be viewed by their neighbours as leaders. At the same time, an attempt was made to understand the problems that most troubled residents of the ward. Need for a day-care centre and provision of rudimentary legal advice were topics most often mentioned in an initial survey. The men and women involved in Handsworth C.A.R.D. had never before been active in any sort of political organization. An advice centre was established, but after the C.A.R.D. organizers left in the autumn, it was discontinued.

As project director, Nandy was struck by the profound gulf that existed between black and white. West Indian distrust of their white English counterpart was great and became more marked the younger the person. To many of these West Indian youths, institutions and participation in formal structures—even such 'informal' structures as Birmingham C.A.R.D.—seemed an irrelevant waste of time: there would be no justice in Britain in any event. All those who were contacted by C.A.R.D. workers—black and white alike— were infused with a race consciousness that made them wary. The members of the fledgling organization defined many of their problems in terms of race and the project workers and director were torn between accepting the views of the participants and trying to redefine some of the problems as they as outsiders saw them (for example, housing, which afflicted both races in the same economic class). Said Nandy: 'To try to educate black and white to some of the salient problems of the area without reference to race is to be paternalist to an extent. And somehow this is what we have to avoid.'[25] His conclusion: the idea of the summer project would have to be drastically altered, C.A.R.D. would have to spend much more time in a community in order to sustain an organization.

## ISLINGTON C.A.R.D.

The sharpest critics of the C.A.R.D. summer projects of 1966 and 1967 were Ian McDonald and Oscar Abrams, members of the C.A.R.D. National Council and leaders of Islington C.A.R.D. This group had generally been regarded as C.A.R.D.'s most successful and active local organization. Its primary role was protesting against housing conditions in North London. Started just after the initial organization of C.A.R.D., by June 1967 the Islington group had a membership of approximately 200, mixed about equally between white and coloured. Most members were working class, with the notable exceptions of Abrams, McDonald, and another founder of Islington C.A.R.D., Nigel Beasley. The main activities of the Islington organization were to make contact with people through careful door-to-door work, to help people to use the 1965 Rent Act, and to march in protest against a landlady who charged excessive rents for her flats, intimidated immigrants, and refused to undertake apartment repairs.

Two salient ideas guided Islington C.A.R.D. One was the need to unite people of the working class regardless of colour by an appeal to their class origins and to class issues. Direct action on a class basis would result. The second idea was the need for individuals to make decisions about their lives themselves, directly and spontaneously, and for leaders to respect and follow the views held by group members. Meetings were held weekly and attempts were made to let discussion flow freely and to have members outline policies and make decisions.

Islington represented the cross-currents of many radical political strains: shop-floor organizations, shop stewards representing workers from a particular factory; tenants associations (Islington C.A.R.D. worked closely with the Islington Tenants and Residents' Association); the 'participatory democracy' goals of the American organizations Students for a Democratic Society and the Student Non-violent Coordinating Committee (as expressed during the

early sixties);[26] and the direct action (protest march) techniques
employed by the Campaign for Nuclear Disarmament.

Out of the welter of influences came a concept of 'community
action' based not on race but on class. McDonald was a white
barrister who considered himself a Marxist (but did not describe
himself in terms of the popular labels, Trotskyite, Maoist, etc.). He
and Abrams (a West Indian architect) believed that the problems
of coloured people in Islington were bound up with those of the
whites of the same economic strata and there should be joint action.
McDonald agreed that anti-discrimination laws were of the greatest
importance; but Islington refused to co-operate with national
C.A.R.D. in testing cases and also opposed the allocation of funds
for summer projects and voter registration. Both men said that for
C.A.R.D. to relate in a meaningful way to Islington residents, it
must confront the problems that concerned people most—poor
housing conditions, bad landlords, and ignorance of the laws.
C.A.R.D. should not try to convince Islington members that anti-
discrimination laws were of the greatest importance. Discrimination,
to McDonald and Abrams, was only part of a larger social problem
in the area. Since immigrants in Islington could not wield any
voting power (the borough is heavily pro-Labour) and since discrimination was not the only determinant (or even a major one)
of bad housing, they were not eager to give money to voter registration or to the summer project (which they viewed as merely
an expensive way of gathering cases to send to the Race Relations
Board). They felt that the money spent on those programmes should
have been given to active, ongoing local groups. Tensions thus arose
between C.A.R.D.'s most active local group and the national
leadership, tensions which were exacerbated by different sets of
political attitudes held by those running Islington C.A.R.D. and
those in control of the C.A.R.D. Executive.

Islington C.A.R.D. provides an archetypal case where the
interests of the local organization were different from the national
group, where C.A.R.D.'s pressure group role at the national level
harmed its relations with a local group. By the summer of 1967,
there was little contact between Islington C.A.R.D. and the
Executive. The leaders at the local level did not take advantage of
C.A.R.D. contacts at the top to make representations to Ministers
on questions of policy affecting the local group. There was little
exchange of information. The latent intertwining of 'class issues'
with 'race issues' complicated by differing theories of organization

and leadership (plus different needs at different levels of operation) surfaced in C.A.R.D. in a substantive way for the first time. Yet the potential antagonism between race and class issues was still latent in Islington. The virulent conflict between lower-class whites and lower-class coloured citizens—which has been so strong in the United States—was not felt during 1967. The conflict was between the local, 'class' approach of Islington and the emphasis through 1967 at the national level on problems—like discrimination—that stemmed from race.

## WEST MIDDLESEX C.A.R.D.

This group grew out of the London-based Complaints Committee. If Islington was based on housing problems that affected people according to class, West Middlesex C.A.R.D. was concerned with testing cases for discriminatory bias according to race. Olwyn Navartne, one of the founders of West Middlesex C.A.R.D., had been involved in an employment dispute with the British Overseas Airways Corporation when he was put in touch with C.A.R.D. He sought legal help to counter an alleged discriminatory policy. After fighting the case, he began to go to C.A.R.D. Complaints Committee meetings and to take along friends. 'These people had not talked about discrimination practised against them before; when given a chance and a sympathetic audience they were soon pouring their hearts out.'[27]

A C.A.R.D. group was subsequently formed to cover the boroughs of Ealing, Hounslow, and Acton. Membership quickly rose to eighty and the organization began to register voters, to test public accommodations, firms, and trade unions, and to recruit membership. The last task was a severe problem. Despite the initial response and an attempt to survey blocks to find out what problems individuals had, the group had difficulty overcoming people's apathy. C.A.R.D. leaders had to counter cynicism and the immigrants' fear of doing something not socially acceptable which might be dangerous.[28] Tension began to develop between Asians and West Indians within the group, not over any specific issue but on matters of style. Indians and Pakistanis were critical of what they felt was the verbal excess of West Indians which was not in turn matched by much action. West Indians were concerned that Asians did not seem open and communicative or understanding of West Indian pride and were potential 'sell-outs'.

From these cases, several major problems that hindered C.A.R.D.'s first (and only) local efforts are suggested. Local groups could desire to keep control of their own domain and yet not be as systematic or advanced as the community action theorists in national C.A.R.D. Starting groups with outsiders and then having these organizations continue with local leadership was an extremely difficult proposition. Local groups could have radically different political orientations from national C.A.R.D. and there could be basic differences about priorities which would inhibit effective relationships. Fear and apathy at the local level could be insurmountable obstacles to organization. Divisions between Asians and West Indians could severely hamper local co-operation. (These difficulties, while hardly subtle, were none the less fundamental, and would have had to be dealt with by a newly energized, locally oriented C.A.R.D. organization.)

## 4. BACKDROP TO THE COUP

During the summer of 1967, the Executive Committee was both excited by the potential of a strong pressure group working at the local level once legislation had been passed and subdued by the difficulties to be overcome in the communities if such an organization was to be developed. For most E.C. members the two basic functions of C.A.R.D. still remained to be performed: C.A.R.D. leaders must represent the immigrant interest to the key points of influence in the political system and develop strategies for change, and a C.A.R.D. structure capturing the support of immigrants still had to be built.

Since C.A.R.D. had successfully helped to initiate new anti-discrimination legislation, the two functions became even more intertwined as the organization began to devote its limited energies to the problems of immigrants at the community level. The paradox of trying to develop community and national power among the 'powerless' remained a numbing contradiction and a puzzle with only tentative, guess-work solutions. 'Community action' as enunciated by Nandy was three-quarters phrase-making, one-eighth sketchy theory, one-eighth experimentation through summer projects. It was hardly a reality. The Nandyites felt that C.A.R.D. would have to become deeply enmeshed in the localities before the prospects of multiracial community action could be evaluated,

A period of exploration lay ahead—the results of field work being fed back to the theorizing apparatus and appropriate new stratagems attempted.

The Nandyites held fast to their basic assumption that immigrants would respond not just to the fact of discrimination (as was supposed in the early days of C.A.R.D.) but to a demonstration that C.A.R.D. could deliver the goods. They felt that they could overcome the brute fact that powerlessness perpetuates itself. Not seeing any significant chance for change in their own lives, people would not choose to press for an alteration of the existing conditions. The expectation that 'things can't be changed' would be reinforced by fear among newcomers that if they challenged a landlord or employer they would lose their flat or their job, a fear that anyone who had worked at a door-to-door level in an immigrant community will remark on. An ambivalence about whether they were British or West Indian, Pakistani, or Indian and whether their home was where they came from or where they were, further undermined the capacity for concerted action by immigrants.

For the Nandyites there was the hope that the ultimate passage of an extended anti-discrimination law would mean that the organization's activities could finally begin in earnest. Then C.A.R.D. could solve concrete problems and gain support in Hackney or Notting Hill or Birmingham's Soho Ward. With the passage of laws and the obvious manifestation of C.A.R.D.'s capacity to settle meaningful problems would come the politicization of the coloured youth who would be more inclined than their parents to participate in a political organization and to seek an equal place in society. They would be British-trained and would respond to C.A.R.D.'s appeal. This was the optimistic vision that the Nandyites, on occasion, allowed themselves during the summer.

Simultaneously, a different group within the E.C. was laying plans for a different future. The immediate goal was not pressure for legislation, but rather a take-over of the C.A.R.D. organization. At the time of the annual convention in November, this group would be comprised of four West Indians—David Pitt, Jocelyn Barrow, Ralph Bennett, and Johnny James. The initiative for the thrust came almost exclusively from James, with an assist by Bennett. The most devoted Marxist within C.A.R.D. and an outspoken admirer of Mao Tse Tung, James aimed at ridding C.A.R.D. of its liberal leadership and redirecting the energies of the organization. Through fortuitous circumstances, the enlistment of new allies, and his own careful groundwork, he was able to achieve, at least, the first of his goals.


## THE NEW MOOD OF MILITANCY

James was aided by a new temper that stirred British race relations during the summer.[29] On 26 July, Roy Jenkins announced the Government's intention to extend the Race Relations Act of 1965 in housing, employment, insurance, and credit facilities. Yet, on that same day, Jenkins banned American Black Power leader Stokely Carmichael from Britain. Carmichael had come to the Roundhouse, Chalk Farm, to address white and black radicals who had called an 'International Congress on the Dialectics of Liberation and the Demystification of Violence'. He had made speeches at rallies in Notting Hill and Brixton, appeared on the B.B.C., and attended meetings of Islington C.A.R.D. and the West Indian Standing Conference.

In preaching the tenets of the Black Power movement which he had spearheaded in the United States, Carmichael emphasized the need for coloured (black) people to control the economic, political, and social institutions in their communities. He also advocated the development of 'black consciousness', the psychological posture of pride in one's own colour and heritage which gave the immigrant (or the Negro in the American context) a sense of self-respect that of necessity preceded self-sufficiency and self-determination. Implicit in his tone and manner, occasionally explicit in his language, was a call for coloured people to use violent means to win their 'liberation' from 'colonial' structures, whether they be in the Third World or in the mother country.[30]

As Carmichael was completing his stay, rioting ravaged Detroit, Michigan, for five days, leaving hundreds injured and forty-three dead. Earlier in July, a clash between police and a Negro taxi driver had sparked a conflagration that engulfed Newark, New Jersey.[31] Both events received wide coverage and were given prominent display by the British Press. Race relations, even in a country where only 2 per cent of the population was coloured, again surfaced as an explosive, major issue.

Also during those last days of July 1967, Michael Abdul Malik (known also as Michael de Freitas or Michael X), the leader of the separatist Racial Action Adjustment Society (R.A.A.S.), was arrested on charges of violating the public order provisions of the

Race Relations Act 1965. Malik was accused of 'stirring up hatred' against whites in Britain during a speech he made in place of Stokely Carmichael before approximately 75 persons in Reading.[32] Immigrant leaders were resentful that Duncan Sandys had not been indicted for stating the day after Malik was arrested that there would be race riots in Britain if coloured immigration was not stopped.[33]

Following the welter of activity in late July, a Biafran playwright and poet, Obi Egbuna, founded Britain's first avowed Black Power group, the Universal Coloured Peoples' Association. Egbuna, who had travelled to the United States in 1966 and become acquainted with Stokely Carmichael, announced the formation of the U.C.P.A. in mid-August and released the group's manifesto *Black Power in Britain: A Special Statement*. The organization was small, comprised mainly of West Indian and African students, and secretive about its activities. The manifesto essentially repeated the three themes promulgated by Carmichael: coloured control of relevant institutions; development of black consciousness and pride; and flirtation with violence as a means for effecting social change, coupled with bitter denunciations of white men and white society.

As the manifesto put it: 'We don't advocate violence. But we do believe that the only way to neutralize violence is to oppose it with violence. We are not initiators of violence. But if a White man lays his hand on ONE of us, we will regard it as an open declaration of war on ALL of us.'[34] Egbuna himself, when announcing the formation of the group, said: 'The Home Secretary declared he wanted to avoid racial riots here. The police are trying to make sure racial riots do happen here.'

As a result of the summer's events, a different set of racial issues began to draw attention. Violence, colour consciousness, Black Power with all its connotations, a world-wide struggle against white, Western society emerged explicitly and loudly from the subterranean murmurings along the fringes of Britain's racial minorities to counterpoint and challenge the concepts of integration, multiracialism, and anti-discriminatory legalisms upon which C.A.R.D. had been built.

Implicit criticism of C.A.R.D. emerged from a much different source in September with the formation of the Joint Council for the Welfare of Immigrants (J.C.W.I.). The aims of the organization were quite limited: to help immigrants entering Britain by providing caseworkers and establishing liaison with Government officials at the ports and air terminals. Those refused entry or unable to gain entry certificates could come to the organization for immediate aid. If the scope of the J.C.W.I. was relatively narrow, support for the organization was broad. On 23 September 1967, more than 100 people representing 74 voluntary organizations met at the Dominion Cinema, bailiwick of the Indian Workers' Association, Southall, to reach an agreement on the constitution of the new umbrella organization. Ratification of the by-laws was unanimous; so was a motion to provide funds for casework.[35] Within several weeks, 115 immigrant organizations, ranging from the militant I.W.A., Great Britain, to the mildest West Indian cultural and social club, had federated to the J.C.W.I.

The impetus for the organization had come from Joseph Hunte, then public relations officer for Standing Conference, and Michael Dummett, of C.A.R.D. Executive Committee. Also active in forming the J.C.W.I. was V. D. Sharma of the I.W.A., Southall, and the C.A.R.D. Executive. The founders wanted to unite disparate groups around a single, sharply focused issue. As they wrote in an early J.C.W.I. document:

The civil rights movement in Britain has not been conspicuous in the past for successful liaison between the various local and national groups, with their varying structures, methods of operation, and ideological backgrounds. To weld them, or even a sizable portion of them, into unity on all fronts would be a long-term task. We felt a single, strikingly successful example of restricted cooperation for a limited purpose would provide a better stimulus to working unity than any amount of exhortation to a more embracing unity under an old or new banner. Here was a project in which all had a common interest, in which all could collaborate without prejudice to their particular ideological position. . . . Any attempt to create an overall unity demands the agreed solution of difficult problems: what is the right tone to adopt in addressing the society at large? what is the right order of priorities? what are the most effective methods of opposing discrimination? . . . the participating groups will not need, for the most part, to debate their varying answers to these questions: they can gain the advantages of unity while by-passing the obstacles lying in the path to achieving it.[36]

C.A.R.D., which had known well its share of obstacles in trying to promote unity, was considered too controversial a vessel for a united effort. C.A.R.D. members, members of the W.I.S.C., and of the competing I.W.A.s could only join around a new and neutral body.

C.A.R.D. had implicitly failed to solve the difficult problems of 'overall unity' and was seen as inadequate for a more limited, if united project. The contrast between the two organizations was made in a telling comparison of the response of C.A.R.D. to the formation of the N.C.C.I. and the response of the J.C.W.I. to the Wilson Committee report on immigration appeals.[37] A concerted response to the N.C.C.I. was not made, the founders of the J.C.W.I. declared. C.A.R.D., by implication, was not able to rally the immigrant community in united opposition to the controversial committee. However, the J.C.W.I. was able to speak with one voice regarding the Wilson report and the whole issue of immigrant appeals:

It is hoped that we have all learned the lesson of this debacle [the N.C.C.I.]. It is this: That any government move, requiring a response from immigrant organizations, is bound to be divisive in just the same way, just because it *is* a government move—unless immigrant organizations can band together to give a united response. . . . Immigrants have said over and over: We are sick of being talked *about*; we want to be *heard*.[38]

The formation of the J.C.W.I. meant that the Government excuse that there was no spokesman for the immigrant interest would no longer be valid, at least on the subject of immigration procedures. The rhetoric sounded as if it had been lifted from memoranda written in the earlier, braver days of C.A.R.D.

IMPENDING CRISIS: ISSUES

During the months leading up to the 1967 convention, tensions within C.A.R.D. were building up. The National Council had ceased to function effectively much to the dismay of Michael Dummett, Oscar Abrams, and Ian McDonald. The Executive Committee was made impotent not by inertia but by division. Little business was actually conducted in the bi-monthly sessions. People went their own ways, continuing projects that had already been started. Nandy was preoccupied with the summer project and long-term community strategy and analysis, Lester with technical and strategic problems associated with legislation. Bennett and James worked, in somewhat desultory fashion, on a voter registration project. Pitt continued to cultivate contacts in the Government.

Since the problems were so immense, there was never any significant objection to the work done by others as long as it did not impinge on one's own efforts. Executive Committee members sniped at their fellows on substantive issues, but battle was never joined on policy matters that might have significant effects on the condition of immigrants (as opposed to the condition of the organization).

Voter registration in Hackney and Stoke Newington, part of David Pitt's Greater London Council constituency, had been accepted less than enthusiastically in December by the Nandyites who felt that it was wasteful to spend several hundred pounds on workers who would have only a few months before the G.L.C. elections in which to put voters on the rolls. But since the chairman had insisted on the project, the issue never was forced, and funds were allotted. Similarly, Ralph Bennett and Johnny James scored the summer project plans, although the funds for it had come from sources outside the normal C.A.R.D. treasury and were in fact especially earmarked for work in Birmingham.

Only the issue of C.A.R.D.'s attitude towards the National Committee threatened to become a full-scale controversy which could divide the E.C. More typical of the rancour which began to characterize relationships on the Executive was the opposition of James to the appointment of V. D. Sharma as C.A.R.D. national organizer during the summer. The money to pay for Sharma's yearly salary had been obtained by Lester from the Hilden Trust and thus did not jeopardize any C.A.R.D. projects. James, while not objecting to the creation of a national organizer, did object to Sharma. His opposition was part of a developing schism within the organization that found the West Indians increasingly isolated and opposed by what was referred to, humorously at first, as the Anglo-Asian axis.

## IMPENDING CRISIS: DIFFERENCES OF PERSONALITY AND PROCEDURE

The mistrust which often bedevils political relationships between Asians and West Indians undoubtedly springs from deep sources: differences in religion, language, and culture, contrasting experiences with British imperialism, divergent attitudes towards organization, differing relative cohesion of the West Indian versus the Indian and Pakistani communities. In C.A.R.D., the immediate origin of mistrust and ultimately antagonism was intraorganizational feuding between the Nandyites and Ralph Bennett over the office and treasury procedures.

H. S. Dhillon, C.A.R.D. treasurer and member of the I.W.A., Southall, had by July become exasperated with the work of Ralph Bennett, the West Indian office secretary. Similarly, Julia Gaitskell, as general secretary, had found it increasingly difficult to co-operate with Bennett. A special finance committee, formed to investigate the problems, decided that some of Bennett's salary (he was C.A.R.D.'s only full-time employee) should be diverted to hire part-time stenographic help. This incensed the Executive's West Indians and prompted Pitt to offer a compromise whereby he would pay two-thirds of Bennett's salary from his own pocket.

Scarcely had this row died down, when Dhillon and Bennett tangled again. The treasurer had been seeking an independent audit of C.A.R.D.'s books and an ordering of C.A.R.D. member-ship lists. To save money an accountant from the I.W.A., Southall, was employed. In late August, Bennett refused to hand over the lists to the man appointed by the finance committee. Julia Gaitskell was forced from the C.A.R.D. office when she tried to prevail upon Bennett. Following this unhappy incident and the continued recal-citrance of Bennett and James, Dhillon resigned. Julia Gaitskell, after seriously considering the possibility, did not.

Bitter wrangling between West Indians on one side and Pakistanis, Indians, and Englishmen on the other began to mark Executive Committee meetings. The depths of pathos and divisiveness were reached at an autumn meeting when one member was accused of being a Nazi. An inhuman order (to turn membership lists over to the auditor) had been resisted as honourable Germans should have resisted during the thirties.

According to one member of the E.C., these almost meaningless disputes were deliberately provoked. In retrospect, it would seem that there had been attempts to divide the West Indians from others on the Executive.[39] Minor issues had become invested with racial overtones.

### THE LIBERAL DEATH WISH: THE ALIENATION OF DAVID PITT

The procedural issue about the audit was unimportant and ulti-mately settled by a compromise. What was significant was the shifting allegiance of David Pitt who had strongly supported Ralph Bennett much to the dismay of Julia Gaitskell, Lester, and Nandy. The C.A.R.D. chairman had always had two sets of allies on the

1966–7 E.C. Firstly, Ralph Bennett, Johnny James, Jocelyn Barrow, Dr. Norman Athill, all West Indians. They had been suggested to C.A.R.D. by Pitt and at various times during the three years of C.A.R.D.'s existence co-opted at his insistence. James and Bennett, as noted, were political workers for Pitt in his G.L.C. constituency. Secondly, Dipak Nandy, Anthony Lester, Julia Gaitskell, and (to a lesser extent) V. D. Sharma. These four had long shared Pitt's parliamentary perspective, emphasizing the need for laws as a first priority. People who were impatient for local development but not alienated enough to quit C.A.R.D., such as Michael Dummett, Ian McDonald, and Gurmukh Singh, had been critical of both groups and of Pitt.

As the year passed, the second group—the Nandyites—began to move away from Pitt. The era when parliamentary pressure tactics could suffice was coming to an end, but Pitt was not creative about local development. He was simply wedded to an old model of political participation through voter registration. The Nandyites felt he was not imaginative or forceful enough in his opposition to the National Committee or the Government. Most damning of all, they felt he was not devoted to C.A.R.D., giving the organization too little time and too little leadership.

The grumblings about Pitt's incapacity were communicated back to him. A member of the Nandyite group in a moment of indiscretion told Ralph Bennett about the loss of confidence in the chairman. Bennett became convinced that there was a plot to rid the organization of Pitt, James, and himself.[40] The slip to Bennett was just a reflection of the sense of despair that had seized people like Lester, Nandy, and Gaitskell. As the summer wore on they were overcome with a sense of failure and foreboding.

The criticism of Pitt was impolitic for the simple reason that the Nandyites had no constructive alternative to offer as chairman. Although they talked in haphazard fashion about opposing Pitt in the autumn convention, no plans were ever laid. It was generally agreed that the chairman had to be West Indian, since an appeal to that group was crucial to C.A.R.D.'s survival. But the young, angry, forceful Trinidadian or Jamaican who should lead C.A.R.D. was not evident. It was agreed that Nandy although young and angry was too intellectual to head C.A.R.D. (and of the wrong nationality). As part of the general feeling of defeat and the wish that their service could somehow come to an end without the appearance of giving up the cause, Lester and Julia Gaitskell decided long before the convention not to stand for the E.C. again. Julia Gaitskell also had no plans to run a second time for general secretary. Work could be carried on in committees or through the National Council.

During the Executive Committee meetings, James began to launch unveiled attacks on white members of the organization, arguing that they could not understand the coloured man's problems and should not be in a position of leadership. The liberal whites took these verbal assaults with resignation. They felt that once racial sentiment was played upon they could do little to combat it. They were white; it was a black man's fight. If their help was not sought, they would leave. As so many hard-working liberals in the United States civil rights movement discovered—men and women who had given much time and effort—as the mood of the coloured man changed, the liberal whites would be prophets of little honour in what had once been partly their own house. Anthony Lester said:

> The series of events in the Executive made us feel that we did not want to continue as workers for David Pitt. I was disheartened to raise money if it was going to keep Ralph Bennett in the office and if the chairman was not going to back our programmes up. We began not to care. . . . We felt it was hopeless.[41]

## THE PREPARATIONS OF JOHNNY JAMES

As the annual convention approached and conditions on the Executive Committee deteriorated, Johnny James brought preparations for the meeting to a crest. He was well placed to play a leading role. He was assistant general secretary for membership and thus in charge of recruiting new groups. He was chairman of the International Committee and therefore responsible for soliciting resolutions on racial matters of international import. And he was also chairman of the conference arrangements committee.

Moreover, James and Ralph Bennett were active in a small left-wing organization called the Caribbean Workers' Movement. From this base, James and Bennett had contact with other small left-wing, pro-Peking organizations in London. In the weeks before the convention efforts were made to bring some of these organizations to the C.A.R.D. annual conference.[42]

### The Caribbean Workers' Movement

Both James and Bennett were officers and founders of this group, which was started in 1965. Bennett was general secretary; James, head of publications. The C.W.M. was concerned with promoting revolution in the Caribbean and introducing 'true' socialism to the island countries.[43] The primary activity of the group was publishing propaganda in Britain. There was a *Caribbean Workers' Weekly*, a penny sheet that usually contained news of political developments in the islands; *Carib*, an irregularly published magazine, containing more lengthy Marxist analyses; and a series of documents called *Caribbean Organization for Mass Political Education*.[44]

The centre of C.W.M. activities was a small, cluttered room near King's Cross in Gray's Inn Road which was shared by the Movement for Colonial Freedom. A battered mimeograph machine churned out literature at a prodigious rate. Membership in the C.W.M. is not known precisely, but was probably not much more than 100 in 1967. The annual expenditures did not exceed £500, most of it coming from donations and party receipts, the bulk of it going to publishing expenses.

### The London Workers' Committee

This too was a small, pro-Peking group concerned primarily with publishing. Its organ was a monthly called the *Workers' Broadsheet* put out by Dr. Alexander Tudor-Hart, a 67-year-old general practitioner from Tooting. Dr. Tudor-Hart believed that the solution to the colour problem in Britain lay in the solution to the class divisions. He felt that a regenerated movement of black and white labourers could bring meaningful socialism to Britain.[45]

Before the C.A.R.D. convention, members of the C.W.M. and the London Workers' Committee met and it was agreed that the representatives of the London Workers' Committee present at the annual meeting would move a resolution calling for constitutional amendments. The resolution was solicited by Johnny James.

### The Universal Coloured Peoples' Association

This organization too was contacted by James. Obi Egbuna affiliated the U.C.P.A. to C.A.R.D. (although whether the affiliation was legitimate is a matter of dispute). He agreed to come with some fellow members to the annual convention.

## The Indian Social Club

In September, Ralph Bennett visited Sardul Singh Gill, president of Southall's Indian Social Club. They talked about C.A.R.D. and shortly thereafter the Club paid £10 to affiliate ten voting members to the organization. Gill had been president of the I.W.A., Southall, in 1963–5, and along with P. S. Khabra, Social Club general secretary, was a rival of the I.W.A. president, H. S. Ruprah, and of V. D. Sharma. Politically, Gill, than a Labour candidate in a Southall ward election, was far to the right of James and the leaders of the other organizations contacted by the West Indian. However, the I.W.A. elections were scheduled for March 1968. Gill, eager to get his faction back into power, was concerned about C.A.R.D. politics and reluctant to have Sharma and Ruprah retain their influence in the organization.[46]

These four organizations—the Caribbean Workers' Movement, the London Workers' Committee, the U.C.P.A., and the Indian Social Club—were for varying reasons to form the nucleus of James's convention effort. In the weeks before the annual meeting, Anthony Lester was deeply concerned because James had submitted resolutions from the International Committee to the Executive, which not only castigated South Africa and Rhodesia, but also attacked Israel (for the June war), the United States, and Britain. To Lester, resolutions that condemned Israel, the U.S., and Britain could not help the C.A.R.D. cause in any meaningful way but might only alienate potential supporters. He was disturbed too because James, as chairman of convention arrangements, planned to display posters of Mao, Kenyatta, and Robert Williams, militant Negro leader of the American Revolutionary Action Movement who was exiled in Communist China.

After a C.A.R.D. delegation met with the Home Secretary to discuss legislation and the implementation of the Wilson Committee report in the days just preceding the convention, Lester, Nandy, and other members of the Executive talked to Pitt in the Lyon's Corner House across from Westminster. Pitt listened to the group's objections and agreed to speak to James about the posters. Pitt also said that he would rule out of order any resolution that was not consistent with the aims and objects of C.A.R.D.[47] At the final Executive Committee meeting on Thursday night before the Saturday opening of the convention, Julia Gaitskell submitted a list of thirty-three affiliated organizations authorized to send voting representatives. Ralph Bennett, Johnny James, and Audrey Cooper, the West Indian regional organizer for the South, were chosen to check credentials at the door.

## 5. THE STRUGGLE FOR THE CAMPAIGN AGAINST RACIAL DISCRIMINATION

### THE FIRST CONVENTION SESSION: THE END AT THE BEGINNING

As the third Annual Delegates Conference of C.A.R.D. got under-way, posters of Robert Williams and Jomo Kenyatta looked down from the walls of London's Conway Hall, site of the first convention two years before. One sign read: 'Black Power means liberation, not integration as third-class citizens.' Another, reflecting an older spirit of the organization, proclaimed: 'Outlaw racial discrimination. Pro-vide effective laws.' The symbolic division was present at the session on Saturday, 4 November, but the brooding presences of Williams and Kenyatta reflected the victory that Johnny James was about to win.

In the hall, often the site of chamber concerts and theosophical debates, the atmosphere was acrid. Mark Bonham Carter, chairman of the Race Relations Board, was greeted with shouts of 'White Liberal' and 'Resign' when he rose to explain the work of the Board. While delivering the chairman's address, David Pitt was heckled with the epithets 'Uncle Tom' and 'house nigger'. V. D. Sharma was also treated to abusive language when he spoke against a resolution late in the afternoon. Two visitors from the American South, inured to the rhetoric, bombast, and plain viciousness of racial meetings, said afterwards that the session was one of the most acrimonious they had ever witnessed.[48] To the Nandyites it appeared that anti-Semitism, and anti-white and anti-Asian feelings were rife.[49]

Despite the uproar, the report of the general secretary was passed with little debate. Energy was being conserved for a controversial resolution that suggested two changes in the constitution. This resolution had been put forward by Paul Noone, a white man, member of the London Workers' Committee, and associate of Johnny James. Around its provisions the forces and antagonisms of the conference were to swirl. Noone's resolution had two import-ant parts:

First, it called for inclusion in the constitution that: 'C.A.R.D.

realizing that racialism, racial prejudice and racial discrimination are manifestations of imperialism, will fight against imperialism in all its forms by all the means at its disposal.'

Second, it said, 'Believing that an anti-racialist organization can only be led successfully by those suffering the effects of racialism, the London Workers' Committee proposes that the leading officials of C.A.R.D., including the General Secretary, should all be immigrant people or indigenous people of coloured origin. The role of the indigenous white . . . people is to support their coloured brothers and sisters in their struggle not to tell them how they are to fight.'

Both parts were strongly opposed by the Nandyites. C.A.R.D. could not permit itself to fight imperialism with 'all means at its disposal' without diverting energy from necessary work in Britain and risking characterization as a radical, left-wing group. (To be sure, for some Nandyites like V. D. Sharma, who was an old line Marxist, the resolution may have been an anathema simply because it came from Maoists.) Further, although most C.A.R.D. members, regardless of faction, wanted coloured leaders in the organization, the Nandyites did not want what they considered a discriminatory clause written explicitly into the constitution.

Late Saturday afternoon, a vote was taken on the 'imperialism' part of the resolution and in the dimly lit hall the Nandyites were defeated by a large majority. At that moment, the balance of power in C.A.R.D. shifted. Although Johnny James had not quite commanded the two-thirds required for a constitutional amendment, he had a clearly demonstrated majority among the 200 plus delegates, which could pass other resolutions and elect officers. A take-over by men who would espouse what the Nandyites considered extreme Black Power and Marxist positions seemed imminent.

When the conference resumed deliberations on Sunday morning, the I.W.A., Southall, delegation, whose ranks had been thin previously, was fully marshalled. An attempt was being made by the Nandyites to recoup. But it was to no avail. The 'Black Power Officer' provision was carried by nearly two-thirds of those present, again not by the votes required to amend the constitution but by more than enough to demonstrate where the strength of the meeting lay. The I.W.A. had come reluctantly to the conference. The conflict over the treasurer Dhillon and the I.W.A. auditor had prompted serious discussion within the I.W.A. executive about leaving C.A.R.D.[50] Now the I.W.A. contingent asked Dipak Nandy, who along with Jocelyn Barrow and Audrey Cooper comprised the

Standing Orders Committee, to investigate the credentials of several organizations from Southall, including the Indian Social Club. While Nandy met with the other members of his committee, the men from the I.W.A. walked out, followed by Anthony Lester and Julia Gaitskell, charging that the meeting had been illegally stacked.

The Standing Orders Committee was confronted with two lists of affiliated groups. One prepared by Julia Gaitskell had thirty-three organizations, the other drawn up by Johnny James listed fifty-two.[51] James's list showed that a number of organizations had affiliated within the past week.[52] The committee decided that the three groups challenged by the I.W.A. were legitimate. Nandy requested that the credentials of many of the others be examined since they had not been registered with the general secretary as required by the C.A.R.D. constitution. The committee, at Nandy's prompting, proposed that an independent inquiry be undertaken by selected High Commissioners from the relevant Commonwealth countries. But despite the fact that he had been ridiculed from the floor by some of the James forces, David Pitt overruled the committee in a crucial (and, to the Nandyites, illegal) decision. Instead, he asked for the election by the full convention of a team from the floor to study the credentials question. To the consternation of the Nandyites this was done and the five-man credentials committee included Bruce Pitt, the chairman's son. Following this decision the Nandyites considered that future decisions of the convention had 'no binding force whatsoever',[53] since an allegedly rigged meeting was investigating itself. The annual delegates conference was then recessed for four weeks pending the investigation.

C.A.R.D. had once again been split apart by words. The crucial, divisive issue was simply the inclusion of several sentences in the constitution. Of course, to the two sets of leaders—the Nandyites and the followers of James (Bennett, Egbuna, Noone, Tudor-Hart)—these phrases were symbolic of different strategies (however vague) and, in some instances, of radically different sets of objectives. In crude terms, the struggle could be seen to have a clear ideological cast: the Nandyites, mainly former Communist party members (Nandy and Sharma) and Labour party liberals (Lester and Gaitskell), opposing the Maoists (James, Tudor-Hart) and Maoist-oriented Black Power proponents.

Yet, despite the broad ideological differences between the two sets of leaders and the various nuances of strategy and tactics that each espoused, the majority of the West Indians at the first convention session were persuaded of two propositions which were emotive but non-ideological. They believed that the control of C.A.R.D. was in the hands of white liberals who, through an emphasis on lobbying, were putting a brake on militancy or preventing black people from deciding their own strategies, or both. They also believed that C.A.R.D. was dominated by its Indian members, perhaps in alliance with the white liberals, and that the Indians were hostile to the interests of the West Indians.[54]

Those who voted with James for the resolutions were: black Maoists, mainly West Indians concerned not just about change in Britain but revolution in the home countries; Black Power advocates, mainly Africans and West Indians, who were relatively well versed in the rhetoric of black liberation as espoused by Fanon and Carmichael; white Marxists; and a number of West Indians who were simply angry at the course of events in Britain and within C.A.R.D.[55] The appeal to these West Indians was based largely on two rumours: first, that Michael Dummett (or Dipak Nandy) meant to depose Dr. David Pitt as C.A.R.D. chairman;[56] second, that the struggles within C.A.R.D. over the national organizer and the treasury presaged a take-over by Indians whose views were seen to be inimical to West Indians.[57]

The old dichotomies between militant and moderate had been called to service again, this time by the James forces. This occurred despite the fact that in terms of work in Britain the Nandyites had been far more 'radical' than any of the West Indians. Pitt had always been one of the most conservative members of the E.C. and James had followed his lead, devoting himself only to the voter registration project.[58] This dichotomy, now overlain more than ever with an emotionally appealing split between 'integrationists' and 'Black Power' advocates, became too potent for the Nandyites at the convention, despite the fact that they commanded the support of a large part of the National Council, more than two-thirds of the Executive, and more than half of the local groups. These groups and individuals did not provide the necessary strength. Alienated from the whites and Asians currently in C.A.R.D.,[59] the West Indians voted behind Johnny James and swept the group that had guided C.A.R.D. for two years from power.

## THE NANDYITES COUNTER-ATTACK

To the Nandyites the forces that had brought off the coup posed two threats to the established objectives of C.A.R.D. First, James and others who advocated a 'world-wide struggle against imperialism' might change the theatre in which C.A.R.D. battled. The organization had always been concerned with discrimination in Britain on the assumption that large numbers of coloured immigrants were going to take up permanent residence in the United Kingdom. To be concerned with promoting social change across the oceans would simply reduce the effectiveness of C.A.R.D. because it would divert resources from a cause that was already weak.

The second implied objective promoted by the Noone resolutions was to move C.A.R.D. in the direction of a separatist, totally 'black' organization. The Nandyites were concerned with developing strategies for gaining power for all coloured people, strategies that would give immigrants and their children an equitable share of influence in decision-making. Radical change would be necessary, but that change had to come by confronting existing social and political structures and attempting to alter them. Black isolation, black enclaves, total separatism were inferred by the Nandyites from the black officer resolution, and this they could not support.

But even if the two parts of the resolution did not imply such a severe alteration of objectives, the Nandyites opposed them because they felt that their inclusion in the constitution would be bad tactics. V. D. Sharma expressed this view when he emphasized that C.A.R.D.'s broad strategy for change depended on developing a coalition to combat discrimination in Britain.[60] Fighting imperialism is not the immediate objective of C.A.R.D., Sharma wrote. It cannot be:

It is quite true that racial discrimination is a manifestation of imperialism. By fighting racial discrimination in Britain we are indeed opposing one of imperialism's objectives—to divide the working class.[61]

An absolutist statement on imperialism would cause others who would support an anti-discrimination movement to hive off, crippling the coalition for change.

Similarly, he opposed passage of the black officer resolution: 'You cannot claim to fight discrimination and not give equal rights to elect and be elected to all members . . . the tactics and strategy of such an organization must be to win the maximum support and sympathy from the 98 per cent who are not coloured.'[62] Sympathetic whites remained absolutely central to the C.A.R.D. strategy.

Moreover, the emergence of Black Power—an explosive phrase imperfectly understood by nearly all parties who heard it and hazily explicated by those who used it—threatened to divide the coloured community in Britain, the Nandyites felt. Many Asians would see Black Power as systematic violence, something they could not condone.[63] Concerned with acquiring property and economic power, many Indians felt 'how silly it is to get something by burning something down and that is the implication of Black Power', as Nandy said. The political hero for many Indians was Gandhi, for some West Indians Toussaint L'Ouverture. Again, given Gandhi's success, Black Power was not an appealing call.

Further, Black Power rhetoric was seen by some Asians as just another example of the verbal excesses of the voluble West Indians. Members of the I.W.A., Southall, for example, resented the vocal militancy of the convention since they believed that they had built a strong local organization which was a significant force for change in its community. The appeal to colour consciousness was not necessarily evocative. Indians and Pakistanis are coloured, but they do not consider themselves black.

Despite signs from James, the Nandyites had not been prepared for the stark challenge at the convention. They had been complacent, defeatist, tired of endless bickering, frustrated with the enormity of the task. 'We should have suspected a coup', said Anthony Lester. 'But we did not really.' Although there were ample warning signals, no counter-measures had been planned. A fundamental pattern had unfolded in the politics of the powerless. C.A.R.D., itself an amorphous agglomeration of groups controlled by wilful leaders, had been infused with new forces (whether they were 'legal' or not is another question) and the new leaders had outbid the ruling powers by going to the left. The established leaders of C.A.R.D. had so far offered their followers little tangible progress in the way of influence, rewards, or progress. The insurgents offered criticism—some of it justified, most of it scathing—and loud promises of a new order. Outbid and outmanoeuvred, victims of the cannibalism of the left, the Nandyites following the convention considered how to counter-attack.

Two paths lay open for regaining control of C.A.R.D. The Nandyites could either wage a legal battle and try to prove the illegitimacy of the convention proceedings or they could try to regroup forces and go to the convention hall in early December to elect their own National Council. However, because the majority against them had been so significant at the first session of the convention, it was felt that a political struggle was hopeless unless an independent inquiry was established and a number of groups discredited. But this meagre hope was snuffed out after a meeting of the Executive Committee on 16 November. The Nandyites told David Pitt that the National Council was the only legal arm of C.A.R.D. with the authority to make decisions between conventions. The credentials battle was a matter for National Council adjudication, not for Pitt to decide. The chairman, during the last, bitter meeting of the 14-man committee, said that he was the only person empowered to act for C.A.R.D. and that his decision regarding the establishment of the credentials committee from the convention floor could not be altered. At that point, ten members of the Executive walked out, leaving Pitt, James, Barrow, and Bennett.[64] The walk-out came during a tumultuous week for British race relations. Dr. Martin Luther King visited Newcastle; Michael Abdul Malik was sentenced to a year in prison; and, most important for the rump of the C.A.R.D. Executive which could lay claim to a share of the credit, the Street report was issued recommending a wide extension of legislation.[65]

With the political route blocked, the Nandyites decided that although they might well win a legal skirmish and keep the name of C.A.R.D., it would not be worth very much. 'Once we had lost the political war there would be no point in winning a legal victory', said Anthony Lester. The Nandyites (with the exception of Michael Dummett) decided on a strategy of aggression. They would try to woo away the local groups from the new C.A.R.D. leadership and have the National Council (1966–7) repudiate the convention proceedings. The aim was to remove the cloak of legality from the new C.A.R.D., undermine David Pitt (who now evoked extreme hostility), and generally isolate C.A.R.D. so that a new movement with a different name could be started.

A National Council meeting was held to gain support for the plan.[66] The local organizations were circularized and asked for their commitment to the established C.A.R.D.[67] The success of the strategy depended on the handling of the reconvened conference. Would it continue along an explicitly Black Power and Maoist path which would frighten away many liberals and whites? Or would it moderate its stance and give the appearance of being the militant, democratic group dedicated to radical change at the grass roots. The outcome depended on the two central figures in the month's developments: David Pitt and Johnny James.

## THE PITT-JAMES ALLIANCE: COMPROMISE

Revolution in the Caribbean and in other parts of the world as outlined by Marx, Lenin, and Chairman Mao was central to the political thought of Johnny James in the years preceding his emergence at the C.A.R.D. convention. His basic orientation, moreover, had always been more towards realizing radical change in the home islands than towards eradicating discrimination in Britain. Most of the political activity carried on by the 40-year-old accountant was concerned with the Caribbean Workers' Movement and its publication, since he was the C.W.M.'s chief propagandist. He met sporadically with small groups of West Indians from the various islands and had in 1966 called a 'Caribbean October Congress' in Britain to discuss political plans for the area. 'The real struggle' was in the West Indies, he told a C.A.R.D. member quite openly in 1967.[68]

James's Communism had been given full verbal rein at the convention; it was marked by hyperbole and vitriol. Flushed with his victory, he began a 9 November Press statement:

Let it be quite clear that I do not like speaking to the white imperialist press reporters, because by nature, they have to lie and distort everything one says to carry out orders and wishes of their white masters.

After referring to the efforts of C.A.R.D.'s international committee, which had received messages of support from eleven countries, James said: 'This solidarity . . . is what is frightening the enemy and its white and coloured running dogs.' In Number 118 of the *Caribbean Workers' Weekly* (published in mid-November) the counter-attack by the Nandyites was described:

They tried posing communism to frighten away Caribbeans, Asians and Africans, this also failed miserably. Finally they have shown their hands by stating to the imperialist press . . . 'WE DEPLORE THE INJECTION OF POLITICAL IDEOLOGY INTO THE MOVEMENT WHICH CAN ONLY DIVIDE US.' This is the nub of the matter, they want BLACKS TO FIGHT empty-headed against an organized, VICIOUS AND BLOODTHIRSTY ENEMY. WE ALL SAY GO TO HELL![69]

The rhetorical overkill reflected a moment of profound hostility towards British society and disaffection from its customary processes which were held to have entangled the coloured man, not freed him. It also camouflaged the fundamental powerlessness in Britain. The deep attraction of hyperbolic language espousing a global movement was that it not only stated important matters of principle but it linked the small coloured minority in Britain to a world-wide struggle that had been joined by millions of comrades and oppressed black brothers. An identity outside the British context shored up those who would assault British society. But the other side of the effusion which produced overstatement was prideful insecurity. 'Do not expect, nor will there be, any wild stupidities', James wrote in the Press statement.

Whether James's prescriptions for C.A.R.D. would be as extreme as his rhetoric was not evident in the days following the first session of the convention. If he wanted to use C.A.R.D. to spearhead radical change in the West Indies, he did not make clear how the organization would do so, other than to issue statements castigating imperialism. In his Press remarks, he scored conditions that afflicted the black man in Britain. But these were aspects of British society criticized strongly by most C.A.R.D. members.[70] If he proposed some new strategy for radicalizing the British working class, consistent with his general political orientation, and yoking racial and class emancipation, these plans were also kept clandestine. In his 9 November Press statement, James pledged that C.A.R.D.:

must become and remain thereafter, a broad, mass, grass-roots organization, in which there will be all races of people. . . .

must be militant and it must be officered by the coloured sufferers of racial discrimination who know the problems and know the way to struggle against it. . . .

[cannot succeed] without attacking the root cause—imperialist oppression —[for otherwise] our struggle will not win support amongst coloured people and/or even natives of Britain.

These objectives were not different from those outlined by James in a proposal for C.A.R.D. development and organization submitted to V. D. Sharma, H. S. Dhillon, and Julia Gaitskell in the calmer days of December 1966.[71] Except for the last, they were such general suggestions that no C.A.R.D. Executive member, past or present, would take issue. James had written in the 1966 memo that coloured people in Britain badly needed politicizing, that C.A.R.D. should work more closely with anti-imperialist groups in the home countries, that C.A.R.D. had so far failed to gain broad coloured support and would do so only if racialism were portrayed as part of the working people's struggle against imperialism.

Fundamentally, the difference between James and the Nandyites —as between the dissidents and the working majority two years before—was how to develop power and gain the support of immigrants who were largely indifferent to C.A.R.D. Disagreements regarding the formal composition of C.A.R.D., leadership, and the language used to analyse social conditions and proscribe change, were key parts of a generalized difference in appeal. This difference, coupled with real personal hostility towards the Nandyites and a much stronger ideological approach, had led James to the virulence which, in the minds of the Nandyites, threatened C.A.R.D. with being classified as an extremist body no longer responsible in the minds of Government, Press, and public.

To halt this movement and to retain power was the aim of David Pitt, the man who had brought James into C.A.R.D. In the months preceding the convention, Pitt had not only been beleaguered by his minority position on the Executive and the break with the Nandyites. He had also been under attack from the Universal Coloured Peoples' Association and other Black Power advocates in London's immigrant community. He had always been seen as one of the least progressive and innovative persons in C.A.R.D. by critics both inside and outside the organization.[72] At the first session of the convention, West Indians and Africans bedeviled Pitt mercilessly and although he was in the chair, he was not in control of the meeting.[73]

Yet, Pitt's role was central, for he made the two decisions that irrevocably swung the balance of power away from the Nandyites. His decision to overrule the Standing Orders Committee on the question of an independent inquiry and his subsequent decision not to recognize the old National Council were calculated to throw support to Johnny James. The choice between his two old sets of allies had been foreshadowed in the days before the convention when he had failed to persuade Johnny James to withdraw the controversial resolutions.

By November 1967, David Pitt, like C.A.R.D., had reached a point of crisis. He had made no secret of his desire to become a Member of Parliament. At that time, it seemed unlikely that he would be given the chance to contest a seat again. He had been rumoured for a peerage. But that too no longer seemed a likelihood. The Nandyites had deserted him, and with the increasing volume of attacks on his alleged conservatism, his West Indian base of popular support seemed to be eroding. Besides his parliamentary ambitions, the lodestar of David Pitt's political life had been his will (and ability) to stay in power. C.A.R.D. as he envisioned it might be the most conventional of pressure groups.[74] Pitt might be a less than tireless leader of the immigrant cause. Yet, he had remained in control, largely because he was a relatively well-known West Indian who had some expertise in elective politics. Now, in a moment of anxiety, he turned to a logical source of support—his own countrymen.

There can be no question that Pitt was both far less radical than James and far more concerned with building a power base in Britain. He wished to become the undisputed leader of the immigrant community, a power broker from a power bloc. None the less, there had been a definite symbiosis between the two men. James had worked in Hackney. He provided a conduit to the working-class West Indians whose support Pitt needed. On the other hand, the C.A.R.D. chairman gave James a respectable front so that he could have some flexibility in using C.A.R.D. for his own ends. Both were concerned about West Indians, one in Britain, the other in the Caribbean. The concerns had usually not seemed inconsistent. Pitt had brought James into C.A.R.D. and often called the tune to which the West Indians in the organization marched. But at the convention it was Pitt who was off balance and James who wielded the baton that aroused or quieted an angry black chorus. He effectively presented Pitt with a *fait accompli*.[75]

Between the two sessions of the annual delegates conference Pitt was able to regain control.[76] He did not condemn the angry men and women who had come to jeer him. He praised the new forces that had emerged in C.A.R.D. and tried to sound as though the organization really had not been changed in the slightest except for being a bit darker in hue, a bit more responsive to the immigrants. The people who had been ousted were simply more divisive than others who had had policy differences in the past but had just left quietly when they were defeated.[77] James agreed to moderate the influence of the Black Power people and to soften significantly his own anti-imperialist stand.

A compromise was necessary for Pitt, and his natural allies were his own countrymen. He had to retain his position and without the West Indians who had been his closest supporters, he was a man with no rank-and-file support. James's reasons were more obscure. Clearly West Indian loyalty and perhaps some personal loyalty to David Pitt played a part in his decision to moderate. He may also have been worried about the attacks on C.A.R.D. in the Press and concerned that he would win over an organization that was so discredited that in kicking out the Nandyites he had only succeeded in destroying C.A.R.D.

## THE CONVENTION RESUMED

The actions taken by the chairman and the black majority at the first session of C.A.R.D.'s Annual Delegates Conference had prevented a military-type coup engineered by those members of the old Executive now out of power, David Pitt told the delegates reassembled in Conway Hall on 4 December. By protecting C.A.R.D. through ascription of all power to himself in the interim, he had protected the organization so that immigrants could lead it, Pitt said with some imagination. 'The policy of this organization', he told 200 people, 'should be based on the experience of the victims of discrimination in this country. If this is not a commitment to black leadership, I do not know what is.'

Pitt was counter-attacking, trying to steer C.A.R.D. back towards the political centre, away from the shoals descried in the organization's course by Nandyites charging that the extremists were taking over. He was careful not to play down too completely the Black Power and anti-imperialist themes (hence the symbology of the Nandyites as militarists) which had emerged at the earlier session. But he, the man most concerned with Parliament, tried to isolate the Nandyites and portray them as unrepresentative leaders who, as had been charged, were more interested in ambling down the corridors at Westminster than working the streets of Wolverhampton.

The report of the Credentials Committee was read. It found that the business of the November session had been properly conducted and there was no evidence of packing the hall. Dipak Nandy, present at the conference with five other members of the old National Council, moved rejection of the report, warning of the disaffiliation of the National Council if there were no independent inquiry. Once this last gesture of defiance had been completed, the conference as expected overwhelmingly voted to uphold the

Credentials Committee. The six from the old National Council walked out for the last time. In keeping with the policy of aggression, Anthony Lester told the Press: 'We fear there is a move for a racialist take-over by people including Trotskyites and Maoists.'[78]

But Lester's charges were an impotent squib, dampened by the subsequent proceedings. The influence of the far left was reduced as the hand of David Pitt again guided the fortunes of C.A.R.D. None of the controversial resolutions still outstanding were considered. The convention just sloughed them off, although several key resolutions—for example, the one charging Israeli aggression—could have been voted on. More importantly, after the elections, the National Council, rather than being the exclusive preserve of blacks or clearly identified supporters of left-wing doctrine, was balanced between nationalities, income groups, and political orientations. Nine Englishmen, eleven Asians, and eleven West Indians comprised the ruling body of C.A.R.D.[79] The Executive Committee selected the following week bore the same moderate, multiracial hue.[80]

The fragile local structure of C.A.R.D. split and began to disintegrate at the second conference session. In the North, C.A.R.D. groups in Leeds, Bradford, Manchester, and Leicester, led by Maureen Burton, northern regional organizer, boycotted the London meeting and gave their allegiance to the old National Council. In the South, the other regional organizer, Audrey Cooper, of West Middlesex C.A.R.D., remained loyal to the new national C.A.R.D. So did her local group, but the price was the break-up of the organization along national lines. Olwyn Navartne tried to take the group out of the new C.A.R.D., but the West Indians in the West Middlesex C.A.R.D. voted *en bloc* for retaining affiliation. Navartne said: 'We are going to set up a new group, one that will not be a trouble-maker with words. As I understand the violence of Black Power, I am against it. Some West Indians were with us, but they could not break away from their fellows during the battle.' One of those West Indians pulled in two directions was Audrey Cooper who had worked closely with Julia Gaitskell and was trusted by the Nandyites. She had been in charge of the door and had thus been one of those people key to James's plan. When the conflict came, Audrey Cooper was swayed by the appeal of her black brothers. Fearful of risking the rude epithets 'Uncle Tom' and 'house nigger' she could not resist the undertow of the Black Power wave, for which she felt strong affinities in any event.

Islington C.A.R.D. managed to maintain loyalty to the new national C.A.R.D. without sustaining a split. With its heavy emphasis on class problems, the group continued to attract members of various nationalities. The country of origin did not play a large part in their attitude towards a reconstituted C.A.R.D. Yet their support of a C.A.R.D. still led by David Pitt was in a sense surprising. Both Ian McDonald and Oscar Abrams had been among Pitt's bitterest and most vocal critics on the old National Council. And, as discussed above, the Islington local organization was most at odds with the C.A.R.D. that David Pitt envisioned and had tried to create. Yet McDonald, deeply committed to radical social change in Britain through the class struggle and deeply in sympathy with the emerging anti-imperialist forces in the Third World, was swayed by the Marxist orientation which the new organization seemed to have. For him, the Marxist approach was not divisive, it was right and long overdue. The new national C.A.R.D. meant to McDonald that the centralizing communists (Nandy and Sharma) and the parliamentary proponents (Lester and Gaitskell) would be gone and the chance for real spontaneity and participation by immigrants in an organization that was part of a genuine social revolution might at last be possible.[81]

Unrepresented at either the first or second sessions of the convention was Handsworth C.A.R.D., the fledgling organization that had grown out of the C.A.R.D. summer project in Birmingham. Its absence was a fitting symbol. The most experimental and, in some ways, the most hopeful developments in C.A.R.D. were the summer projects and yet they had not been sustained, shrinking from modest beginnings to insignificance. The Nandyites had been deeply pleased at the end of the summer when West Indians in the Soho Ward came together to make plans for continuing the summer's work. In December, the C.A.R.D. group in Birmingham —the city itself a symbol of Britain's troubled spirit over race— had died, and with the events of the second session, the troubled spirit of C.A.R.D. was *in extremis*.

The newspapers offered their condolences. *The Economist* said C.A.R.D. was Britain's 'only effective non-official pressure group against colour prejudice. . . . C.A.R.D. for all its occasional failures . . . has proved the most positive channel of protest against discrimination.' The *Guardian* on 4 December called the division within C.A.R.D. the 'silliest dispute of the decade. In the three years since it began, C.A.R.D. has been a militant, democratic, multi-racial organization. . . . For a small organization this [its role in legislation] is an impressive record. No other group has been so effective in illustrating the danger of complacency in race relations.' The editorial continued:

The change could not have come at a worse time. With the draft of the government's new anti-discrimination laws about to be published, there is an urgent need for effective lobbying to see that strong and practical legislation is passed this time. Only the opponents of racial equality in Britain can benefit from this split in C.A.R.D.

The shift in C.A.R.D. had come almost three years to the day after Dr. Martin Luther King, Jr., had met with immigrant leaders in London and served as the catalyst for a new organization. In 1964, the prospect for legislation was looming; the race climate was tense; politics was stained by the colour question; and the need for strong, outspoken leadership on racial matters was great. Three years later, all the needs were the same. Legislation again loomed; building in the communities was still of the essence; immigrants were still without power. But a critical element had changed. C.A.R.D. as it had been known was ending, not beginning. As a unified front for all immigrants, fissured and finally collapsed, the immigrant community would have to devise new forms of leadership.

## NOTES

1. V. D. Sharma, C.A.R.D. vice-chairman, was general secretary of the Indian Workers' Association, Southall, at the time. As a leading member of Britain's most potent coloured community organization, he was thus the exception to the general rule that C.A.R.D. members, even coloured members, could not sway the immigrant masses.

2. Author's notes, C.A.R.D. National Council Meeting (30 October 1966).

3. Members of the 1966–7 Executive Committee were, from the first Executive: Pitt, Lester, Singh. From the second: Barrow (West Indian, teacher), Gaitskell (C.A.R.D. staff), Ennals (of the N.C.C.I.), Nandy (Indian, lecturer at the University of Kent in English literature), Sharma (Indian, bus conductor). Serving for the first time: H. Dhillon, treasurer (Indian, factory worker), Ralph Bennett (West Indian, C.A.R.D. staff), Michael Dummett (Fellow of All Souls, Oxford), Johnny James (West Indian, accountant), Olwyn Navartne (Ceylonese, engineer), Robert Souhami (doctor), Len Squire (union official), Norman Athill (West Indian, doctor). The Nandyites, a descriptive term used by the author, included everyone but the West Indians. They tended to vote together on the E.C. Michael Dummett later on tried to be a bridge between the groups.

4. He urged the Information Panel to make a number of recommendations to local authorities regarding provision of interpreters, recruitment and training of immigrant personnel, refuse collection, education in race relations, planning for

future problems, use of research in formulation of policy, publicity for race relations. Other areas outside his panel's jurisdiction would obviously deserve mention, not the least of which is the provision of council housing which, as demonstrated in the P.E.P. report, p. 12, rarely goes to immigrants, 'in marked contrast to the section of the white population with similar occupation levels'. See also Burney, op. cit., for an analysis of the relationship between immigrants and local authorities and the problems coloured persons have in getting public housing.

5. Dipak Nandy, 'An Illusion of Competence', in A. Lester and N. Deakin (eds.), op. cit., p. 40.

6. Interview with Nadine Peppard (2 June 1967). See also Foot, op. cit., Chapter 10.

7. Of forty-three V.L.C.s in operation by May 1966, twenty-seven had paid liaison officers. Seven were Standing Committees of the Councils of Social Service (one being significantly in Leicester where Nandy was chairman of the Leicester Campaign for Racial Equality). Two had originally been promoted by the Council of Social Service but were independent. Seventeen existed in towns with a Council of Social Service. Seventeen existed in towns where there was no Council of Social Service. See *Analysis of Voluntary Liaison Committees* (London, N.C.C.I., June 1967).

8. *Draft Constitution for Voluntary Liaison Committees* (London, N.C.C.I.).

9. Nandy's analysis of the voluntary liaison complex was not shared by Nadine Peppard who had been involved in its development for nearly a decade. Miss Peppard told the author (interview, 2 June 1967) that as she conceived of the V.L.C.s they should have five functions: provision of information about immigrants to the local community; education of public opinion about requirements, advantages, duties, and responsibilities of living in a multiracial society; provision of welfare services for immigrants; consulting with the local authority, getting the local authority to accept the 'committee as the authority for briefing'; working against discrimination.

She said that in the developing years of the V.L.C.s the first three functions were emphasized; that there would be increasing emphasis on the last two. Interestingly, the first three functions were outlined in the objects of the *Draft Constitution for Voluntary Liaison Committees* circulated by the National Committee, while the last two were not. Further, Miss Peppard, as general secretary of the National Committee, had the responsibility for co-ordinating the efforts of the V.L.C.s. She could not command them to take action. Thus, it is certainly possible that Nandy's analysis of the situation would be compatible with Miss Peppard's hopes for the future. With V.L.C.s in forty-three localities there would obviously be great variety of response to the racial situation.

10. See Chapter Two, and Rex and Moore, op. cit., Chapter VI.

11. Dipak Nandy, *C.A.R.D. Summer Project 1967* (London, C.A.R.D., 1967).

12. Interview with Dipak Nandy (20 May 1967): 'With the exception of the I.W.A., Southall, very few groups have patronage that they can distribute. Leadership is always unstable. The only hold on the following is through the creation of a home atmosphere; transferred nationalism, the effect of which is to turn immigrants away from the here and now and concern them with the reproduction of the politics of Trinidad, or the Punjab. That takes a lot of time and energy and prevents a group like C.A.R.D. from using their strength in local situations to tackle local problems.'

13. The problem of research—both doing it and assimilating work already completed regarding urban areas—is of extraordinary significance in a field as complex as planning for social change regarding race relations in urban communities. A strong 'research arm' of any local group, possibly provided in part by the national organization, would seem both a necessity and a rather idealistic dream.

14. The work of Saul Alinsky and his Industrial Areas Foundation is widely known in the United States. His objectives and the uses of conflict are described in Charles Silberman, *Crisis in Black and White* (London, Jonathan Cape, 1964), Chapter 10. Alinsky was one of the first to develop 'community organization' techniques as the term is used today. For C.A.R.D. members, the theory for much 'community action' work envisioned in 1967 was taken unashamedly from the United States' experience. Interview with Dipak Nandy (30 April 1967). For a history of community action as an idea adopted by the United States Government and put into effect as part of the Economic Opportunity Act, see Marris and Rein, op. cit. For a summary of governmental efforts in the United States and a discussion of objectives and assumptions see *Focus on Community Action*, Report of the National Advisory Council on Economic Opportunity, March 1967. A detailed bibliography regarding governmental programmes is included. For a critique of the 'community action' concept and a post-mortem on the governmental programme, see Daniel Moynihan, *Maximum Feasible Misunderstanding* (New York, Collier-Macmillan, 1969).

Typical tactics are rent strikes, formation of tenant or welfare rights unions, and boycotts of local merchants suspected of price gouging.

15. Interview with Dipak Nandy (20 May 1967): 'We have not been in the field long enough to have models of how it ought to be done. We are on the brink. There is a C.A.R.D. idea of local organizing; but no one is quite sure what it is.'

16. Interview with Ralph Bennett, C.A.R.D. assistant secretary (19 May 1967). C.A.R.D. records of membership, as with records of affiliated organizations, were badly kept. There was no systematic breakdown available regarding nationality. Nor on the growth of the organization. Nor a very precise geographical distribution. Significantly there were very few C.A.R.D. members—perhaps fifty or sixty—in the West Midlands. Nor were there any figures available on occupation or income breakdowns. Rough guesses were that the organization was half coloured, half white.

17. Membership in C.A.R.D., as mentioned in Chapter One, was of two types: affiliated organizations and individual members. Presumably, once a group paid its subscription fee, then its members were technically part of the C.A.R.D. structure. Yet C.A.R.D. could make no claims on these people either to help in activities or contribute money. Very few members of, for example, the Indian Workers' Association, Southall, paid individual subscription fees to C.A.R.D. The evolution of local groups, technically called area committees, indicated areas where C.A.R.D. membership had grown. These organizations were supposedly comprised of individual C.A.R.D. members—those who had paid their individual subscriptions. Yet the leadership of a given local group would often be informal about the collection of the subscription fee.

18. In the period from 1 June 1967 until the convening of the Annual Delegates Conference, six more local C.A.R.D. groups were formed. See note 108, p. 110, for the first nine. The new six were in Acton, Bristol, Handsworth (Birmingham), Huddersfield, Stoke Newington and Hackney (one group), and Wandsworth.

19. Interview (29 May 1967).

20. When asked about his personal activities in C.A.R.D., Pitt listed: conveying people's complaints to higher bodies ('I do this most of all'); talking to M.P.s to solve specific problems; work for the extension of laws ('I've been tremendously involved here'); public speaking; Press work, writing letters, talking to reporters; planning C.A.R.D. strategies. Under the last topic, he responded to a query about C.A.R.D.'s priorities by mentioning: gaining new legislation; making legislation work through using contacts in Government; giving victims of discrimination legal defence; changing immigration policy; exercising political influence through voter registration. This suggested that although Pitt vaguely wanted local development

he did not feel a personal responsibility to foster it and would probably not take an active lead in stimulating local growth.

21. Interview with Dipak Nandy (20 March 1967).

22. Ibid.

23. *Summer Project Report 1966.*

24. *C.A.R.D. Summer Project 1967: A National Plan.* Nandy felt that any summer strategy had to meet three requirements. Active interventionism: C.A.R.D. had to reach out to people in need and get them to claim their rights. Moral autonomy of the immigrants: to avoid paternalism, C.A.R.D. had not only to involve immigrants in the decision-making and execution of the programmes, but to take account of their perceptions of their own problems and needs. A balance had to be struck between the needs of the community as seen by the project leaders and as seen by the people being served. Conflict: C.A.R.D. had to recognize that the project was not an exercise in community relations since no community existed, but rather could involve conflict in securing rights.

25. Michael Banton, op. cit., p. 368, raises the issue of colour consciousness in Britain in a correlative way: '. . . because someone is coloured it is assumed that he is different; indeed, being coloured seems to be more important than whether or not he is really different—for if he is treated as different he will become different. In this respect the white man creates the role "coloured man" and all those who are forced into it develop common interests.' (And, one might add, develop a conception of the role of the 'white man'.)

26. See Landau and Jacobs, op. cit., for early documents.

27. Interview with Olwyn Navartne (14 May 1967).

28. Navartne had a number of threatening letters, including one warning that he would be killed.

29. Colin McGlashan, 'Black Power Leader Leaves Mark on Britain', *Observer* (6 August 1967); also interview with Nicholas Deakin (7 January 1968).

30. Carmichael said on B.B.C.'s Panorama programme (17 July): 'When the question of violence is ever brought up I say that white western society ought to be the ones you talk about. For coloured peoples around the world to be truly equal with white people they must feel that they can just as easily shoot down a white man. That sounds violent. It happens to be a fact.'

Carmichael had actually left Britain before the edict banning him was issued.

31. *Report of the National Advisory Commission on Civil Disorders* (New York, Bantam Press, 1968), Chapter 1.

32. The audience in the Rainbow Hall, Cheapside, Reading, was mixed. Malik was quoted as saying: 'White people are vicious and nasty. Don't try and beat the white man with the English language because he will beat you every time. You had better try and play some other game. . . . If you ever see a white laying a hand on a black woman, kill him immediately.' *The Times* (30 September 1967).

33. *Daily Telegraph* (25 July 1967). Sandys suggested that the Government pay the fares of all those immigrants who wished to return to their homelands. He also deplored the rise in mixed marriages: 'The breeding of millions of half-caste children would merely produce a generation of misfits and create increased tension.' No public censure of Sandys was made by the Government.

34. *Black Power in Britain: Special Statement* (London, publisher not given, 1968). The pamphlet was written in highly generalized prose, replete with grandiose imagery. The aims and objects of the organization as contained in the manifesto were:

To set up advice bureaux to investigate and act upon problems affecting our people.

To take immediate action for the establishment of nurseries for coloured children; and to encourage coloured people to participate in the administration and uses of this facility.

To introduce organization, education, and clearance of the Ghettos of our people.

To undertake all such activities which will promote the emancipation of our sisters all over the world.

To provide legal aid to all coloured people who find themselves oppressed by the racial persecution of Anglo-Saxon society.

The establishment of study groups for our people to recognize their racial interest.

To establish cooperatives in pursuit of the economical and social interests of our people.

The training of coloured people, by education and practical discipline, to be representatives of our people.

To provide protection, guidance, and discipline to our people who suffer because of their colour, faith or unwarranted racial disturbances.

To propagate solution of our problems on international levels.

The manifesto said: 'These are but a few of our domestic objectives.'

35. *A United Voice of Immigrants on Immigration* (London, Joint Council for the Welfare of Immigrants, 1967).

36. Ibid., pp. 3–4.

37. The Committee of Enquiry on Immigration Appeals, headed by Sir Roy Wilson, issued a report (Command 3387) in August 1967.

38. *A United Voice of Immigrants. . .* , op. cit., p. 7.

39. Interview with Michael Dummett (19 January 1968).

40. Interview (17 January 1968).

41. Interview with Anthony Lester (8 January 1968).

42. Evidence for this section is based on interviews with members of these small groups, documents of the Caribbean Workers' Movement, and events that took place at the convention. When I returned to England in January 1968, I was able to speak twice with Ralph Bennett. Johnny James would not grant me an interview, nor would David Pitt.

43. The aims and objects of the organization as outlined in a 1966 fund raising appeal were: To campaign for national independence and ultimately socialism based on scientific socialist philosophies oriented to our people's way of life and living. To serve generally the interest of the working people, specifically the Caribbean and Latin American working class, their political movements and their party organizations in the struggle to defeat the common enemy—imperialism, led by the ruling classes of the U.S.A., Britain, France, and others.

To play a leading role in bringing about as quickly as possible greater Caribbean-Latin American unity and linking this to the Afro-Asian and other anti-imperialist forces to defeat the common enemy.

To participate in all anti-colonial, anti-imperialist, and anti-fascist activities for the benefit of working classes in all parts of the world, thus playing our proper role in the international working class movement against imperialism.

44. Sample documents in this series are: Caribbean History, *A Caribbean Concept of Scientific Socialism*, and *The Caribbean Socialists Review: A Marxist/Leninist Theoretical Journal*, with articles by a 'Haitian Comrade', a 'Jamaican Comrade', etc.

45. Interview with Dr. Alexander Tudor-Hart (12 January 1968).

46. Interview with Sardul Gill (15 January 1968).

47. Interview with Anthony Lester (20 January 1968).

48. They were Clifford and Virginia Durr of Birmingham, Alabama.

49. Interview with Anthony Lester (8 January 1968).

50. Interview with V. D. Sharma (15 January 1968).

51. Matters detailing the conduct of the Standing Orders Committee are related in a letter from Dipak Nandy to Bruce Pitt (29 November 1967). Pitt, son of the chairman, was a member of the Credentials Committee elected to study the controversy.

52. Ibid. Included on James's list were a number of small student groups, not recognized by activists in British race relations, e.g. the Uganda Students Union, the Garvey Group, the Afro-Asian Liberation Front, Tanzanian Students Zimbabwe.

53. Dipak Nandy in a letter to Bruce Pitt (29 November 1967).

54. Part of this analysis stems from a paper written by Michael Dummett in December for submission to the C.A.R.D. National Council entitled, 'The C.A.R.D. Crisis'.

55. The proportions of each group of supporters can only be surmised from a very rough guess since records were not kept and James would not talk. The working hypothesis of observers present was that more than 50 per cent fell into the last category. These would for the most part be London-based.

56. Michael Dummett had been nominated for chairman by a West Indian member of Manchester C.A.R.D. Although Dummett did not want to be C.A.R.D. chairman he did not withdraw his name for two reasons. First, he did not want to do so without speaking to the man who had nominated him. Second, he and the Nandyites felt that it might serve some purpose to put pressure on David Pitt. Dipak Nandy could not stand for chairman since his name had not been submitted properly under the constitution.

57. The conflict between H. S. Dhillon and Ralph Bennett was one example cited by those promoting the rumour. Other charges were that Sharma's salary as national organizer was being paid by the United States' Central Intelligence Agency or by a pro-Zionist organization. The Nandyites charged that these rumours and the anti-Asian atmosphere were part of a general take-over strategy that had been used in Guyana. Both James and Ajoy (or A.J.) Ghose, a leader of the Universal Coloured Peoples' Association, were Guyanese and active in the politics of that country (which are marked by bitter Indian-West Indian conflict). Whether the Nandyites' charge was true or not, it is clear that at the C.A.R.D. convention the two nationalities were antagonistic.

58. The three substantive C.A.R.D. projects in 1966-7 which could be considered most 'innovative' or 'radical' or 'militant'—the complaints committee, the summer project, the developing antagonism towards the National Committee—had stemmed from the Nandyites. Neither Pitt, Barrow, James, nor Bennett had ever been deeply involved in the planning or execution of any of them and in fact had been cold to the effectuation of the projects.

59. Whether they were disaffected from whites and Asians in general would be indicated at the resumed delegates conference in December (see below).

60. In an article in the Morning Star (5 December 1967).

61. Ibid. Sharma also wrote: 'For me the battle against imperialism started at 14 in India, when I went to jail for three months. In later years I served a total of 3 and a half years in jail as well as periods in illegality [sic], with a price of 2,000 rupees on my head.'

62. Ibid.

63. Interview with Dipak Nandy (21 January 1968).

64. They caucused at a near-by restaurant and at midnight issued a statement repudiating the chairman's ascription to himself of the role of arbiter of the constitution. 'The issue is not between militancy and moderation, nor between black and white, but between concentrating our energies on fighting racial discrimination here in Britain or dissipating our energies in fighting anti-imperialist battles abroad. We shall always believe in a militant movement, democratically based, fighting for the rights of black people and for racial equality.'

65. Street, Howe, and Bindman, op. cit.

66. A resolution passed by the National Council, 25 November 1967, said:
The proceedings of the November 4-5 conference were suspect because a number of organizations affiliated shortly before the convention without informing the

General Secretary, because certain groups present and voting are alleged to have contravened the constitutional prohibition against affiliation by political party organizations, and because certain individuals present and voting did not appear to accept the constitution of C.A.R.D.

The atmosphere was deplorable, charged with 'rabid anti-white, anti-Asian and anti-Semitic feeling of a kind which disgraced the ideals of C.A.R.D.'

An independent inquiry must be conducted.

'Unless these measures are taken it will dissociate itself entirely from any gathering purporting to be the Annual Delegates Conference and will recommend all affiliated organizations to do likewise.'

67. In the general secretary's 1966–7 report, fifteen local C.A.R.D. groups were listed: Acton, Brent, Bristol, Croydon, Glasgow, Handsworth, Huddersfield, Islington, Leeds, Manchester, Newcastle, Sheffield, Stoke Newington and Hackney, Wandsworth, West Middlesex. Three groups—Bradford, Leeds, and Manchester—indicated immediately that they would disaffiliate. Six others—Brent, Islington, Newcastle, Sheffield, Stoke Newington and Hackney, and West Middlesex—indicated that they would remain within the C.A.R.D. structure. The remainder by January 1968 were still undecided or divided.

68. Interview with Michael Dummett (19 January 1968): 'He told me that racial discrimination in Great Britain was not the great problem. When revolution came in the Caribbean, then people would go back there. He felt that people in Great Britain should be taught about revolution and should be prepared to go back to support such activity when it occurred.'

69. This issue was subtitled 'Militants vs White Liberals and Household Slaves'. On the front page was a picture of David Pitt above a caption reading: 'leading CARD with wisdom, relying on the masses of members'. The walk-out was staged by the S.O.B.W.L.s (an incomplete acronym for 'son of bitching white liberals') and by 'their tame blacks', the pamphlet said.

70. James listed discrimination, discriminatory laws, police brutality, and double standards applied to racial hate language. These would have been criticized by all factions. Two other sources of his anger—attacks 'against our women-folk' and Press attacks on the working people of Britain—would not have drawn unanimous support.

71. Johnny James, 'Proposals for CARD Programmes and Organizational Development' (5 December 1966).

72. Such diverse people as Selma James, Jeff Crawford, Michael Dummett, and Dipak Nandy had all been sharply critical of Pitt, usually for the same reasons: his authoritarian manner, his insistence on tight central control, his lack of energy, his failure to innovate, his habit of sharpening conflicts so severely that the losing party would be forced out of the organization, his commitment to regular Labour party and parliamentary channels.

73. Michael Dummett who was sitting next to Pitt on the platform during the meeting described the scene: 'Pitt would call for order and no one was responding. People were insulting him, calling him a Tom or Tshombe. Then James would issue orders and the people quieted down. He asked me, quite innocently it seemed: "Why does someone else have to keep order not me?" There seemed to be a nightmarish quality for him, as if the familiar landmarks had been uprooted and torn away.'

74. Pitt's views following the events of the year and the changes in national mood and within C.A.R.D. were expressed in an interview on the B.B.C. (2 January 1968): 'What I always tell them to do [coloured people]—two important things —join their trade union and join a political party. . . . It is only through the existing political machinery that we will be able to influence Parliament, and influence political affairs and get representation.'

75. The question should be raised at this point: Was Pitt the ultimate power in the take-over plan? The balance of evidence that I was able to accumulate suggests no, despite the fact that Pitt knew of the Nandyites' resentment. That resentment allowed Pitt to swing fully to the side of James and left no hand in defence of the Nandyites. But it does not seem to have been the motivating factor in a coup masterminded by the chairman. The main argument for Pitt's lack of leadership (as opposed to his acquiescence) was the first convention session when James was clearly running things and Pitt was sitting by helplessly. The thesis is that Pitt had had some warning, was not deeply aware of the full extent of the new forces, had not specifically planned to force all the Nandyites out (and probably did not want them to leave), but was willing to ride the events as they happened.

76. Interview with Michael Dummett (19 January 1968). Pitt told Dummett that he and James were far apart on some political questions: 'I am well aware of the danger of Johnny James.'

77. B.B.C. broadcast (2 January 1968). Pitt referred to Richard Small and Marion Glean, dissidents in C.A.R.D.'s first phase. They might have found his praise ironic.

78. *Guardian* (5 December 1967).

79. Interview with Ralph Bennett (10 January 1968).

80. The new officers of C.A.R.D. were: David Pitt, chairman and press officer; Jocelyn Barrow, vice-chairman; S. S. Gill, vice-chairman (Indian); Frank Bailey, general secretary (West Indian, head of Tower Hamlets Voluntary Liaison Committee); V. Davis, treasurer (West Indian); Johnny James, assistant secretary and organizer; Ian McDonald, legal adviser (British); S. Ennis, social organizer (West Indian, also associated with the Caribbean Workers' Movement); D. R. Banger (Indian); S. Morris (West Indian, staff of the N.C.C.I.); Dr. A. Tudor-Hart; Rev. A. Campbell (West Indian); Ralph Bennett; Audrey Cooper; Joseph Hunte (West Indian, newly elected chairman of the Standing Conference); Mrs. M. Tsele (Indian); Guy Elliston (West Indian); John Hatch (British); Roy Shaw (British); Zacharia Choudhury (Pakistani, associated with the Federation of Pakistani Associations).

By early January, three prominent members of the Executive were threatening to quit: Frank Bailey, S. S. Gill, and Joe Hunte. Bailey quickly became frustrated at what he termed the 'total ineffectiveness' of Ralph Bennett and the C.A.R.D. office, and angry at David Pitt for his lack of leadership (interview, 15 January 1968). Gill, too, was anxious about the divisions within C.A.R.D. and unhappy with the ideological leanings of some of the leading C.A.R.D. members (interview, 15 January 1968). Hunte was being strongly challenged by the Standing Conference to quit C.A.R.D. since the W.I.S.C. had formerly disaffiliated from C.A.R.D. Bailey subsequently resigned from C.A.R.D.

81. Interview with Ian McDonald (8 January 1968). Stokely Carmichael had visited an Islington meeting in July and left his imprint. Members were impressed with his theories of antagonism and polarization by coloured people as a prelude to power.

CHAPTER SIX

# Conclusion

The short history of C.A.R.D. was marked by long, bitter, and divisive arguments. The split in the formative period between the working majority and the dissidents, the conflict between C.A.R.D. and the Standing Conference of West Indian Organizations, and the fervid antagonism between the Nandyites and the forces marshalled by Johnny James, overshadowed and drew energy from the substantive, though limited, progress that the organization was able to make in the three years of its existence. The wrangling of November and December was an indicator of the general atmosphere of bitterness that again plagued British race relations, but it was also the dissonant rendering of *Dies Irae*, for C.A.R.D. never regained much momentum. Its local structure fractured and its national voice stilled, C.A.R.D., to most observers, seemed dead, a rump organization that occasionally went through rote liturgy against discrimination while waiting for the final break-up.[1]

In C.A.R.D., powerlessness perpetuated itself through faction. The bringing together of people with widely divergent backgrounds and political orientations to embark on an enterprise of great difficulty and commensurate frustrations, had perpetually produced paralysis and anger. Given its ambitious goals, C.A.R.D. always had little progress to show. Thus, those with different theories about organization and processes of change, representing tiny constituencies, contested for titular control of an essentially powerless institution that had almost no power in the general political world and little influence in its own universe, save force of personality or clarity of thought. Antagonism escalated and substantive work diminished as people were driven off. The name of C.A.R.D.— once a rallying point for the immigrant cause—became, in the end, a brush with which those concerned about changing the conditions of life for immigrants did not want to be tarred. Events never kindled the unity that might come from defiance of severe repression or from an unambiguous and embittered battle against a larger outside foe. During the three years of its existence, C.A.R.D.'s antagonists in British society—those reluctant to grant the coloured man equality—were too amorphous to sustain the organization.

## 1. THE NATURE AND CAUSES OF FAILURE

In one obvious sense, C.A.R.D. failed. It did not survive as a viable, functioning organization attempting to implement its own explicit goals; it did not become a united mass movement of coloured people.

Even during its life, attainment of its stated goals proved elusive.[2] C.A.R.D. made only a tiny dent on racial discrimination against coloured people in Britain. It was not involved at all in the elimination of discrimination against other minority groups in Britain. It was not effective in implementing its concern 'about the struggle of oppressed people everywhere'. It was unable to co-ordinate the work of other private organizations attempting to combat racial discrimination and it had never been an effective clearing-house of information for such groups. It was unable, in 1968, to oppose with any weight at all the new Commonwealth Immigrants Bill restricting coloured entry to Britain. Other organizations—like the Joint Council for the Welfare of Immigrants—had to bear the burden of the protest.[3] As we have seen, C.A.R.D. could claim some credit for the shape of the Race Relations Act 1965 and had been valuable in preparing the way for introduction of new anti-discrimination legislation. But when the critical period for overseeing the passage of the legislation through Parliament came, C.A.R.D. had left the field and a specialist organization with no roots in the immigrant communities, Equal Rights, was responsible for lobbying to alter the Government's proposal.[4]

Beyond the failure to implement what it had set out to do explicitly, C.A.R.D. also failed to articulate theories of social equality and cultural diversity, and a set of goals to give concreteness to these broad principles. It, thus, necessarily failed to implement the implicit task which had been set for it by many of its members who realized how inextricably bound up were the concerns of coloured immigrants and Britain's poor.

### THE PROBLEMS OF LEADERSHIP: INDIVIDUAL DILEMMAS

If C.A.R.D. could ever have overcome the obstacles in its path, the organization would have needed strong leadership. Yet, given the nature of C.A.R.D.'s dual functions, an immigrant leader would be torn between his two broad constituencies, the immigrants and the British. As C.A.R.D. chairman, David Pitt attempted to be the all-purpose coloured leader who faced two ways. For the immigrants, he would be the great prestige figure who could understand coloured problems and yet could also have access to the inner councils of white society where he would tell the power brokers what they must do to please the coloured population of Britain. For whites in the Labour party (and in other structures of power), he would be the 'responsible' black man who understood the coloured community, could give advice on how to deal with that community, and yet, at the same time, would understand the political 'realities' within which the white man operated.

To perform successfully the delicate balancing act, a leader would need a firm grasp of the nature of politics and a subtle understanding of political consciousness in the many facets of both constituencies. Yet Pitt was not particularly sensitive or knowledgeable about the politics of the Indians and Pakistanis. Nor, more importantly, was he attuned to the problems and aspirations expressed by the more politically active (and often more radical) West Indian organizational leaders. Although he had been a radical West Indian anticolonialist thirty years before, Pitt, during C.A.R.D.'s lifetime, was wedded to a fairly conventional approach to immigrant politics—use of electoral power, centralization of command, allegiance to a major political party.[5] He did not seem to realize that a platitudinous appeal to party and electoral politics, without more, was not going to raise immigrant, especially West Indian, political consciousness and dispel apathy. In contrast to Neville Maxwell, he seemed unconcerned about the cultural and economic life of the coloured communities.[6] Pitt's dominant life-style had been to adopt British folkways, accept British institutions, and try to become a 'black Englishman'. This approach to British life may have blinded him to the basic psychological, economic, and cultural needs of West Indians. It certainly siphoned off energy he might have devoted to C.A.R.D. (as he sought status in British institutions) and aroused the enmity of other West Indians.[7]

Pitt's inability to master the demands of the double role may thus have been a basic cause of his failure to act as a cohesive agent.[8] It must be reiterated that C.A.R.D.'s functions of pushing for legislative change and creating a militant grass-roots organization were so fundamental as to be unexceptionable for all members of the organization at all times. Yet again and again these aims were lost in the clamour of internecine warfare.

The problems of facing towards both the immigrants and the British structure of power bedeviled other important C.A.R.D. leaders too. If the prime 'individual' responsibility for the failure of C.A.R.D. lies with David Pitt, then the roles of three middle-class intellectuals—Julia Gaitskell and Anthony Lester especially, and Dipak Nandy, to an extent—are suggestive about the problems middle-class whites (Gaitskell and Lester) and intellectuals (all three) have in an immigrant political movement; for, paradoxically, the three were responsible for much of C.A.R.D.'s short-term success (such as it was) and yet they were also responsible for, at least, arousing some of the divisive forces always latent in C.A.R.D.

As lobbyists and strategists, Gaitskell, Lester, and Nandy were viewed with a suspicion that could easily evolve into distrust by people with different backgrounds and different functions within the organization. As liberals, Gaitskell and Lester were similarly suspect in the eyes of persons further to the left. In addition to their many tasks within C.A.R.D., a centrally important one, therefore, was to assuage the hostility that would have existed almost by definition.

Yet, the impact of the duality on them personally was probably a primary cause of their inability to dampen the conflict that surrounded them. If Pitt's failing was that he exercised too little constructive leadership, the 'failing' of Gaitskell, Lester, and Nandy was that they exercised too much. Even though they knew that immigrants must lead C.A.R.D., they none the less found it necessary to assume more and more responsibility if C.A.R.D. was to operate as effectively as it could under the circumstances as perceived by them. This inevitably stirred up resentment. Further, although Gaitskell and Lester were obviously (at times painfully) aware that they had no roots in the communities they were trying to serve, they could not—because of their efforts—help but become possessive about the organization. Such possessiveness sometimes led all three to be impatient with personalities opposing them and, more importantly, to exclude all but their own approaches to immigrant politics.[9] Although both Gaitskell and Lester gave much, they could not give the fundamental sacrifice that was demanded by the angrier West Indians and more radical Asians—verbal salvoes, renouncement of ambitions, tolerance of doctrinaire statements.[10] Suspended as they were between the immigrants and the British,[11] they had no secure position of power and no clear role when some of the immigrants become anti-white. Similarly, all three, being vulnerable to the charge of intellectuality, could not argue from positions of strength with others who would contest their strategies and claim greater experience in the local immigrant community (although Nandy, of course, had had local experience in Leicester). In sum, all three were unable to perform the exceedingly delicate and difficult task of giving substantive guidance to the young organization while at the same time helping immigrant leadership to emerge.[1]

## THE FORCES OF DIVISION

Yet even if Pitt had been a more creative and charismatic leader and even if Gaitskell, Lester, and Nandy had succeeded in dampening the resentment and distrust that they engendered, it is highly doubtful that C.A.R.D., as originally conceived, could have survived. Put another way, it is misleading to talk solely (or even primarily) about individual responsibility because of the obstacles C.A.R.D. faced, first, in simply surviving as a coalition organization and, second, in implementing enormously ambitious goals. In simply surviving as a coalition—of immigrants and sympathetic British, of individuals and organizations—C.A.R.D. would have to overcome significant, even profound, forces of division. As stated at the outset of this volume, these forces made C.A.R.D. unique as a pressure group, shaped the definition of the organization, dictated its two basic functions, and yet were ultimately responsible for the break-up of the organization.

To summarize, C.A.R.D. had tried to:

1. Join white and coloured races when, because of actions by the British Government, the writings of national liberation authors, and world events, there was increasing 'race' consciousness and growing suspicion of whites by activist coloured people.

2. Join classes of coloured citizens when the distance between the life of an intellectual, London-based immigrant doctor and an immigrant labourer in Newcastle would be enormous, both psychologically and in terms of life-style.

3. Join generations of coloured citizens when the younger coloured citizens (either young immigrants or the second generation) were beginning to question old styles of leadership and action.[12]

4. Join three different nationality groups—Indian, Pakistani, and West Indian—at a time when suspicion (at least between the Asian groups and the West Indians) was growing.

5. Join sub-groups within the nationality types that identified themselves according to regions or islands, not nationalities.

6. Join individuals who as part of basic nationality groupings would differ according to language, religion, and basic elements of life-style.

7. Join coloured immigrants when some of those people were uncertain whether their migration was temporary or permanent.

8. Join coloured immigrants whose levels of political consciousness—even political consciousness solely directed towards participation in the British political system—was of different levels.

9. Join immigrants and whites of different political beliefs and ideologies at a time when race itself was becoming both a political issue in Britain and an ideological one internationally.

10. Join communities of coloured citizens that were geographically dispersed when information about those communities—let alone communication between them—was not good.

11. Join organizations founded on the basis of nationality lines when such organizations were themselves weak and subject to some of the same forces of division which beleaguered C.A.R.D.[13]

Needless to say, the forces of cohesion were much less potent. The founders of C.A.R.D. had always hoped that talismanic phrases like 'anti-discrimination' or 'coloured' or 'need for social equality' would, somewhat magically, bring together those otherwise divided or disorganized. C.A.R.D. never had significant financial resources and was never able to generate any—and thus the sheer fact of money could not act as a cohesive agent. The successes of C.A.R.D. in lobbying and gaining Press attention were only great enough to make the organization attractive for take-over or destruction. The initiative of community action, delivering the goods, was never tested as a cohesive force.

Thus, underneath the many divisions and debates lay significant forces of division. It is, unfortunately, easier to list the potential forces of division than to detail precisely how they operated. All were operative—though at different times and in different relationships any one may have been most 'important'. For example, at the beginning of C.A.R.D., political ideology divided C.A.R.D. members, while at the end of the organization's life, race consciousness was divisive, albeit a race consciousness that was part of a newly emerging political ideology (i.e. Black Power, a collection of thoughts not as important in 1965—if they were articulated at all—as in 1967). Some Indians and Asians were joined because of ideology; others were divided because they disliked the other nationality's perceived characteristics. Thus, however difficult it is to delineate the precise effects of the forces of division, that is, to say that one particular force was the most divisive, there is no denying their cumulative potency. Without power, or the clear prospect of gaining power, creating the mutual self-interest necessary for union among members, an organization subject to these divisions was, almost necessarily, rent by them.

As has been shown, C.A.R.D. rarely faced hard choices about allocation of scarce resources; the antagonisms generated by the forces of division none the less generally manifested themselves in apparent debate about forms of political action. In the United States, a charismatic leader like Martin Luther King had trouble keeping the civil rights movement from splitting apart. It is hardly surprising that David Pitt, a man who did not demand the label 'charismatic' and who faced divisions perhaps more profound than those that faced King following the passage of anti-discrimination laws in the United States, would not be able to shore up the would-be coalition called C.A.R.D.

INFLATED GOALS

C.A.R.D.'s ambitious goals also led to the 'failure' of the organization. First, as suggested, there was the simple fact that C.A.R.D. did not succeed in implementing those broad goals to any significant degree, a fact stemming in part from the nature of C.A.R.D.'s efforts, but also from the difficulty in meeting the tasks set. But, second, almost more important, was the amorphousness of those goals and the expectations that they aroused. C.A.R.D. was organized to have a significant impact on critical problems. When it did not have such an impact, when it could not organize a mass demonstration, or could only alter slightly a crude piece of anti-discrimination legislation or could not repeal a discriminatory immigration law, then its critics could always charge that it was not doing enough (for it never was). The actors in the organization were themselves always discouraged by the enormity of the task that they had set themselves and by the knowledge that they would not get plaudits, even for hard work. As Dipak Nandy said: 'If nothing could count as success, there was no way of keeping up morale.' It was almost as if the founders of C.A.R.D. had believed that since they were going to weld together the improbable—somewhat grand—coalition projected in 1964, they would have to pronounce goals worthy of such an armada. Yet the very improbability of realizing the dream with any immediacy meant that limited successes, which might under other circumstances have served to attract people and organizations to C.A.R.D., were only seen as evidence of C.A.R.D.'s failure and thus served to discourage people who desperately needed hope that the organization would make a difference.

## INTERNATIONALIZATION[14]

The impact of events overseas only compounded C.A.R.D.'s difficulties, aiding the forces of division and keeping up pressure for ambitious (though somewhat ill-defined) goals. As suggested, the main pressure of overseas events came from America. C.A.R.D. had been founded as an almost explicit attempt to emulate the civil rights movement; yet the distorting effects of the division within that movement in America affected C.A.R.D. even in its early days. As C.A.R.D. organized to be a parliamentary lobby for the fight in 1965, part of the organization, sensitive to developments in the Student Non-violent Coordinating Committee at the time were concerned about letting immigrants set priorities and determine tactics. This was a bitter source of division. Similarly, in 1967, when C.A.R.D. was turning to some ideas of 'community action', on a multiracial basis, that movement had been superseded in the United States (in terms of publicity given to it) by the Black Power writers and activists who were much more militant in their rhetoric, much more antagonistic to white society in their desire to develop an independent sense of pride and self-sufficiency among black Americans. America again provided the language and the example for the forces of division. The break-up of the civil rights movement, in short, could not help but have an effect on C.A.R.D. since those involved in the British group were constantly aware of developments in the United States. The divisions that caused the break-up of the movement in the United States were felt and to a limited degree repeated within the civil rights analogue in Britain. Further, although their impact was less obvious (at least to me), other events in other parts of the world probably aided the forces of division.[15]

Internationalization also had an effect on the goals of C.A.R.D. Many of the tasks facing the organization required long and difficult hours; analysing the distribution of power in an urban area;

organizing in those areas; actually delivering the goods; preparing for the legislative battle over the amendments to the Race Relations Act 1965. Yet there was a daily regimen of racial drama carried in the British Press. The urban riots in America; the struggle of a coloured people for national liberation in Vietnam; the development of nationalism in Africa, these all loomed as events of world import, moments of high drama. They made the difficult task of transforming the immigrants' conditions of life pale by comparison (at least in terms of the action that was being carried on in Britain in 1967). There was always an incentive and an audience for a would-be leader who would cite an international example and require that C.A.R.D.'s efforts be that dramatic or that sweeping.

### THE IMMEDIATE RESULT OF C.A.R.D.'S FAILURE: SINGLE-ISSUE FORMATIONS

With the new and apparently final splintering of C.A.R.D., the inherent weaknesses of local immigrant organizations and the renewed factionalism in the major immigrant organizations, the guiding ideal of C.A.R.D.—the creation of a mass united front for immigrants and their children—seemed beyond attainment. The multi-purpose, multiracial pressure group was no longer an immediate possibility after C.A.R.D. had lost its momentum.

In place of C.A.R.D.'s efforts a new pattern of immigrant political activity began to take place. Given the diversity of the immigrant group universe and the many tensions that existed between various groups and between the various nationalities, a single-issue approach seemed the only practical course open to those who wanted to gain as much support as possible among immigrants in pushing for social change and for restructured policies. The Joint Council for the Welfare of Immigrants was the striking example of an organization that came into being for a single purpose and tried to gain strength by encouraging all those who felt strongly about a single policy—immigration appeals and procedures and policies regarding the entrance of immigrants into Britain—to join together.

A second organization, dedicated to lobbying for acceptable anti-discrimination legislation, also came into existence as C.A.R.D. was fracturing. Equal Rights was formed late in 1967 to work outside of the National Committee and to avoid the wreckage of C.A.R.D. in providing an independent, non-official rallying point for experts on legislation and their supporters. Led by Roy Marshall, a West Indian professor of law at Sheffield University, the group attracted many who had been involved in legal work for C.A.R.D.[16] Equal Rights aimed at broadening the scope of new legislation to its furthest point and making the enforcement machinery as potent as possible. Although leaders of the group wanted to elicit broad expressions of support from the immigrant community, it was mainly a technocratic enterprise, hoping to persuade through detailed legal presentations and to use the Press contacts of its members to argue its case in the media and in Westminster during the legislative debates. A continuation of C.A.R.D.'s general public policy protest function could be discerned in the formation of the Black People's Alliance, a union of militant Pakistanis, the Standing Conference of West Indian Organizations, London Region, and the left-communist wing of the Indian Workers' Association of Birmingham.[17]

## 2. THE IMPLICATIONS OF C.A.R.D.'S DEMISE: PROSPECTS FOR THE POWERLESS

### THE LIMITS OF SINGLE-ISSUE FORMATIONS

Although single-issue organizations may have been the only stratagem available at the time of C.A.R.D.'s disintegration, this pattern was of limited value in performing the two basic functions of C.A.R.D. At the level of national policy formation, a group like Equal Rights could not muster large numbers of immigrants in an attempt to co-ordinate its lobbying with a demonstration of support for strong anti-discrimination legislation through a peaceful protest or even civil disobedience. It was the dock workers marching in support of Enoch Powell on the issue of immigration who received public attention and shaped the tenor and dimensions of the debate on race relations in early 1968.[18] Moreover, the Joint Council, although it could speak out strongly in opposition to the new immigration Bill, could not organize for protest action or wield power in any other significant fashion to put some muscle behind its objections to the new round of discriminatory legislation. The variegated groups that comprised the Joint Council simply were not strong enough nor firmly enough welded together to do much more than register written protest through a co-ordinating committee. Similarly, the Black People's Alliance could issue strongly worded denunciations of the Government but because of its left-wing orientation could not attract broad immigrant support for concerted action against the Government's immigration policy.

Of course, as single-issue organizations neither Equal Rights nor the Joint Council set out to build up a mass organization of coloured immigrants and their children, so that function of C.A.R.D. was simply ignored. The Black People's Alliance, comprised as it was of groups that existed at the time of C.A.R.D. and which were still beset by the same problems that had plagued them then, showed no signs of building a mass base of any significant proportions nor even of working very closely or very effectively in tandem. It had come into existence over immigration policy and the legislative debate, but it did not seem to be able to transcend those events and evolve into a more permanent and substantial organization.[19]

Single-issue formations were possible when the task was to join groups together to issue a statement of disapprobation of some Government failure. Yet, without more substantial organizations and systematic development of a power base, they could not be too effective even at that. Moreover, without organization, they could not carry on other critical tasks. For example, at the level of national policy-making, there was not a group, after the fall of C.A.R.D., to effectively police the Race Relations Board or oversee and criticize the effectuation of the Government's Urban Programme.

At the local level, the single-issue approach was even less promising. The whole effort of planning, applied research, and counter-bureaucratic techniques was derailed in large part when C.A.R.D. ceased to function effectively. Conservative immigrant and community groups—with a few exceptions like Islington C.A.R.D. or some of the I.W.A.s—who had little conception of the political nature of community organizing would not be stimulated by C.A.R.D. techniques and ideas applied in their locality. And it seemed highly unlikely that there would soon again be a working agreement among a wide range of bodies at the national level on the necessary strategies for change at the local level. Most community groups, assuming that they were political at all, would again be relegated to independent foraging, with few resources and little chance for mutual support or feedback or cross fertilization in their attack on discrimination and other sources of inequality at the local level.

Essentially, C.A.R.D.'s two major functions—building a mass movement and altering public policy—could have been reinforcing.

The cumulative effect of the performance of different functions *might* have given strength to an organization trying to represent the powerless. Surely the single-issue approach, although perhaps a necessary expedient, seemed less promising, for it only further divided the immigrants. A show of strength that joined many organizations might occur, yet such effects seemed destined to be short term; the processes of accumulating strength that is central to building an organization could not really occur; and the type of influence developed would be largely the registration of protest—only occasionally could the single-issue formation live long enough and develop the resources necessary to negotiate with the executive. The performance of reinforcing functions would have seemed a better route to developing a political institution to speak for immigrants in Britain. Yet, because of the forces of division and their frequent tendency to set the mass organization and public policy roles in opposition, it seemed unlikely that a multi-purpose, multiracial organization, even on the scale of C.A.R.D., would exist again for some time.

Let us turn briefly, now, to the four issues posed at the end of the Introduction.

## THE CONTINUING NEED

First, the need, which had stimulated the formation of C.A.R.D., continued to exist. Despite legislation, discrimination was still prevalent in Britain. The conditions of life for immigrants were often grossly substandard.[20] At the political level itself, the rise of Powellism, the 1968 Commonwealth Immigrants Bill, the faltering Urban Programme, and the somewhat disappointing Race Relations Act 1968, all indicated that a strong political counter-pressure operating independent of Government on behalf of immigrants, was necessary if discrimination was to be eradicated, attitudes changed, and conditions altered.

## SECTIONAL OR PROMOTIONAL POWER

To return to the second of the four questions posed about the pressure group system in the Introduction: How would a group like C.A.R.D. attempt to gain and exercise power? As a unique experiment in British politics, C.A.R.D. had tried both to promote a cause and to develop power for a distinct section of society. With the C.A.R.D. take-over and collapse of its operations, the two routes to influence separated. The effective performance of the promotional role had always implied the successful establishment of a coalition of British and immigrant forces. The successful performance of the sectional role had been dependent upon the formation of a cohesive coalition comprised of the members of the three major immigrant nationality groups. As we have seen, tensions within the immigrant forces and between white and coloured ultimately underlay the C.A.R.D. break-up.

With the disintegration of C.A.R.D., the promotional route seemed closed off except in the single-issue situations. Coalitions between national white groups and a national immigrant organization were not possible when no national immigrant organization existed. Further, important national pressure groups like trade unions gave no evidence of supporting the cause of immigrants. At the local level, such patterns of alliance might be brought to bear upon local authorities or local V.L.C.s, but since both the authorities and the V.L.C.s were often without the requisite power to alter conditions this strategy had limited value.[21]

The sectional route to power, if not blocked, was not clearly delineated. C.A.R.D. had hoped to represent the section of the population characterized as immigrants. But C.A.R.D.'s founders had never been clear on the nature of the power that would be used by C.A.R.D. at all the various possible levels of interaction with authorities and other forces with influence. Like the civil rights movement in the United States, C.A.R.D. had at the outset not tried to exercise influence as a part of the system of functional representation, failing to develop strategies as either a consumer or producer group. Rather, as a combination sectional-promotional group, it had tried to appeal to the reason and conscience of men in power and of those other groups—functional producer groups and voting blocs—to whom the Government responded. Of course, in the early days, C.A.R.D. leaders always thought they had in reserve the tactics of mass protest or civil disobedience; thus, neither economic nor formal electoral pressure was ever discussed with much seriousness. Even the concept of organizing at the neighbourhood level through 'community action' and 'delivering the goods' had depended on the fact of agglomerating sheer numbers of immigrants in an organization (and thus having the latent power of protest) and/or appealing to the reason of the local authorities. The local strategy, as it had developed in 1967 (whether on a class or race basis), did not contemplate with much sophistication (though it did not preclude) the development of economic power or electoral influence as a means of gaining sanctions. Nor did 'community action' as devised by C.A.R.D. strategists contemplate some form of 'community' or 'immigrant' control by which *official* governmental power in an urban area would be devolved to a neighbourhood largely comprised of immigrants.

Whether a group or groups of immigrants could gain power as either a 'consumer' or 'producer' group in relation to the party system, Parliament, the executive, or local authorities, and whether that power could be used to eradicate discrimination, change the pattern of public policy, affect basic social conditions, and simultaneously start a shift in attitudes, is of course problematical. An electoral strategy for immigrants has not been devised and evaluated critically. Similarly, a strategy of gaining political power through economic function—either through participation in the labour movement or in terms of ownership by immigrants of productive resources—has not been devised very seriously. Nor, to move outside the pressure group frame for a moment, have strategies been advanced for control by immigrants of official institutions, at least on the local or neighbourhood level through formal decentralization.

## THE NEED FOR GOVERNMENT TO HELP ESTABLISH AN IMMIGRANT PRESSURE GROUP

If a group like C.A.R.D. could not gain power given existing policies and practices within the pressure group system as presently structured and operated, should special support be given to the effort so that a group or groups of immigrants might succeed in operating within the pressure group universe?

A key assumption which lies behind an affirmative answer to that question is that the exercise of *group* power by immigrants is necessary if as *individuals* they are to gain those basic rights of British citizenship—political, civil, and social—which have broadly served as the frame for evaluating the nature of the immigrants' advance. The problem with formulating the desired objectives in terms of acquiring 'rights', however, is that the word 'rights', because of its individualistic bias (individuals customarily have rights; groups do not) may hide the need to transfer power to groups. The adoption of Marshall's classification of the rights of citizenship, in short, does not give sufficient emphasis to the needs of individual immigrants to ally themselves to sub-groups and to gain power, not as individuals within existing British institutions, but rather within uniquely immigrant organizations that might be organized along class, race, or nationality lines.

A brief argument in favour of the assumption might run as follows. If social rights involve access to social benefits and services —to education and economic security and the range of services associated with the Welfare State—then such rights may also entail the right to live according to diverse cultural norms in a multi-racial society. In most of the policy decisions taken in the past, the consent of the minority has been assumed: but there is the possibility that it 'can no longer be taken for granted'.[22] Yet, the dimensions of a cultural diversity that would be subsumed under a broad concept of social right has not yet been discussed very exhaustively:

. . . what degree of pluralism can our society, its homogeneity already under attack from other directions tolerate. The separatism of Indian and Pakistani communities has been the subject of both criticism and defence: criticism on the grounds that it constitutes an impermissible degree of communalism, and defence on the grounds that the phenomena involved are of a temporary nature and have a certain exotic value in terms of style of life. In neither case has the problem of separate institutions and the extent to which they can be conceded parity of esteem been considered. . . . One difficulty about charting a secure passage through these rocks is that the debate on cultural diversity has so far taken place on such a superficial level.[23]

Thus, if one wished to help immigrants secure social rights, one might be concerned with aspects of social inequality that affect white and coloured disadvantaged alike. One might just as well argue that given a concept of cultural diversity that is contained within the broader concept of social right and given the need for immigrants to perhaps 'realize their potential' in a group setting (that is, to gain the full meaning of social rights in a group setting), immigrants and their children should be treated differently by Government, should be given special opportunities to attain social rights not as British citizens who happen to be Indian, West Indian, or Pakistani but as British Indians, British West Indians, or British Pakistanis. If such differentiation were thought desirable, rather than 'universalist' policies that dealt with coloured and white alike, the social policies that followed would *not* be 'colour-blind' or 'nationality-blind'.

The experience of C.A.R.D. was only the beginning, not the end, of developing a normative perspective on both the proper role for immigrants in Britain (the nature of cultural diversity) and how to obtain that position (the proper exercise of power by immigrants). To even begin to make headway on those difficult questions requires important empirical undertakings.[24] Yet whether social rights are guaranteed by government according to policies of 'strong universalism',[25] or policies that explicitly deal with groups according to nationality or race or treat geographical areas in which there is likely to be a concentration of a type of person relatively disadvantaged, the need for political institutions comprised of immigrants (either wholly or partially) seems critical. The dimensions of the social rights that government might—in a more hopeful time—try to insure must gain meaning through definition by the people involved.[26] Further, the mechanisms of welfare must not be used by government to induce further dependence and disability among those it is supposedly serving. To counter both potential ills, a political group is necessary. The social policies administered by government alone (assuming government could even be pressured into undertaking such policies) will not be sufficient to insure social rights; the exercise of political power by groups of immigrants will be necessary if government is to define and effectuate policies that will be of service, and not disservice, to the powerless. The emphasis on the role of government in *Colour and Citizenship*, while understandable in terms of the need to make clear the importance of that role, seems significantly overstated, or, at least, disturbingly unqualified.[27]

Thus, given a broad definition of social rights that includes some concept of cultural diversity, the attempt by government to guarantee social rights for all citizens—regardless of race—may require more than a *redistribution of social benefits*: it may also require a *redistribution of power* through which groups of immigrants can participate as political equals in a collectivist, pluralist political system, since the fact of political activity will, it has been argued, be necessary both for the definition of social rights and for the attainment of certain conditions of existence—a sense of autonomy, self-sufficiency, responsibility for one's own affairs—which are concomitants of those rights. The paradox of developing power for the powerless was that the route to influence was always eroded by the lack of power; the forces of division could not be overcome unless there was the attraction of significant power to render those divisions less potent, yet given the divisions, power could not be developed, momentum not obtained. The challenge to government is to share power as a means of developing the organizations or institutions for immigrants and their children.[28] Yet, the obvious and confounding paradox is that government will be reluctant to do that without pressure; even if it had goodwill, it would be restrained by other groups whose interests might be injured by a transfer of power to immigrants and their children. In America, even the threat of the uninhabitability and deterioration of the nation's great cities, has not yet produced a meaningful sharing of power with black Americans. The situation in Britain is not yet seen as being so dire, nor has a sharing of power as a solution been confronted directly and alternatives considered seriously.

## CHANGING THE STRUCTURE OF INFLUENCE

Even if the central government wished to 'share power' with groups of immigrants, there would be a variety of problems. As suggested, there would be the opposition of influential groups whose interests were being affected (or who thought their interests were affected). But beyond the practical constraints (which are obviously more complex than I have indicated), there are problems of principle. If the government somehow was going to give groups of immigrants (whether organized by class, race, or nationality) special subsidies or benefits to build them up as a political group (and assuming—a large assumption to be sure—that the government would do this in a fashion that would create relatively autonomous groups, not puppets), how could the action be justified? By what principle could government buttress its favouring of one class of people? The advantages of 'strong universalism' in a 'sharing power' sense are that distinctions can be drawn in terms of the only mildly controversial categories of lower income class or relatively disadvantaged group or relatively disadvantaged area (categories which apply to all races and nationalities in principle though they may apply, in fact, to particular races or nationality groupings) rather than in terms of the more controversial and untraditional categories (in the British political culture) of particular ethnic blocs as a private group. There would inevitably be the further problem for government of determining which private groups were 'legitimate' recipients of public benefits.

An alternative to an attempt to share power by building up ethnic pressure groups at a national level so that they could in turn bargain with and pressure government for policies more in their interest would be to devolve power to local levels and to alter the structure of power so that governmental institutions had the resources and responsibility necessary for altering the conditions of the people in those areas. This would entail decentralization of resources to either the local or neighbourhood level and the creation of new institutions. Such a change—which would be of significant proportions—would necessarily alter the patterns of collective influence as now exercised through the British political system. Such changes may be necessary from a normative perspective in order to insure the rights of citizenship guaranteed both to coloured minorities and to the lower classes of British society, though that complicated argument has only been hinted at here and not developed. Whether the power could be mustered for such a change, is necessarily problematical. To be sure, the distance of such thinking from the initial efforts of C.A.R.D.—a small group of individuals lobbying at Parliament for anti-discrimination laws with reason as their source of influence—is great. The common thread being followed, however, is the attempt to unravel and understand the processes by which the powerless may gain sufficient power to live with dignity in Britain.

## NOTES

1. There has been virtually no activity within the organization since autumn 1967. David Pitt, however (as of autumn 1969), still referred to himself as the chairman of C.A.R.D.

2. For the original statement of aims and objects, see p. 21.

3. Standing Conference and the Indian Workers' Association, Birmingham, were other immigrant organizations vocal in their opposition to the Bill.

4. For a brief account of events surrounding the passage of the 1968 Race Relations Act and the specific role of Equal Rights, see Rose *et al.*, op. cit., pp. 615–21. No full account of these events has yet been published.

5. During my second visit to England in January 1968, Dr. Pitt refused to grant me an interview. My analysis of him is based on an interview of several hours in spring 1967, attendance at a number of C.A.R.D. meetings at which he was present, and the observations of many persons listed in the table of interviews, pp. 233–4.

6. Pitt's major concern, outside his medical practice, was clearly elective politics; he desperately wanted to be Britain's first coloured M.P., a goal he was unable to attain. Pitt was defeated in the Stoke Newington constituency during the 1970 general election.

7. Perhaps like the black *bourgeoisie* described by Franklin Frazier, Pitt was in a sense uprooted from his 'racial tradition' and, as a consequence, had no 'cultural

roots in either the Negro or the white world'. (Franklin Frazier, *The Black Bour-geoisie* [Glencoe, 1957], Chapter V; '. . . But more important still the black bour-geoisie has rejected the folk culture of the Negro masses. . . . As a consequence of their isolation, the majority of the black bourgeoisie live in a cultural vacuum. . . .') This rootlessness is accompanied, Frazier writes, by a capacity for self-delusion about one's own influence. While not denying that voter registration and an active political role within a political party could have real importance for immigrants and for the second generation, one can seriously question Pitt's narrow concern with electoral politics as a tactic of first priority and see elements of self-delusion in his belief that *he* could both *organize* immigrants as a voting bloc and *make* that bloc effective in swing constituencies, as he had often said that C.A.R.D. should.

As the C.A.R.D. crisis reached a head in November, people close to Pitt found him increasingly short-tempered, as his own political dreams seemed to have gone smash and C.A.R.D. itself seemed to be spinning out of control. There were elements of individual pathos at the first session of the convention when Pitt was bewildered at being jeered by coloured radicals, but it was pathos for C.A.R.D. as well. Johnny James, by contrast, while playing a double game at the tactical level, was much more single-minded than Pitt in his fierce desire for West Indian inde-pendence and his strong dislike for things British. Whatever one thinks of James's tactics, there can be no doubt that he was a man of substantial political conviction. His deep commitment to the idealistic qualities of Communism plus his desire to have West Indians liberated within the Caribbean, on his own terms, comple-mented his dislike of Britain. Although I was not able to gather much biographical material about James, his response to the C.A.R.D. situation might be seen in part as representing the extreme passion of West Indian politics; the frustration of a first-generation immigrant who, if he is politically aware, realizes that the promise of equality would not be fulfilled for him and possibly not for his children; the sense that powerlessness could be dissipated by aligning oneself with great inter-national forces.

The problem of West Indian commitment to life in Britain was expressed by James's ally, Ralph Bennett: 'We don't know if we are bloody Jamaicans or bloody British. Blacks here have no stability. We don't have a chance as in Cleveland to elect a Negro mayor.'

8. C.A.R.D.'s chairman was more a reactive agent (and at times a reactionary one) than an innovative leader, more a member of distinct factions than a man who could weld groups together by artful listening and creative reconciliation of issues through redefinition of problems that troubled different groups. Head of an organi-zation which was to eradicate discrimination, attack prejudice, and itself practise tolerance in order to attract the necessary multiracial multitudes, Pitt precipitously forced people out of C.A.R.D. rather than respond to their real (if not always ar-ticulate) concerns.

9. For example, as Tassaduq Ahmed, a friend of all three, said: 'In a way the last convention was their failure, for they put people off. If a mass movement has no people then who are you going to perform services for? After the six walked out of the second convention session, they said "it just shows how ungrateful the organization is". But that has got to be the wrong perspective. For two years instead of drawing all sorts of people in, they have put people off. In a group like C.A.R.D., there must be a place for everyone. I was put off—even someone like me who had at all times been loyal to them.'

10. The distrust of and dislike for doctrinaire statements from the far left doubt-less stemmed in part from their view of the divisions within the Labour party during the years before the 1964 general election. Lester was a professed admirer of Julia Gaitskell's father.

11. Julia Gaitskell could always go back to the job she had left with the B.B.C.

Lester could have had a much more lucrative law practice and made no secret of his activities in his local Labour party and of his desire to go to Parliament. Both had escape routes that most immigrants could not traverse. A curious resonance developed. Lester and Gaitskell were charged with wanting to use C.A.R.D. only for their own advancement. Hurt by these charges, they would consider out loud the things they could be doing if they were not devoting time to C.A.R.D. They were seen by some immigrants as part-time campaigners and yet they were also seen as being among the most effective members of the organization and, therefore, a challenge to the competence of the immigrants. Mutual defensiveness between white and coloured meant communication might be diminished.

12. The experience of C.A.R.D.'s 1967 summer project uncovered either a profoundly apolitical spirit or a distrust among the young of the leadership of their elders.

13. Even as C.A.R.D. was going through the throes of crisis, other 'major' immigrant organizations were being divided and altered. The Indian Workers' Association, Southall, was girding for an election campaign that promised bitter factionalism and in which subsequently S. S. Gill, former I.W.A., Southall, president who had been expelled from the organization in December 1968 for his role in the C.A.R.D. take-over, ousted the faction of which V. D. Sharma, former C.A.R.D. national organizer, was a member. The Indian Workers' Association, Great Britain, split apart, although both factions remained antagonistic towards the I.W.A., Southall. The split within the organization resulted after a Maoist-inspired attempt in West Bengal to throw over the left-wing government of the region. Within the I.W.A., G.B., the pro-Peking faction, including J. Joshi, was ousted, although as of this writing Joshi seems to have regained his position. The National Federation of Pakistani Associations began to be energized by young left-wing radicals, Abdul Martin and Zacharia Choudhury (a former member of the C.A.R.D. National Council who was re-elected to the body under the rules in effect at the reconvening of the C.A.R.D. convention in December 1968). But the more moderate members of the Pakistani community remained distant. Tassaduq Ahmed hoped to start a new, British-oriented Pakistani 'civil rights' organization. This failed, but Ahmed's allies recaptured the Pakistani federation subsequently. In Standing Conference, Joseph Hunte was elected chairman after Neville Maxwell decided to accept a job in Africa, and Jeff Crawford, who along with Maxwell had tried to prod Conference into more political positions, refused to stand for the office. Hunte, who in 1966 had tried to get Conference to join the N.C.C.I. after the West Indian organization disaffiliated from C.A.R.D., and who in 1967 was a member of the N.C.C.I.'s Legal and Civil Affairs Panel, was subsequently on the C.A.R.D. Executive Committee. To Crawford, this was a reprehensible act, since Conference had officially separated from C.A.R.D. After more division within Standing Conference, Hunte resigned his post with the C.A.R.D. rump. If Hunte represents (like Pitt) the West Indian leader who is seeking an accommodation with British institutions and acceptance and status within the more formalized structures of British life, albeit the race relations structure, and if James represents the West Indian in Britain who is concerned fundamentally with the Caribbean, then Crawford is a third 'type' of West Indian leader. He is a man dedicated to change in Britain, but who also draws his strength and sense of purpose from his 'negative identification' with Britain, from his opposition to it, and its rejection of the kind of changes he hopes to effect. At its most extreme, Crawford's relation to Britain is seen by him in dramatic terms linking him to martyred coloured leaders of the past: 'When they succeed in burying Jeff, there will be a lot more Jeffs to be buried; they [the British] can't shoot us all.' Even the tiny Universal Coloured Peoples' Association, in existence only a few months, splintered: Roy Sawh, a West Indian rival of Obi Egbuna, left the U.C.P.A. to form another group.

14. See Preface, *supra*, pp. ix–xi.

15. As an American, I was naturally sensitive to events in America that would have affected actors in Britain. I was, admittedly, not as sensitive as I might have been to other events that would also have had an impact. For example, the Indian-Pakistan War, the divisions within the Communist movements in India and Pakistan, the antagonism between Asians and West Indians in Guyana, the rivalries between islands in the West Indies.

16. Roger Warren Evans, an early member of the C.A.R.D. legal committee, and Nicholas Deakin, a member of the first C.A.R.D. Executive Committee, were among the founders of the group. Tassaduq Ahmed was active in it. So, subsequently, was Anthony Lester. Dipak Nandy became its secretary in the spring of 1968.

17. Rose *et al.*, op. cit., p. 620.

18. Ibid., Chapter 29.

19. Ibid., p. 620.

20. The argument presented in the Introduction, pp. 10–12, still obtains.

21. For a more detailed analysis of this problem, see Rose *et al.*, op. cit., Chapter 15 and pp. 663–4.

22. Ibid., p. 662.

23. Ibid., p. 663.

24. For example, a critical question is whether West Indians, because of discrimination and the poor conditions prevalent in Britain's twilight zones, are going to be pulled under by the pattern of cumulative inequalities which has so injured black Americans. See, for the most widely read account of the American situation, K. B. Clark, op. cit. A corollary of the analysis put forward by Clark of ghetto pathologies is that the psychological and social deprivations of ghetto life must be countered by exercise of community (ethnic group) power to break the cycle of injurious cumulation.

25. Rose *et al.*, op. cit., Chapters 15, 29, 31.

26. For example, how, in a culturally diverse society, should the educational content of schools for coloured children be determined. Education may be an essential social right, but critical to the realization of that right is its definition. Or, if resources for social services are scarce, who is to decide which service should be emphasized, which relatively neglected.

27. Rose *et al.*, op. cit., Chapter 33. Rose *et al.*, recognized the importance of immigrant leadership and were aware that the consent of the coloured minorities cannot be assumed (pp. 662–3), yet they did not emphasize the need for the creation of strong immigrant political organizations.

28. Perhaps through a 'community action' component of an expanded Urban Programme, an elaborate system of grants would be developed to aid those organizations that, on a non-partisan basis, qualified to be social service or advocate planner organizations for Britain's coloured citizenship.

# Appendix

## PRIMARY SOURCES

INTERVIEWS
*Members of the Campaign Against Racial Discrimination*
(Following each member's name is his highest position in C.A.R.D. and the date he assumed that position. For example, the Executive Committee was elected in mid-year, so that the date will indicate the year of election. Executive Committee and National Council members could have been selected four times: when C.A.R.D. was first founded [those persons will be designated members *pro tem.*], 1965, 1966, 1967.)

Oscar Abrams, National Council (1966, 1967), Islington C.A.R.D.

Tassaduq Ahmed, National Council (1966).

Hamza Alavi, vice-chairman (*pro tem.*, 1965).

Ranjana Ash, recording secretary (*pro tem.*), Executive Committee (1965).

Frank Bailey, general secretary (1967, resigned January 1968).

Maureen Baker, regional organizer (1967), Leeds C.A.R.D.

Jocelyn Barrow, vice-chairman (1966–7), general secretary (1965).

Ralph Bennett, assistant secretary (1966–7).

Audrey Cooper, regional organizer (1967).

Nicholas Deakin, Executive Committee (*pro tem.*).

H. Dhillon, treasurer (1966).

Anne Dummett, National Council (1966).

Michael Dummett, Executive Committee (1965–6).

Martin Ennals, Executive Committee (1966).

Julia Gaitskell, general secretary (1966).

Robert Gillespie, Glasgow C.A.R.D.

Nick Howard, Sheffield C.A.R.D.

Selma James, organizing secretary (*pro tem.*), National Council (1965).

Anthony Lester, Executive Committee (*pro tem.* to 1966).

Ian McDonald, National Council (1965–6), Islington C.A.R.D.

Dipak Nandy, Executive Committee (1966), Leicester C.A.R.D.

Olwyn Navartne, West Middlesex C.A.R.D.

Eithne O'Sullivan, Brent C.A.R.D.

David Pitt, chairman (*pro tem.* to 1967).

V. D. Sharma, vice-chairman (1966).
Gurmukh Singh, treasurer (*pro tem.* to 1965), Executive Committee (*pro tem.* to 1966).
Richard Small, press officer (*pro tem.*).
Robert Souhami, Complaints Committee.
Len Squire, National Council (1966–7).

*Others*

Clem Byfield, past president, West Indian Standing Conference.
Jeff Crawford, secretary, West Indian Standing Conference.
Felicity Bolton, British Caribbean Association.
Obi Egbuna, president, United Coloured Peoples' Association (1967).
David Ennals, Home Office.
Reginald Freeson, (then) Ministry of Power.

Jack Howard-Drake, Home Office.
Joseph Hunte, Public Relations Officer, West Indian Standing Conference.
DeWitt John, author.
Jagmahan Joshi, general secretary, Indian Workers' Association, Great Britain.
Joan Lestor, M.P.
John Lyttle, Race Relations Board.
Neville Maxwell, chairman, West Indian Standing Conference.
Colin McGlashan, the *Observer*.
Nadine Peppard, National Committee for Commonwealth Immigrants.
R. E. K. Phillips, Jamaican High Commission.
Eric Silver, the *Guardian*.
Tony Smythe, National Council for Civil Liberties.
Keith Webster, general secretary, Standing Conference of West Indian Organizations, Birmingham.
Shirley Williams, (then) Department of Education and Science.

INTERNAL DOCUMENTS OF THE FOLLOWING ORGANIZATIONS
(*This source material is on file at the library of the Institute of Race Relations.*)

Campaign Against Racial Discrimination.
Caribbean Workers' Movement.
Indian Workers' Association, Southall.
London Workers' Committee.
National Committee for Commonwealth Immigrants.

National Federation of Pakistani Associations.
Standing Conference of West Indian Organizations, London Region.
United Coloured Peoples' Association.

# Index

Soskice, Sir Frank, 113, 124, 138, 155*n*; concessions on Race Relations Bill, 119–20
Souhami, Robert, 132, 204*n*, 234
Southall, 173; discrimination, 133; *see also* Indian Workers' Association, Southall
Southan, Malcolm, 128
Sparkbrook study, 9
Squire, Len, 159*n*, 204*n*, 234
Standing Conference of West Indian Organizations, London Region, 18, 19, 23, 30, 59, 60, 97, 102*n*, 103*n*, 127, 182, 211*n*, 221, 229*n*, 231*n*; activities, 73–4, 105*n*; affiliated organizations, 72, 104*n*; and C.A.R.D., 57, 61–5, 82–4, 85, 88–90, 99; conflicts of aims, 105–6*n*; desire for independence, 84–5; development, 65–75; officers, 107*n*; organization and leadership problems, 66–7, 75–82, 85–6; white officials depart, 68
Standing Orders Committee, 191–2, 208*n*
'Statements of Future Work', 25
Statutory commission, C.A.R.D.'s proposals, 154*n*
Stewart, 14*n*
Stoke Newington and Hackney group, 184, 206*n*, 210*n*
Street, Harry, 137, 159*n*, 209*n*
Street Committee Report, 140, 159*n*, 196
Student Non-violent Coordinating Committee (SNCC), 25, 28, 53*n*, 219
Summer projects, 171, 173–5, 184, 207*n*, 209*n*, 231
'Survey of Race Relations in Britain', 69, 127

Tajfel, H., 103*n*
Tanzanian Students Zimbabwe, 209*n*
*Teamwork*, 69, 81, 103*n*; editorials, 77–8
Thornberry, Cedric, 113, 134
Thorneycroft, Peter, 119
Tilden, Francis, 56*n*

Townsend, Peter, 13*n*, 106*n*
Trade unions, 59, 130, 140, 160*n*; and C.A.R.D., 153; attitude to race legislation, 158*n*
Tsele, M., 211*n*
Tudor-Hart, Dr. Alexander, 188, 192, 211*n*

Uganda Student Union, 209*n*
Underhill, Evi, 113
United States, discrimination patterns, 131, 135; sets patterns for U.K. race relations, viii–xi
Universal Coloured Peoples' Association 181, 188, 189, 199, 231*n*
Urban Programme, xii–xiii, 232*n*

van den Berghe, Pierre, 10, 15*n*
Vigilante groups, 74, 75, 108*n*
Villier, F. N., 72
Voluntary liaison committees, 145, 149, 160*n*, 224; and C.A.R.D. local groups, 172; role, 164–5
Voter registration campaign, 160*n*, 184

Waddilove, E., 158*n*
Wallace, George, viii
Wandsworth group, 206*n*
Webster, Keith, 234
Welfare, 13; and C.A.R.D. local groups, 165–6; overemphasis on, 164, 165; and social rights, 226–7
West Indian Student Union, 18, 72
West Indians, activists, 89–90; attitudes, 174–5, 231*n*, 232*n*; colour and class, 106*n*; cultural identity, 71–2, 80–1, 86; integration or assimilation, 69–70; distrustful of whites and Asians, 174–5, 177–8, 184–5, 193; organizations, 72–3, 75–82, 105*n*; and West Indian politics, 193, 197
West Indies Federation, 65–6, 67, 174
West Indian Standing Conference, London Region (W.I.S.C.), 61, 182, 211*n*; *see* Standing Conference of West Indian Organizations